The Good Temp

The Good Temp

Vicki Smith
Esther B. Neuwirth

ILR Press
an imprint of
Cornell University Press
Ithaca and London

First published 2008 by Cornell University Press

Printed in the United States of America

Library of Congress Cataloging-in-Publication Data

Smith, Vicki, 1951–
    The good temp / Vicki Smith, Esther B. Neuwirth.
        p. cm.
    Includes bibliographical references and index.
    ISBN 978-0-8014-4580-4 (cloth : alk. paper)
    1. Temporary employees—United States.   2. Temporary
help services—United States.   3. Temporary
employment—United States   I. Neuwirth, Esther B.
(Esther Batia), 1966–   II. Title.

    HD5854.2.U6S64 2008
    331.25'7290973—dc22

                                        2007050246

Cornell University Press strives to use environmentally responsible suppliers and materials to the fullest extent possible in the publishing of its books. Such materials include vegetable-based, low-VOC inks and acid-free papers that are recycled, totally chlorine-free, or partly composed of nonwood fibers. For further information, visit our website at www.cornellpress.cornell.edu.

Cloth printing   10 9 8 7 6 5 4 3 2 1

CONTENTS

ACKNOWLEDGMENTS

We are grateful to the individuals at the organizations we studied and hope that we did justice to them in our effort to analyze the complexity of their world.

Many thanks to our colleagues for contributing important insights on various versions of this work: Chris Benner, Fred Block, Sean O'Riain, Eileen Otis, Jennifer Reich, Preston Rudy, Ellen Scott, Bindi Shah, Eva Skuratowicz, Maureen Sullivan, Mridula Udayagiri, and participants in the Power and Inequality Workshop at the University of California, Davis. Others who provided invaluable support include Dorothy Duff Brown, Janet Gouldner, Larry Greer, Patricia Keller, and Carolyn Shaffer. Sarah Ovink's work as research assistant made it possible to complete this manuscript in a timely way. George Gonos gave us valuable advice on the material in Appendix II. And special thanks to Fred Block for intellectual engagement with this project from the start and for his invaluable insights over the years.

This work benefited from partial financial and institutional support at various stages of the research and writing from the University of California Institute for Labor and Employment (now known as the Labor and Research Fund), the Social Science Research Council's

Program on the Corporation as a Social Institution, and the University of California, Davis Consortium for Women and Research.

Finally, we are indebted to our editor Fran Benson for her support and encouragement.

We dedicate this book to our families. From Vicki a dedication in the memory of Steve Smith, and to Steve and Molly McMahon. From Estee a dedication to Michael Stein, Rachel, and Simon, for giving my life greater meaning, and to my parents, Rutie and Arieh Neuwirth, for their love, support, and encouragement.

The Good Temp

Chapter One

The Temporary Advantage

Introduction

The story of the explosion of temporary employment and the challenge to the permanent employment contract in the last half of the twentieth century has been told many times. Researchers from a variety of academic disciplines have written about it, as have activists who organize to help American workers maintain a decent standard of living and a modicum of dignity, and policy analysts who fear the degradation of the employment relationship that seems to be a foregone implication of temporary work. They have focused on different units of analysis: workers who desire permanent jobs but can't find them, workers who have lost out as companies have downsized and restructured, businesses and their myriad reasons for using temporary workers as a solution to their profitability and competition problems, and the temporary help service industry (THS) itself.

The Good Temp takes a different tack to explain these developments in labor market institutions and behaviors. Specifically, we look at how the THS industry in the United States reinvented temporary work in the second half of the twentieth century and examine how individual THS agencies continue to manufacture and market this reinvented product—the good temporary worker—today. It is a customized, historically specific make and model whose marketability rested on two selling points: that temporary employment could be a viable alternative to permanent employment and that the workers on whom the system of temporary employment relations depends could be as good as permanent workers and sometimes better. The historical and social construction of "the good temp," we show, was embedded in THS-industry profitmaking strategies and relied on the diffusion of new norms about what constituted acceptable employment practice. Now entrenched, these norms underpin our current employment relations in the United States which many, if not most, of us experience as precarious and contingent, even when we have so-called permanent jobs.

The Good Temp builds on but goes beyond previous analyses in several ways. First, most researchers have implied that the THS industry has simply been in the business of producing generic temporary labor, even when their studies have inadvertently documented otherwise. We argue, in contrast, that the industry developed and continues to promote an image of a very particular brand of temporary labor wherein workers are effective and efficient, even committed. This product branding has been the competitive motor of the THS industry. *The Good Temp* documents the rise of a new ideology about employment, taking a historical view of industry and personnel management rhetoric about temporary workers as a productive and, surprisingly, quality commodity.

Second, we add a new piece to the picture of temporary employment relations by showing how the THS industry must market itself to two customers: not only to the client firms in which they place their temps but to temp workers themselves. A straightforward way of thinking about the latter is this: When hunting for a temporary job, what leads a clerical worker to choose Office Angels over Kelly Services, a pharmaceutical worker to choose RxRelief® over The RxGuy, a paralegal to choose Legal Temps over Special Counsel, Inc., an assembler or warehouse worker to choose LaborFinders over Volt? We show how THS agencies try to increase the chances that job seekers will choose their services. Having to sell themselves and create demand for their products on two fronts leads many for-profit agencies not only to try to supply quality temporary workers to client companies but to supply decent services and jobs to temporary laborers.

In telling the story of the good temp we show how temporary placement agencies today strive to insulate temps from gross mismanagement and help improve their wages and working conditions. Yet we don't mean to suggest that temporary help agencies are in the business primarily to serve workers or help them with their long-term career goals. On this point, we agree with other researchers who have been concerned for what temporary agencies *don't* do for American workers (Benner, Leete, and Pastor 2007; Rogers 2000). Nevertheless, because they need to attract and maintain workforces of good temps, agency representatives have a genuine stake in encouraging client companies to develop decent temporary jobs—though this process is not without its contradictions and rough edges.

Third, looking in depth at how one agency serves its two sets of customers—companies and workers—provides a micro-level perspective that complements the global stories of the THS industry which dominate the literature on temporary employment. *The Good Temp* goes beyond general or aggregate accounts of the THS industry to show how agency staff create and sustain an employment relationship that is fraught with insecurity, ambivalence, turmoil, and anxiety, in their office and on the multiple sites of hiring companies.

Fourth, combining historical analysis of industry and personnel management rhetoric with the fine-grained picture of contemporary agency practices allows us to represent the social construction and institutionalization of a labor market for temporary labor across time. As economic sociologists have noted, markets, including labor markets, are not primordial strata on top of which layers of social organization are mechanically deposited. Instead, they are built up from complex social organization and by interactions between people and organizations (Block 1990; Fligstein 1990; Krippner 2001). Labor markets, in particular, emerge when corporate managers and personnel experts circulate new ideas about how they can employ workers; reconfigure traditional forms of employment; and identify new populations of people as suitable for particular jobs and employment relationships. The rise of temporary employment is an ideal case for a "deeply historical" study of the *process* of making labor and labor markets in the United States (Peck 1996; Tilly and Tilly 1994). We show how what appear to be purely "market-mediated" employment relationships are constructed by those who possess industry power and in the negotiations and contestations between personnel from labor market intermediaries, line and human resource managers, and workers themselves.

This study of the THS industry's market-making activities is important because when the industry encouraged a new set of employment relationships and work conditions, it also encouraged the normative and structural erosion of good, permanent jobs. As temporariness in employment became more pervasive, expectations for permanent, attached employment simultaneously declined. Across the middle part of the twentieth century, corporate managers in many large, bureaucratic, and profitable companies endeavored to build internal employment systems that would provide incentives to employees to work hard and remain loyal to their employers. The THS industry directly challenged this traditional orientation just as global economic conditions were opening up opportunities for new employment practices to take hold. In much mid-twentieth-century rhetoric, experts applauded temporary employment and disparaged permanent or regular workers. In so doing, the THS industry played a critical role in undermining the stable, permanent employment contract. In the early twenty-first century, temporary workers and temporary jobs have, improbably, become a permanent feature of our employment landscape, as have insecurity and destabilization for workers in so-called permanent jobs.

There are several kinds of employment situations involving temporary workers in the United States today (besides those employed by agencies) which don't make their way into this book.[1] For example, our findings would not necessarily pertain to the practices of outsourcing firms that hire "contract company employees" and place them inside other firms on a time-delimited basis (such as Sodexho does with food service and facilities management workers, Pinkerton with security and emergency services workers, or Xerox with document production and mailroom staffing workers). Nor would they necessarily hold for the situations of companies that hire temps directly, bypassing temporary placement agencies, agencies that recruit and place well-paid, high-level contract workers, or agencies that place day laborers only. Further, the conditions and practices we analyze don't map conveniently onto the employment experiences of seasonal agricultural workers; adjunct academic lecturers (including "freeway fliers" who teach one course on one campus and two courses on another campus every semester); or informal-sector workers who earn wages off the books (such as child-care providers, housecleaners, or day laborers in construction and landscaping), who are poorly paid and work on intensely insecure and unpredictable terms.

Our research findings concern the practices of established private-sector temporary agencies that place workers across a spectrum of entry-level, often low-skill positions.[2] Job seekers can find these agencies listed in the yellow pages of the phone book, Help Wanted ads in the classified sections of newspapers, or on Internet Web sites. The agency issues a paycheck to the temp, pays state and federal taxes, and contributes to worker compensation insurance and unemployment funds. In-depth research on such agencies is vital, and for that reason we focus on agency practices rather than on the experiences of temporary workers, about whom substantial research already exists. It is important to note, however, that the percentage of all workers employed by this kind of temporary help agency was 2.3 percent in April 2006, statistically small but socially, culturally, and economically meaningful (Mishel, Bernstein, and Allegretto 2007, 239, fig. 4T).[3]

Although there is absolutely no doubt that most of these temporary jobs are disadvantageous compared with permanent jobs,[4] we agree with others that THS agencies can improve the situation of their temporary workers. We further concur that many workers benefit from access to temporary jobs, depending on and relative to their other labor market options. (On both these points, see chapter 6.) Yet allowing for these points does not require us to sacrifice the goal of striving for better employment for American workers. It forges a middle path between seeing temporary employment as exclusively negative (the oppressive model) or exclusively liberating (the free agent model) and points to the political value of pressuring agencies to embrace a higher road of employment practices than is typically expected of them. It is no small irony that the industry that has played a critical role in increasing the precariousness of employment—an industry that is both cause and effect of the restructuring trends of the last four decades—weaves a layer of such protection by virtue of the way they manufacture their product: the good temp.

Temporary and Permanent Employment across Time

Since the 1940s there has been a paradigmatic shift in the way firms use temporary workers. In the immediate post–World War II period, temporary employment was a marginal labor market practice. A temporary worker was typically a white woman clerical worker with children, hired by a company to fill in for a permanent employee who needed time off from work—for a vacation, illness, or, more rarely, for childbearing (Moore 1965, 555, 558).[5] The temp would leave when the permanent worker returned to the job. The "Kelly Girl" exemplified this temporary worker; the jobs she took were, for the most part, truly temporary, and her weak attachment to the labor force was taken for granted. Companies hired temporaries as a stopgap solution to cover short-term needs but otherwise kept permanent workforces on their payrolls that were large enough to handle the maximum workload (Henson 1996; Rogers 2000; Vosko 2000).

The permanent "good" worker of this earlier economic era was male (typically white), expected to work full time and continually; companies relied on his loyalty to the firm and, in the primary part of the labor market where he was employed, expected him to be attached, committed, and employed across his entire work career. Researchers from a variety of perspectives and proclivities have scrutinized this historically specific good worker, ranging from Whyte's (1956) argument about the bureaucratically oriented "organization man" to Riesman's (1965) "other directed personality," fundamentally shaped by stable bureaucratic social relations of the firm (see also Edwards 1979, chap. 8). Contemporary feminists also weighed in on the organization man, reminding us that not everyone could attain this type of career.[6] Specifically, feminist scholars pointed out, the "male career model" privileged white men's labor force participation and excluded most white women and people of color.[7]

In the 1960s these conventional understandings about temporary jobs, temporary workers, permanent jobs, and good permanent workers began to shift. In a new paradigm, the notion of using a temp as individual stopgap shifted to a view of using temporary workforces as a collective labor or staffing solution (Vosko 2000). Temporary workers wouldn't merely substitute for regular workers in permanent jobs; they would work in positions that opened up but were then eliminated on a regular basis, in accordance with fluctuations in demand for the firm's products.

The new "staffing" paradigm of temporary employment calls for company managers to continually recalibrate the size of their workforces and employ permanently only the number of people necessary to handle a minimum work flow, rather than maintaining a larger workforce that could handle a maximum work flow; when and if it came, managers would hire groups of temps for the additional work. Here, the temporary stint is not coupled with a permanent position or worker. Both people and positions are temporary, and managers use temporary workers in a planned and systematic rather than an impromptu fashion. In addition, whereas in the postwar era the vast majority of temporary workers were women, by 2005 men were 47.2 percent of temporary agency workers (Mishel, Bernstein, and Allegretto 2007).[8] Instead of Kelly Girls, the firm is now called "Kelly Services," and the "permatemp" is now a standard term in the business and academic press and in everyday conversation. Today, temporary workers, men and women alike, work in a wide variety of occupational positions that are temporary themselves, often on an open-ended basis, which will never be classified as permanent or regular.

By the end of the twentieth century, the postwar, hegemonic model of the good worker with the stable permanent job had vaporized, both demographically, normatively, and experientially. As it turned out, the permanent job and the male career model were inextricably linked to historically specific labor markets and organizational structures. The corporate and employment restructuring of recent years has radically challenged earlier conventions about jobs and careers.[9] Now, people who want permanent, full-time jobs and to work in the same companies for the long haul are more often viewed as complacent, unproductive, lacking in initiative and the capacity for innovation. The highly valued—good—workers in our economy are, in the eyes of many, the "free agents" who crave variety, diverse work environments, and the flexibility to pursue new and different careers (Reich 2000; Smith 2001a, chap. 6).[10]

The Good Temp adds two more chapters to this long story. The first addresses how, in mid–twentieth century, new ideas about using temporaries were articulated, circulated, and diffused, promulgated to destabilize traditional employment practices and institutions and pave the way for and normalize new ones. The second analyzes how, once the new paradigm of temporary employment was legitimated normatively, these employment relations have been built and sustained in the trenches: specifically, in temporary help placement agencies. To be sure, many researchers have discussed temporary help service agencies in the course of focusing on temporary workers. But we lack ethnographic, in-depth case study research focusing on temp agencies which would parallel, for example, targeted studies of temporary and contract workers,[11] of corporate/organizational determinants of the use of temporary workers,[12] or of the temporary help services *industry*.[13]

Barley and Kunda's (2004, chap. 4) analysis of agencies in Silicon Valley is a notable exception but they focus on agencies that serve professional and technical workers rather than agencies that place production, warehouse, assembly, and clerical temps. Agencies are the third corner of the triangular temporary employment relationship, a population of labor market intermediaries that has assumed considerable power in negotiating labor market conditions and opportunities for American workers. *The Good Temp* fills in the third corner of this three-way, symbiotic relationship (Rassuli 2005).

We focus on historical and contemporary processes found in the market for lower-level (i.e., low-skill, low-wage) temps, an important distinction. Many who study contingent or nonstandard employment differentiate between high-level contract workers (well-educated professional, managerial, and technical workers who possess specialized skills and often earn spectacular wages for their work) and low-level temporary workers (those who typically lack much formal education, possess general skills, earn fairly low wages, and have virtually no bargaining power) (Cohany 1998; Kalleberg, Reskin, and Hudson 2000, 273; Levenson 2000; Osterman 1999). Temporary employees constitute the majority of contingent workers (working in assembly, laborer, clerical, materials movers, and warehouse jobs, to name a few); comparatively fewer managerial, professional, and high-tech contractors are represented in this workforce (Bureau of Labor Statistics 2005b; Dey, Houseman, and Polivka 2007; Kilcoyne 2004, table B1).[14] Thus, the dynamics, processes, and social relations discussed in this book are particular to the agencies that place the great majority of temporary workers in the United States today.

We show how, over the course of the last part of the twentieth century, the THS industry constructed a unique product: the good temp. The concept of the good temp has specific historical meaning that few have fully appreciated to date, even though clues are present in much of the earlier research. As temporary and other forms of contingent employment have become widespread, so has the concept of the good temp: a person with a fair work ethic and a modicum of skill who requires minimal supervision; and one who will be satisfied with a temporary job and may even consent to stay in a stable pool of workers who are willing to work in temp positions on an ongoing basis. These attributes constitute the minimal bar that agencies hold for their temporary workers, and agency staff construct practices that will maximize the chance that most of their temps will clear this hurdle.

But importantly, the good temp is an ideal, an image, a notion, a sales pitch, a source of competitiveness for a temporary help services firm. Sometimes temporary workers measure up to this ideal, sometimes not.[15] Sometimes temporary workers want to be good temps, but not always. Our point is that the desirability of selling good temporary workers is a driving, profit-maximizing logic of the THS industry, leading it to adopt practices that will improve its ability to stand behind its product.

As is true of other products in a market-based economy, the good temp did not spring out of thin air. It is a commodity that was imagined, produced, and marketed just as surely as Apple designs, manufactures, and persuades us to buy iPods, or Starbucks develops its winning coffee formulas and convinces us to part with our hard-earned money for a double soy vanilla cappuccino—light. This concept—good temp as commodity—is particularly puzzling and worthy of analysis because the idea of a good temp is counterintuitive: why *should* temps be good, committed, or do quality work? Many studies of temporary employment have noted the negative stereotypical views held by managers and by the public: the belief that temps don't care about doing quality work because, after all, there is little incentive to care; that temps drag down permanent workers' productivity and efficiency; that they are just a set of warm bodies with poor work ethics. When interviewed, temporary workers commonly report feeling stigmatized by their temporary status: they assume that people look upon them as deadbeats, as "just a temp" unable to hold down a "real" job (Henson 1996, chap. 6; Parker 1994, chap. 4; Rogers 2000, chap. 5).

Indeed, temporary workers themselves often criticize other temps and try to dissociate from them. Smith, for example, in a study of a high-tech firm, found temps who felt that some of their temporary coworkers were "bad," "deviant," and "immature" and made it clear that they did not identify with such workers just because they all shared the same employment status (2001a, 115). Rogers similarly discovered that temps told "bad temp" stories and tried to establish themselves as different and separate from allegedly mediocre temps (2000, 87–88).

Some firms (hiring companies) have institutionalized their assumption that temps won't be good.[16] For example, companies signal their distrust and low expectations when they apply a different set of policies to temps, spatially segregate them from permanent workers, stigmatize them and mark their difference from permanent workers (requiring temps to wear different color smocks or identification tags, such as Microsoft's "orange badge" policy: Bishop 2005; DuRivage 2001, 385–86; also see Schoch-Spana 1998), or formally restrict their participation in on-site social events (Smith 1998, 2001a). Ikea, a hugely profitable and popular retail merchandiser, communicates its distrust to customers by suggesting that temps provide the brawn but not the brain of the job. In Sacramento, California, Ikea outfitted its temporary workers, hired to help out in the business crush of the first few weeks after its grand opening, in bright yellow T-shirts stating emphatically in large blue lettering "Temporary Co-Worker. Don't ask me any hard questions" (observed February 2006).

Furthermore, American popular culture reinforces negative images of temporary workers, portraying them as employees of last resort. Hollywood movies portray temps as psychotically ambitious (*The Temp*); ambivalent and mediocre, a threat to corporate success (*Haiku Tunnel*); or provocateurs (*Clockwatchers*). In the social–commentary comic strip *Dilbert*, aggravated office workers occasionally deal with bumbling temporary workers hired by their inept, pointy-haired boss; the resident temp in the 1990s was a rodent, Ratbert.[17]

Given employers' intuitive distrust, the rise of the good temp must be explained. This worker is not a disembodied individual who materialized in response to abstract laws of the market, an explanation put forward by those espousing the "market-mediated" approach (Capelli 1999). In their view, the growth of the temporary workforce was a more or less straightforward outcome of supply (of temporary workers) meeting demand (from employers). To be fair, others have taken a social constructionist perspective and examined the ways in which the THS industry has worked to create demand for their services and workers (Ofstead 1999; Barley and Kunda 2004; Finlay and Coverdill 2002).[18] But left to be fleshed out is the "market-making" work (Benner, Leete, and Pastor 2007; Peck 1996), the way the industry paved the way for the normalization of temporary employment and for the belief that using temps could be desirable and advantageous, vis-à-vis permanent workers. Also left to be explained is how and why agencies construct the *supply* of temps or the precise type of temporary worker that the industry strives to market: workers whom firms will agree to hire because they will accept the terms of temporary employment, turn in quality, reliable work, and possibly even be loyal to the companies where they labor.

The normalization of the good temp and of temporary employment by the beginning of the twenty-first century is a contemporary project that this book explains. And it is a project that cannot be understood, first, without analyzing historical discourses about temporary workers in relation to permanent workers and, second, without a microscopic examination of how agencies impress their product on the companies who "buy" their temps, assuage the fears and anxieties that hiring companies have about using temps on a broader scale, cultivate workers to become part of a laborforce of good temporary workers, and manage what is nearly universally seen as a precarious and risky employment relationship.

Current Social Science Research about the New Paradigm

Reinventing and promoting a well-known product presents particular challenges to business leaders, as Howard Schultz noted when writing about "reinventing" coffee and building Starbucks into the megacorporation it is today.

> *"Yes, you can reinvent a commodity...."* Conventional business wisdom tells you that the most attractive business start-ups have a proprietary idea or technology—something to offer that no one else has. Notable examples are Apple's computers, Intel's microchips, and Microsoft's operating system. If you hold a patent to your product, so much the better. It's less risky if you can erect some barriers to entry, to prevent a dozen competitors from popping up and grabbing your market away from you before you can establish yourself. We (Starbucks) had no lock on the world's supply of fine coffee, no patent on the dark roast, no claim to the words *"caffè latte,"* apart from the fact that we popularized the drink in America. (Quoted in Schultz and Yang 1997, 75–76)

Temporary help service agencies have existed in the United States since early in the twentieth century (Moore 1965). Indeed, employment bureaus existed long before that and employers have hired workers on a temporary basis since the early days of industrial capitalism (Licht 2000). In the 1960s, temporary workers were standard issue—albeit a very small segment of the workforce—who worked on a stopgap basis to cover for regular workers. But the industry has experienced a pattern of substantial—some say explosive—growth since 1960. A series of well-documented, mutually conditioning events have contributed to this change, fueled by pressures on both the demand and the supply side of the equation. On the demand side, structural and global conditions were ripe for a new approach to employment relations to take hold. American corporations experienced massive profit squeezes in the late 1960s, and from there on, American capitalism has grappled with many challenges to its economic hegemony. The rise of international competitors meant that American companies had to fight to maintain strong market positions. Businesses moved their operations overseas, where the overall cost of production was lower, given the availability both of cheap labor and of lax labor and environmental laws. Firms not only displaced their manufacturing workforces but began to engage in massive layoffs of managerial and professional employees as well, a historically unprecedented act. Many industries attacked their unionized workforces, and organized labor—champion of the permanent job that paid a living wage—became a scapegoat for America's competitive ills.[19]

Across the board, corporations turned their attention to the "problem" of labor, especially what THS industry leaders began to call "the true cost of labor" (see chapter 2). As large corporations dieted to become lean and mean—by reducing the size of permanent workforces, attacking unions, depressing wages, finding more productive ways of creating goods and services, and getting rid of excess bloat, whether in the form of humans or bureaucratic layers—THS industry leaders spied an opportunity to manufacture a new product that enabled firms to shed even more pounds. Current research shows at least three ways in which the industry accomplished this.

Changing Hiring Companies' Employment Practices

Social science researchers have documented the institutional, market-making work that the THS industry undertook in order to exploit this opening, to stoke demand for its product, and strengthen its standing as a growing industry. Their studies make a compelling case for the claim that the THS industry has been an active and purposeful collaborator in the restructuring of American employment relations (Gonos 1997; Peck and Theodore 2002).

For one thing, industry representatives had to persuade managers at hiring firms that employing temporary workers was a viable business strategy. Ofstead (1999), for example, has documented how temporary staffing agencies had to appease hiring managers' anxieties about the logistical complexities of bringing in temps and to overcome their reluctance to change long-standing practices of hiring workers on a permanent basis. Vosko (2000, chap. 4) similarly noted that representatives from the Canadian THS industry, one that modeled itself on its U.S. counterpart, "sold" temporary workers by convincing employers that temporary employment could be a normative employment *alternative*, not just a *supplement*, to the traditional model of full-time, permanent jobs. Employers had to be convinced that using temps would not compromise trade secrets, that the costs associated with training and retraining workers would not be prohibitive, and that temps could be loyal to the companies that employed them (Vosko 2000, 149).

Because managers in hiring firms historically were concerned that temporary workers would not be reliable or productive, their level of distrust and suspicion was high. The prevalent stereotype that employers initially held of temps was that they were deficient, flighty, lazy, dishonest, or (at best) secondary wage earners who weren't capable of succeeding at "real work" (Henson 1996). One way that the "labor market entrepreneurs" in temporary-placement firms assuaged these concerns and built ongoing business relationships with hiring companies was by promising to send their best temps back to the companies as "repeat placements" (Ofstead 1999, 291).[20] Throughout this process, Ofstead argues, agency representatives continually adapted their "product offerings"—the quality and type of their temps—to better suit local labor market conditions (1999, 287). Introducing their own agencies as labor market intermediaries (as entities that would routinely recruit, screen, and manage temporary employees), garnering hiring companies' consent to use temps, and building legitimacy for this new employment institution constituted a historic stage in creating the triangular relationship that is the hallmark of temporary employment (see also Parker 1994).

Ofstead studied employment relations in transition and the difficulties that the temporary-placement industry faced in carving out demand for its product, showing how it constructed demand for temporary employees; her account contains the seeds of the practice of marketing "good" temporary workers. Although she doesn't fully articulate this point, such workers would be the foundation for the long-term success of the industry. Her study, however, raises an unavoidable and nagging question: with so much riding on their sales pitches and marketing strategies, how did the industry ensure that it could maintain a supply of dependable, quality temps? How did agencies attract the workers who would become part of their labor pool, their marketable product? Not only did agencies struggle to generate demand from hiring companies; they had to create demand for their services from employable temps. What, after all, led a worker to choose one agency over another in an era in which agencies were plentiful and multiplying?

Changing Employment Law and Exploiting Trends
in Employment Litigation

In related developments, representatives of the THS industry intervened over time to reshape labor law, hoping both to generate demand for their product and to improve the competitive conditions of their industry. Temporary-placement companies had existed since the early twentieth century but only after World War II, George Gonos (1997) argues, did the THS industry emerge, spearheaded by Manpower, Inc., and the National Association of Temporary Services (NATS). The THS industry lobbied and worked through state and federal courts to become legal employers of temporary workers and to embed itself deeply in the contemporary employment relationship.[21] This accomplishment had two profound implications: it meant that the temporary agency, rather than the hiring company, became the employer of record, so that firms rid themselves of legal obligations to a subset of their workers. Given that managers in hiring firms did not actually have to fire temps themselves, given that they could simply inform agencies if they didn't want certain temps to return or if they needed a fresh supply of temps, the corporate world gained great latitude over their use of labor. The new temporary-help formula "became a key mechanism for the dramatic restructuring of employment relations that began in the 1970s, that is, for the break-up of...the New Deal model of industrial relations" (Gonos 1997, 86).

Changes from other quarters of the legal system fueled the efforts of the industry. For example, with the rise of litigation over wrongful termination in the second half of the twentieth century, employers became less willing to enter into permanent employment contracts with workers (Autor 2003).[22] At-will employment—the un-limited discretion that an employer *or* an employee has to terminate the employment relationship at any time—has been eroded, since employees have successfully sued companies when they are termi-nated. By hiring temporary workers whom they can scrutinize and "test" for permanent hire, client firms are "contracting around the risks" in Autor's terms (2003, 7). If they decide that a temp will not be acceptable as a regular worker, the client firm incurs no liability when it declines to invite the worker to return to the job or refuses to hire the temp for a regular position.

Autor makes the dramatic claim that changes to the at-will employ-ment doctrine—the "try before you buy" practice (Peck and Theodore 2002, 169)—over the last several decades accounts for 20 percent of the growth of employment in temporary-help services and that as of the year 2000 it had accounted for 365,000–530,000 additional workers employed in THS on a daily basis (2003, 3). In striking ways, the burden and cost of at-will employment has simply been shifted from the hiring firm to the temporary-placement agency, a policy shift embodied in temp-to-perm programs that the THS industry has been all too willing to exploit and manipulate. With such programs, companies hire temps for a probationary period and then transition, or convert, them into permanent workers (Smith 1998).

Changing Compensation Practices

The THS industry gained further traction by dismantling the fee-splitting system that was widely used up through the mid-twentieth century. Gonos's analysis of the demise of fee splitting and the in-troduction of the markup system touches on a pivotal point in the transition to nonstandard employment relations. Under the earlier fee-splitting system, each placement that an agency made generated a one-time-only fee, paid by the worker herself, which would be split between the agency and the hiring firm. The markup, in contrast, was the "secretive" practice by which a hiring company, in negotia-tion with the temp agency, agreed to pay temps an hourly wage, plus a certain amount per hour which went to the agency and constituted the agency's profits. The markup system allowed agencies to mask the degree to which they were profiting from temp placement. The client firm paid the fee directly to the temp agency rather than to the temp worker, leaving the latter out of this primary transaction. Furthermore, agencies were not required to post or report their markup schedules to temps (Gonos 2000–2001, 2001).

The hourly markup system also provided the underpinnings for what we now think of as permatemps: temporary workers who work in single positions for a long period of time. Because agencies continually profit from the temps' labor (agencies are now compensated for every hour that a temp works, not just the initial hire), agencies have no reason to move temps around from job to job. Neither the agency nor the hiring firm could profit from routinely letting go of temps and bringing in new ones.

Unanswered Questions

To a large degree, scholars have demonstrated, temporary help service agencies have stabilized the regulatory and the institutional environment for their product.[23] But two issues remain understated and unproblematized. First, throughout the period that Ofstead, Gonos, and Autor discuss, what was changing at the broader cultural level—the level of business norms, ideals, and philosophies—that would have eased the fears and doubts of business managers about temporary workers? How did employers come collectively to grasp and trust that the temp was no longer simply a stopgap measure and that using a temporary workforce was a reliable staffing strategy? To be sure, agency representatives could try to sell temporary workers to managers at hiring companies by meeting with them and talking about the "temporary advantage." But spot visits, we would expect, would be effective only if they took place in an environment in which ideas and values about employment were shifting and pervading business culture as well.

Second, how does the THS agency work to stabilize its supply of good temporary workers? Gonos's important research, side by side with Ofstead's work, shows how an industry continually and systematically pressed for industry advantage, created demand for its product, and constructed one of the most important labor market practices of the contemporary economy. Once the THS industry had created more suitable market and legal conditions for the new temporary employment relationship, however, where was it to find the reliable temporary workers on whom the success of the industry depended?

Both Ofstead's and Gonos's work suggests an important problem facing the THS industry. Given that THS agencies must compete with other agencies to survive (as does any enterprise in a capitalist market economy), they must manufacture a steady supply of their product. Moreover, an agency must market a competitive product, one that gives hiring firms clear reasons to use *its* temporary workers. These competitive dynamics give THS firms a strong incentive to manufacture a quality product: a steady supply of good temps. They are selling able-minded and able-bodied individuals, to be sure, but they are also selling their own ability to deliver a pool of temporary laborers, temps-in-waiting.

Part of the answer to the question of where temporary workers come from lies in the changing nature of the contemporary economy. Although a fair number of people choose to work in temporary positions because they want to, more and more workers in the United States have no choice but to use temp agencies because they have either been displaced or are unable to find permanent jobs. The majority of those who hold temporary jobs would prefer to have permanent jobs, but in an era when permanent jobs are in short supply and when many jobs repel workers because they pay only minimum or low wages, a temporary position in a decent company can look attractive.[24] It doesn't take much in the way of sophisticated advertising or false rhetoric to establish the appeal of temporary employment, and having an agency that seems to be working for *you* can feel like a positive buffer from the worst of the job market.

Even Richard Bolles, the guru of job hunting and author of the best seller *What Color Is Your Parachute?*—the leading advice manual for people who want to find their dream jobs—acknowledges the nature of the changing economy, advising his readers, "If you are having trouble finding a long-term, full-time job, you certainly want to go register at one or more of these [temp] agencies" (2007, 199). It seems that Americans have taken this advice to heart: the American Staffing Association claims that, according to a survey they contracted, over three-quarters of staffing employees in 2006 saw temporary and contract work as a path to a permanent job and believed that their temporary positions enabled them to gain new skills and expertise; almost 60 percent of them said they believed that a temporary job would help them get a foot on the bottom rung of a permanent career ladder (American Staffing Association 2006b, fig. 5).

In this sense, agencies clearly can play on workers' insecurity when they search for new recruits, and unquestionably, there is considerable structural pressure on workers today to seek out the services of temporary help agencies. This pressure—coupled with the fact that throughout the twentieth century the THS industry actively worked for legitimacy and a hospitable legal environment for the agencies' services and products—has been well established in the vast literature on temporary employment. But still missing is a picture of the active work in which agencies engage to recruit a particular type of temp and maintain a stable, ongoing workforce of good temps. Understanding this requires a detailed explanation of what drives competition in the temporary help service industry.

Understanding Competition and Profitmaking in the THS Industry

Temporary help service firms earn their profits in a variety of ways. They sell their expertise and ability to assist with human resource administration, recruiting, screening, hiring, placing, monitoring, and firing temporary workers (Pfeffer and Baron 1988; Smith 1997; Vosko 2000); take over payroll management (temps are on the agencies' payroll, not the hiring company's payroll); set up on-site offices from which they interact with and oversee temps ("vendor on premises" arrangements: Benner 2002; Vosko 2000); and engage in secondary sourcing, wherein agencies contract with other agencies who can provide a back-up supply of temporary workers in times of high demand (Benner 2002). Requiring little capital to establish an office (Moore 1965, 564), and with franchise ownership making entry fairly easy, this industrial field has been wide open for expansion along these lines.

Fundamentally, THS firms can compete on quantitative terms *and* on qualitative terms. Quantitatively, they can offer smaller markups than those of their competitors. If an agency fills an order for a high volume of temps or for temps who will work on a long-term basis, it may agree to lower its markup rate (Gonos 2000–2001); however, this is a risky strategy because the markup is a lucrative source of profitability for the agency. Barley and Kunda (2004, 73) note that agencies that place high-level contract workers will often allow their contractors to bargain down the percentage of the markup that goes to the agency, thus increasing the percentage that goes to the contractor, but theirs is a unique case because contractors typically have some degree of leverage over the agency; they have skills that are specialized, scarce, and in high demand. Keeping a coterie of contractors who span a wide range of skills and knowledge bases gives agencies an important competitive edge which losing them can undercut. When agencies primarily deal in the market for temporary workers with general, not specific technical or professional, skills, however, they will be less willing even to discuss the size of the markup, let alone to negotiate it, given temps' minimal leverage.

Qualitatively, agencies have various options for increasing their competitiveness. They can expand the array of services they offer for sale, for one thing. Some have argued that the practice of establishing on-site offices, or "vendors on premise," is one way agencies have gained a lead over their competitors (Benner 2002; Peck and Theodore 1998). When agency representatives can conduct orientations for temps and can coordinate, control, and iron out problems with their temporary workers at the site of work, they bring an advantage to the management of the temporary workforce; in business parlance, they "add value" to the firm. In recent years, agencies have added new services that enhance their marketability: helping companies develop and manage temp-to-perm programs, sending representatives to "spot check" sites as a way of monitoring the work of their temps, and even transporting temps to their work sites (Vosko

2000). Yet these services may prove to be of marginal or debatable dollar value to agencies. To take one example, Vosko believes that agencies dislike the temp-to-perm service because "it has the potential to deplete their supply of high-calibre workers in the short run" (2000, 152).

Agencies can compete with one another by offering these transactions and services, but they can also compete by promising reliable temporary workers. The driving dynamic of the THS industry is the competition among agencies to supply and place temporary workers. Temporary workers are the grist of the THS mill, a field that is dense with agencies all striving to place their product first.[25] Within the industry, THS firms need to differentiate themselves from one another in order to compete on the market, and one way they have done so is to create good temps and work to keep them.[26] This point is latent in much of the extant research, but many studies touch openly on it. Also, agencies have an incentive to offer good services to temporary employees because temps have three (admittedly modest) grounds for leverage, vis-à-vis agencies.

First, temps can register with multiple agencies and ultimately will accept the placement offer of whichever agency best meets their needs and preferences (Gottfried 1991; Rogers 2000). By thus decreasing their dependence on any single agency, they increase interagency competition. Second, any given agency theoretically should "do right" by its own temps: since agencies have been known to raid the best temporary workers from their competitors (Rogers 2000, 109), each agency must be wary about alienating or frustrating its better temporary workers and attentive to the kinds of opportunities it can offer them. Third, temps can walk off the job or refuse to return to a "bad" job, thus draining the agency's pool of reliable workers, not to mention undermining its credibility.

Hiring companies play their own role in pressuring agencies to produce a good pool of temps. They threaten to use the temps of other agencies if they are not satisfied with what they're being given (Benner 2002; Peck and Theodore 1998; Rogers 2000). Companies may demand "good" quality temps because they are concerned with productivity, skills, effort, and motivation (Nollen and Axel 1998, 138). As Peck and Theodore (1998, 660) note, the constant threat that a hiring company might change its primary agency is meaningful because agencies' "profit is derived from giving employers what they want." Further, the success of temporary agencies depends on their quick response time (Moore 1965; Peck and Theodore 1998). To maintain consistency with the raison d'être of temporary employment—that it gives companies a way to rapidly expand their workforce when there is unexpected demand for products—any given agency must be able to fill an order for temps quickly, a strong motivation for having a just-in-time pool of good temporary workers.

What constitutes the ideal type of worker who, in theory, embodies a bundle of characteristics that an agency would want and a hiring company would prefer? Multiple dimensions can come into play in making someone not simply a good worker but a good temporary worker. The first concerns willingness, cooperation, and consent. Successful temporary workers need to understand and accept the terms of temporary employment. When individuals arrive fresh to the world of temporary employment, it is imperative that they are, or become, familiar with the facts of "at-will employment": that there is no job guarantee; that any given stint might be just a few days or just a few weeks; that it might be a dead-end job; that the wage they seek undoubtedly is not the wage they will receive; that a client can dismiss them without advance warning; that flexibility means flexibility for the firm and not for the temp;[27] and that the agency, not the client firm, is their boss.

These terms may be troubling to the individual who is dead set on landing a permanent job. Such an individual, with the predictable resentment, anxiety, and possible confusion about having to accept temporary employment, very likely would be a difficult person to place and keep on the job, for future temps need to accept the high odds against their being converted from temporary to permanent work. Typically, temps have no guarantee that they will be converted to permanent status and if this liminal status is not acceptable, they might not accept the position. And if they accept the position, the quality of their work performance could be in question.

The second dimension of the good temp has to do with the capacity to labor in a fashion that is minimally competent, responsible, and adaptable. A temp ideally would be able to walk into a variety of situations and get right to work. Materials handling, for example—delivering materials and supplies to different production units in a workplace—might be thought of as requiring primarily physical strength and endurance but in reality, it could entail greater complexity (such as social-relational competencies) than would be obvious on first blush. Language competencies might be essential in such jobs, as might the capacity for teamwork.[28] Individuals with previous experience in an environment characterized by despotic, hierarchical management might be ill equipped to survive in a production setting that stresses participation and initiative. Someone who has worked in a law office may feel qualified for a white-collar work environment but might be very frustrated and resentful at having to work in a back-office, mass-production setting repetitively entering data. And technical skills do not automatically translate into social-relational and other "soft" skills.[29] For these reasons, we might say that a good temp would be minimally multivalent.

Aside from adaptability and capacity, are employers usually looking for temps with particular skills? Typically not in this low-level niche, yet a number of researchers who have interviewed temporary workers find some of them are frustrated because they feel "overqualified" for the positions in which they are placed. One senses an assumption that this mismatch is inexplicable, an oversight by the agency that is injurious to the temp: Why would an individual be sent to an assignment for which he or she was overqualified? The temps, as well as the researchers, however, may be missing the point. The primary commitment of the temporary placement agency isn't to match workers to their ideal jobs; it is to match workers to the company's definition of a suitable temp. Companies that hire temps often don't need specific technical skills; they need more general work habits and aptitudes. Evidence of stable employment experience, no matter whether blue- or white-collar, semiprofessional or assembler, can simply be a proxy for punctuality, cooperativeness, and a positive frame of mind, all of which can matter much more to employers than particular skills. Indeed, this expectation holds true for employers across the board today, not simply for those looking to hire temporary workers. Capelli, in his influential article on the "skills gap," argues that "employers see the most important consideration in hiring and the biggest deficit among workforce entrants as being the attitudes that they bring with them to their jobs" (1995, 110).

THS agencies possess explicit and implicit understandings of ideal-typical good temporary workers, and they face a formidable task in "manufacturing" them, a process that has been taken for granted in previous studies. Researchers who examine temporary work have mentioned the "signifiers" of good temps without asking how they are constructed or acquired. Table 1.1 lists qualities of good temporary workers, typically posited but not explained, which we cull from the foundational studies about temporary workers employed by agencies.[30]

The ghost of the good temp has hovered throughout these studies, its ethereal existence occasionally floating into view but dissipating if one tries to look at it too closely. *The Good Temp* brings this ideal-typical worker out of hiding. It analyzes how the THS industry manufactured the image of good temporary workers over the second half

TABLE 1.1
Characteristics of The Good Temp

Reference	Description
Chun 2001	Needs minimal supervision and/or possesses a self-starter work ethic (134); good at working in teams
Henson 1996	Will save the boss from his or her own errors (153); multitasker, goes beyond the minimum (152); acts like a perm–will "pass" (150); willing to accept long-term assignments, indeed, seeks them out (154)
Parker 1994	Personally flexible (89); trustworthy, dependable, open-minded, willing to get along, outgoing, personable, works well with people (90)
Peck and Theodore 1998	Not too slow (660); not belligerent but compliant (662); does quality work, won't be gone tomorrow, is reliable, committed, and stable (663); can adapt to the culture of different firms (668)
Rogers 2000	Cooperative; flexible about the assignments he or she will accept (75); works even though aware of receiving lower wages; has a proper work ethic; goes over and above the call of duty; works like a "supertemp" (93)
Smith 2001b	Valued, the glue that makes the production unit work (17); part of the team
Vosko 2000	Productive and willing to stick with repetitive work; flexible (175)

of the twentieth century and how agencies create corporeal workers in this image today.

Our Methods

To understand the temporary help industry from a historical perspective, Smith conducted a content analysis of close to 300 articles from personnel and THS industry magazines, taken from a larger database of articles on the industry that were collected for the decades of the 1940s through 1990. This part of our study shows how new ideas about temporary workers and temporary employment developed over time, forming an ideological underpinning to larger structural and legal changes. Appendix I supplies a detailed explanation of how the database was constructed, themes were identified, and articles were coded.

The insider's view of agency life that is at the heart of this book was acquired on the job. Neuwirth was employed full time for four months as a placement specialist at Select Labor (SL), a pseudonym for a for-profit staffing firm in the Silicon Valley.[31] As a participant observer at SL, Neuwirth was trained directly by its branch manager. In her job, she interviewed and placed applicants in temporary jobs, conducted skills training tests with them, worked with managers and human resources specialists in hiring companies, went through SL corporate training seminars, attended industry-relevant workshops and job fairs, and, in general, engaged in all aspects of agency life.[32] She also visited the sites of client firms, interacting with line and human resource managers there, and observing temps on the job.

Our understanding of local labor markets and labor market processes, and of agencies such as SL, is bolstered by an additional four months of participant observation that Neuwirth conducted in 2001 in a nonprofit, labor-supported placement agency, also located in Silicon Valley.[33] She directly interviewed company line and human resources managers about their use of temporary workers, as well as twenty temporary workers who used the services of the nonprofit agency. (A fuller discussion of the nonprofit agency can be found in Neuwirth 2004, 2006.) These interviews round out our analysis of temporary employment. In all, Neuwirth logged approximately 1,400 hours of participant observation and collected massive amounts of industry data for our study.

Neuwirth conducted field work at Select Labor in the year 2000, a time when the high-tech economy of Silicon Valley was hot, robust, and had a considerable amount of churning in the labor market for temporary workers. For understanding the dynamics of temporary employment, the timing was perfect, as it meant that the full range of agency practices and agency-to-firm relationships was in play and observable. Because the labor market in the Valley was tight, however, hiring companies' dependence on the agency may have been greater than normal, giving the latter greater leverage over the former (Houseman, Kalleberg, and Erickcek 2003). Further, a tight labor market may have forced agency representatives to craft more beneficial policies for temps in order to attract them. The "tight labor market" of the Valley was somewhat deceptive, masking a tremendous amount of labor market turmoil and instability (see chapter 3). We weave these issues throughout our discussion of the production, buying, and selling of good temps.

As is common with single, qualitative case studies, there are limits to the degree to which we can generalize about THS agencies today. In this book, we discuss a single agency and a single region— Select Labor in Silicon Valley. Studying single cases doesn't allow systematic comparisons that might have helped us explain patterns in organizational processes. Nor can we claim that the cases are representative. We were driven to do research by theoretical concerns but had to be opportunistic when it came to deciding *where* to do it. Silicon Valley was a likely region because of its geographic proximity; Select Labor was a likely agency because Neuwirth succeeded in finding employment there. Given her extensive fieldwork in the Valley, however, and our reading of the now-voluminous literature on temporary employment, we have a fair degree of confidence that the practices of Select Labor were extremely similar to those of other moderately sized agencies.

One might of course ask whether the case of Silicon Valley is atypical, since it is the heart of the high-tech industry and might be particularly volatile. Yet the temporary labor market there is probably more typical than one would expect. Benner, Leete, and Pastor, for example, comparing labor market intermediaries in Silicon Valley with those in Milwaukee, Wisconsin, concluded that "intermediaries are likely to be just as important throughout U.S. regional labor markets and have their roots in market transitions that transcend regional developments, particular technologies, or volatility per se" (2007, 124).

Select Labor is a midsized private agency that has been in operation for over two decades. With a host of branch offices in California and a corporate office that manages the combined business of the individual branches, this agency, like many others, was rapidly expanding when Neuwirth began her field research. The SL branch office where she worked was among the largest and most profitable of all SL's branches. Its staff of nearly ten comprised a branch manager, sales people, and recruitment/placement specialists. Neuwirth also worked with staff in nearby Select Labor branch offices that specialized in vendor-on-premises arrangements: on-site accounts with hiring firms (there was extensive collaboration between the various SL offices). The majority (approximately 85 percent) of Select Labor's corporate profits was generated by temporary placements, a figure extraordinarily close to the national average for the industry.[34] Select Labor very likely typifies any number of staffing agencies that would be found around the country today; examining its practices and networks gave us great purchase on the making and selling of good temporary workers. Neuwirth's extensive fieldwork and archival research, interviews and observations of temporary workers conducted by Smith in the 1990s (Smith 2001a, 2001b), and content analysis conducted by Smith of personnel magazines across the middle of the twentieth century all combine to provide data about the historical construction and contemporary reproduction of the good temp.

Organization of the Book

Drawing on these multiple data sources, the chapters of the book proceed as follows. Chapter 2 looks at how personnel and THS industry leaders constructed and disseminated the idea of temporary workers as good workers and of temporary employment practices as advantageous to business. Past research takes for granted that temporary employment simply grew on its own, its rise reflecting a shift in the global economy (increased competitiveness, the need for reduced costs, increased flexibility, speedier production, and so forth) and subsequent adjustment of employment relations and labor market institutions. But, we ask, how did such a shift happen, at the level of business culture and ideology? Such dramatic structural and institutional changes rarely occur mechanically but often are produced and inspired by the spread of new ideas about how to manage business organizations.

We track changes in discourse and beliefs about temporary employment by analyzing personnel and business articles published between 1960 and 1990, paying particular attention to the diffusion of new norms in temporary employment and to the rhetorical devices that writers used to normalize and legitimate it. Personnel and temporary help service experts framed temporary work as a necessary trend that could offset and reduce the costs of permanent employment, discussed ways to integrate temps into corporate workplaces, and expanded the definition of who could be a good temporary worker. Changes at this level of rhetoric and discourse were part and parcel—and, indeed, lubricated the way for the rise and intervention—of the temporary help service industry. These normative changes, we argue, were integrally linked to the larger shift in employment culture in the United States.

Chapter 3 shifts to contemporary times and analyzes the strategies used by staff at Select Labor, a successful temporary agency, to manufacture good temps. By the end of the twentieth century, employment relations had changed notably. Given that fact, it is important to look at how these relations are enacted and sustained on the ground, in and between agencies, hiring companies, and temporary workers. Accordingly, we analyze how staff in one agency selectively recruited applicants for their pool of good temps, maintained networks with job development specialists, coached temps to build both their technical and their cultural capital, and realigned temps' aspirations and mobility goals in order to place them effectively. Predictably, not everyone *wanted* to be a good temp: agency staff encountered reluctance (workers resisted taking temporary jobs over permanent jobs; they complained, requested a transfer if they considered a temp job bad, walked off the temp job, and on occasion treated agency personnel contemptuously). Yet the routine and fundamental logic in the agency was to try to maintain a pool of good temporary workers, even if this ideal could not always be realized.

In chapters 4 and 5 we turn our focus from agency staff efforts to build and maintain a good temporary workforce to their interactions with managers in hiring firms. We discuss two types of intervention whereby agency staff engaged to promote and protect temps. They were more likely to succeed in keeping a pool of good temps if they succeeded in rationalizing and stabilizing work at the point of production (the subject of chapter 4). In so doing, they created "good enough" temporary jobs: jobs that, even though they didn't necessarily pay a living wage, were decent, not harmful to one's physical or mental well-being, and rationally rather than capriciously managed.[35] Good temp jobs emerged in the nexus of give-and-take (conflict and cooperation) between agency staff and line managers. Agency staff helped create good temp jobs by reining in overtly destructive management behavior. They also helped craft reasonable job descriptions for temps, conducted job evaluations, made recommendations for workplace safety, advised on wage rates, and taught line managers how to think about the temp-to-perm hire.

Line managers' ability to maintain a hospitable environment for temporary workers was shaped and constrained by a higher level of policymaking. In chapter 5 we move to the higher level and analyze how agency staff attempted to rationalize and gain some control over human resources (HR) management policies. HR managers are critical actors in the implementation, coordination, and stability of temporary hiring systems, and much has been made of the challenges they face in dealing with the massive changes precipitated by temporary employment. Some industry experts have been particularly concerned that HR is "disappearing," rendered obsolete by the externalization of HR management. The chapter enters this debate by analyzing how the introduction of temp agency staff challenged, assisted, and reconfigured HR managers' work.

Line managers and human resources staff in hiring companies, we argue, were hamstrung around the use of temps, giving agency staff considerable leverage. As temporary work is institutionalized (both in structure and in budget practices, cemented by the fact that managers and supervisors often are only authorized to hire temps, or can get authorization to hire temps fairly quickly), managers and supervisors increasingly become dependent on creating desirable temporary jobs. They *have* to care about the retention and the quality of temps. In-house managers and HR personnel often lacked the time and resources to manage their temp workforces and depended on agency representatives to help them do it. Chapter 5 thus links relationships and events at the point of production, and the agency's pursuit of good temporary workers to the practices of human resources managers.

In the final chapter we step back from the historical and contemporary details of how good temporary workers are constructed and maintained to address some of the larger issues swirling around temporary employment. Drawing on the study of Select Labor as well as other studies in the fields of sociology and labor economics, we argue that agencies for temporaries are important for creating *transitional opportunities* for many people. We would be remiss, however, to neglect the downside of temporary jobs, and so we also discuss the disadvantageous aspects of temporary employment for low-paid, low-level temps and for employment relationships across the board. We ask what remedies and solutions might counterbalance some of the worst aspects of temporary employment today.

In particular, we are intrigued by Barley and Kunda's (2004) and Benner, Leete, and Pastor's (2007) suggestions that it could be effective to apply pressure to THS agencies to protect the jobs of temporary workers and make them decent. Barley and Kunda found that high-level contractors (the more privileged of the temporary workforce) have developed a strong sense of good and bad agencies. They flock to the good and try to avoid the bad, circulating information within their occupational community about which agencies to avoid. Such choices on the part of temporary workers may pressure more agencies to follow the high road of temporary employment (such as it is), as workers increasingly utilize agencies that are known for superior practices. Finally, we identify some important topics for future research that could shed greater light on the historical and contemporary manufacture of good temporary workers.

Labor markets represent the energetic efforts of employers and states to organize work and employment. Understanding the historical conditions under which these efforts take place is important because it allows us to see how we might create and support markets that advantage workers and fight market arrangements that disadvantage them. Accepting employment systems and labor markets as inevitable can trap us in a pessimistic view in which workers around the world are consigned to accepting low-wage jobs, jobs that lack security and benefits, that are dangerous, and do not afford dignity. Instead, we'd like to think about ways to create greater opportunities for and extend a sense of agency to people, both as individual workers and as a collective movement. Much as labor markets of the vast part of the twentieth century were constructed within the nexus of power, inequality, and social change, so too are the insecure, temporary labor markets of today historical constructions that can be critically analyzed and targeted for social change.

Chapter Two

The Social Construction of New Markets and Products

We may find business more willing to buy people's services
for near-term duration. The application of temporary help on
a project basis has yet to be accepted by business, but there
are signs that such acceptance might be realized by the end of
the decade.

Guy Millner, President, Norrell Services and National
Association for Temporary Services, 1972

In the mid-twentieth century the temporary help service industry succeeded in recasting temporary employment from a marginal
to a normative practice. But, as argued in chapter 1 institutional
and legal market-making activities can't fully explain this success.
Rather, industry writers disseminated novel views of temporary and
permanent employment as part of an effort to promote the new market paradigm. In articles published in personnel and business magazines, these writers attempted to shape the terms of a new labor
market and persuade readers of the value of their new product by
reiterating five key issues: (1) how new THS industry practices differed from traditional practices, (2) the "true" and "hidden" costs
of permanent labor, (3) templates for using temps and agencies efficiently, (4) finding out who has the capacity to be good temporary
workers, and (5) identifying new occupations, industries, and task
niches where temporary workers could be used. Taken together,

these articles portrayed temporary workers as legitimate, reasonably qualified, even desirable employees.

We have analyzed archival data to document changing personnel doctrine about temporary and permanent employment systems. By conducting a content analysis of several hundred articles in personnel and other industry magazines published between 1960 and 1990, we document the rise of the "staffing" paradigm. This new outlook called attention to the benefits of jobs organized on a temporary basis and of good temporary workers, while criticizing the "traditional" model of employment based on full-time, permanent jobs and workers. Tilly and Tilly (1994) argue that capitalists purposely create new labor markets by emphasizing new norms and values. In this spirit we show how the normative construction of the new paradigm on the part of personnel and THS professionals was an integral part of shaping a new labor market for temporary jobs and temporary workers. This discourse sets the stage for chapters 3–5, where we look at agency practices on the ground and examine how agency staff actually sustain this unique employment relationship.

Many who study historical transformations at work, whether of management theories and ideologies (Barley and Kunda 1992; Bendix 1956), internal labor markets (Dobbin et al. 1993), legal edicts (Edelman, Fuller, and Mara-Drita 2001), or "fashions" such as quality circles (Abrahamson 1996), argue that the diffusion of new ideas throughout the business world provides important indicators of employment change. Rhetorics—discourses that reflect beliefs and theories about how things can or should be done, how they can or should look, or what values should prevail—invite analysis because they "provide both the locale (or venue) and the rationale for trends in organizational management (and) usually precede or develop along with the implementation of ideas by firms" (Edelman, Fuller, and Mara-Drita 2001, 1592). Professional personnel journals in particular have contributed to the diffusion of new ideas, but they also "provide documentation of their evolution" (Edelman 1990, 1410), with personnel professionals being the "engine" driving the diffusion of new ideas about management and employee governance throughout the twentieth century.

We cannot claim that the rise of a new doctrine in personnel publications actually caused employers to start using temps on a widespread basis. Rather, we suggest that the new doctrine slowly contributed to a hospitable business environment for the new practice. Authors of these articles showed how using temps could be safe and provided formulas for using them, thus demystifying the practice. Tempting though it may be to try, new managerial rhetorics cannot be singled out as either causing or resulting from workplace practices; rather, they are both the harbingers and the footprints of social change.

Managerial rhetorics are promulgated through a variety of sources. The "media" (Edelman, Fuller, and Mara-Drita 2001, 1601) of management rhetoric consist of professional and industry periodicals, meetings, workshops, and, in contemporary times, Internet Listservs. Bendix's classic *Work and Authority in Industry* (1956), for example, drew on one arm of the management media—personnel magazines and mass-market books that popularized management practices—to analyze ideologies about the use of authority in business enterprises. Such publications provide a venue for promoting new ideas about managing people, organizing work, using technology, restructuring organizations, implementing legislation, building worker commitment, and otherwise achieving organizational goals.

Personnel writers use a variety of strategies to promote new doctrines. In order to increase the competitiveness of their ideas, they may emphasize the failure of previous models of management or organizational structure. They may highlight examples of successful cases in which new techniques or approaches have yielded positive effects: specifically, increased organizational efficiency and profit (Edelman, Fuller, and Mara-Drita 2001, 1601). Abrahamson (1996) additionally notes that these "fashion setters" will highlight "performance gaps" that organizations typically experience; managers are urged to use new practices or approaches to close those gaps. One way to persuade business managers, Abrahamson argues, is to frighten them, threatening "managerial demise" if they ignore the gap and the proposed solution (1996, 268). Those trying to introduce new ideas may use "mythical statistics" (Smith 2001a)—memorable, quantified sound bites repeated and circulated until they gain the status of undisputed fact. In general, fashion setters' rhetoric will succeed when it convinces managers that incorporating a given idea into everyday practice will help the business organization progress toward rational business goals.

Personnel industry journals and business journals that published articles on personnel management proved to be an excellent source of data for understanding the diffusion of new ways of thinking about temporary labor and temporary workers. Articles in these magazines reveal that personnel and THS leaders targeted the costs of traditional workplace organization, proposed new formulas and templates for organizing workplaces, challenged deeply held assumptions about permanent employment relationships, and identified new labor market practices. The pages of these journals constituted a domain of ideas and the makings of a business culture wherein the THS industry endeavored to promote its product, the good temp, and to build a market for that product's consumption. The advice in these articles made it possible, we argue, for employers to rethink their most fundamental hiring practices.

We analyzed 263 articles on temporary employment (found through a search of articles listed in the Business Periodicals Index, originally the Industrial Arts Index) from the 1960s, 1970s, and 1980s. Appendix I provides a methodological discussion of this database and the content analysis. Thematic coding of these articles shows that the THS and personnel industries went for the hard sell, undertaking a major educational campaign to persuade managers to use temporary workers and to convince them of the good quality of those workers. The sales pitch grew over those decades, from 46 articles published in the 1960s to 160 articles in the 1980s (see Appendix I, figures 1 and 2); further, 185, or 70 percent, of the total 263 articles we coded, addressed one or more of the five topics listed above, usually emphasizing several at once.

The Industry Distanced Itself from Previous Practices and Embraced the New

How did the personnel and THS industries begin the national rhetorical conversation about its changes and its new goals? At the commencement of this three-decade period many articles explained how "new" temporary employment compared to the traditional (immediate postwar) variety and spoke broadly to readers of how industry strategies were changing. Writers of these articles often adopted a self-reflective and self-critical tone, scrutinizing THS market practices and suggesting that the industry had the capacity to reform itself. They reassured readers that the industry was rationalizing and stream-lining and used new taxonomies about its history to prove the point. Ultimately aided by the proliferation of personnel magazines in the 1970s and '80s, leaders of the THS industry had ample opportunity to spread the word.[1] Indeed, 35 percent ($N = 64$ of 185) of the articles on these five themes were written by THS industry leaders, includ-ing presidents of for-profit firms such as Kelly Services, Manpower, and Norrell Services, and presidents of THS industry professional as-sociations, such as the National Association of Temporary Services (NATS).[2] In addition, industry leaders were regularly featured in and interviewed for articles on the industry.

To take one example, Nathan Picker, president of a temporary firm called Echelons, noted in *Office* in 1963 that the temporary industry was becoming big business. Interviewed for "Supplying Tested and Rated Temporary Office Help," Picker reflected on how his company was experiencing growing pains, systematizing its practices, and changing its market goals: "We reorganized our methods from top to bottom, and that took a great deal of time, effort, and money. We changed our name from Office Temporaries, Inc. to Echelons, and we had to educate our various publics about a revolutionary new con-cept."[3] Reinforcing a view that his was an industry capable of adapta-tion, improvement, and innovation, he emphasized:

> The key to success in the temporary field is the use of a quality standard to accomplish two things....First, we must attract and test qualified applicants; second, we must provide employers with specific information on how to order the people they need. The spectacular growth of the industry in a relatively short time has created many problems and a great deal of confusion, but we be-lieve we have found the solution....In the past, too much depended on interpretation. What one man considered a typist, another con-sidered a secretary. *Our method allows virtually no margin for error.* (*Office*, March 1963, 104, 108; emphasis added)

As part of this image transformation, many writers went to great lengths to distinguish how new ways of using temps differed from traditional ways. Offering a historical taxonomy to the business community, two authors—one, a director of marketing at Kelly Services; the other, a president of Western Temporaries—wrote, in separate articles, about the "third revolution" in the THS industry. In the immediate postwar period or first generation of the industry, they pointed out, temporary workers were used to cover for absent regular employees or in emergency situations; this is what we have been calling the traditional or stopgap paradigm. In second-generation deployment, according to personnel and THS experts, managers realized that they could lower their operating and production costs by using temporaries to supplement their regular workforces. In this early articulation of the staffing paradigm, cost-conscious personnel administrators were urged to use temps to avoid overstaffing their firms. In the third generation, both writers claimed, the industry began to diversify, sending temporaries into new occupations and industries, developing new services (such as payroll), or helping firms find workers who would start as temps and move on to permanent status (*Management Review*, December 1974; *Office*, December 1974). A writer in *Administrative Management* (May 1974) agreed with the concept of three waves in the industry, likewise referring to the "third revolution" in temporary help.

Indeed, the staffing paradigm was articulated as early as 1958, when one writer bragged about the benefits of using temporary workers to deal with unexpected orders and unpredictable surges in demand (*Dun's Review and Modern Industry*, September 1958). Other business articles asserted that companies should hire temporary workers in order to cut the costs of recruiting, interviewing, and training; to lower the risk of making a bad permanent placement; to avoid payment of fringe benefits; and to eliminate unnecessary direct costs for labor when a job was done (*Office*, September 1962).

Typologizing the history in a somewhat different way, a president of NATS and of Tempositions (a THS firm) applauded the contemporary (late 1960s) rise of a "second generation of instant people." He summarized the shifting paradigm in the following way:

The use of temporaries has moved far beyond merely throwing them into the breach in emergency situations. Management and the temporary personnel contractors have developed a broad spectrum of services that temporaries can perform more efficiently and more economically. Instead of waiting for emergencies to develop, temporaries are used on a *planned* basis. The entire temporary personnel industry is moving into its second generation. (*Office*, January 1967, 92; emphasis added)

In self-conscious efforts to effect an image change, writers deliberately evoked "old-fashioned" symbols of temporary employment and workers, juxtaposing them against emergent, modern realities of the industry. Nineteen percent (N = 35) of the articles addressing our themes contrasted new THS industry practices with the traditional Kelly Girl/clerical work model. Industry leaders had to convince client firms and the business public that new uses and new efficiencies were possible. Helga Tarver, president of a THS professional association as well as the private-sector Tele Sec Temporary Personnel, Inc., was clearly aiming to do so in her article "Understanding Temporary Help." In directing her comments to employers, customers who might purchase her firm's temporary services, Tarver attempted to demystify the contemporary goals of the industry, which was so visibly expanding, and gain the goodwill of future customers by assuring them that the THS industry had truly changed:

> Our function is widely misunderstood, perhaps because we gained broad experience so quickly. Perhaps it is because in our formative years we were frequently "desk space" in a regular employment agency. Perhaps it is because there are still marginal one-desk operators who jumble public stenography, duplicating, employment functions, and temporary personnel services together and confuse the picture. (*Office*, January 1969, 95)

Her points suggest that not only had temporary *work* changed, but that the industry was changing its practices, as well, by modernizing, separating itself from employment agencies more broadly, and establishing its own market niche. But some emphasized that the THS industry had to actively bring this modernizing message to managers.

Guy Millner of Norrell Services tackled this issue directly by saying, "The leadership within the temporary help industry itself will need to take a more active role. The industry has a rather low profile and, before acceptance of a business service can be accomplished, much greater education is needed by our buying public" (*Office*, December 1972, 41).

Fortune magazine was another important voice in the promotional efforts of the THS industry, introducing an article on how temps were being used all across the occupational spectrum with an image from the past:

> Not so long ago, the typical temporary-help agency was a modest local operation dispatching a handful of typists and stenographers out of a small, back-floor office. Today the purveying of temporary help has developed into a booming industry, with the leading firms running networks of offices throughout the country and offering scores of job skills. (*Fortune*, October 1968, 164)

The contrast continued to be made on into the 1980s: Mike Kutka, regional manager of Temporaries, Inc., wrote, "Gone are the days when temporary employees were looked upon as a stopgap measure, and the prevailing attitude was 'If they can answer the phone and don't touch anything else, fine!'" (*Management World*, September 1980a, 10). His comment distances his industry from two images: first, that temp workers were too untrustworthy to do anything but the simplest tasks; second, that temps were brought in for just a very short time, used only on a stopgap basis.

Mirroring the claim that temporary help services were keeping up with corporate and business changes occurring in the national and global economy, one author wrote to dispel any notion that the industry was just dumping warm bodies on the market without regard to the quality of its product or to the needs of the customer. In "The New Economics of Temporary Personnel," readers learned that

> competition among temporary services has never centered much on price—most services charge about the same. Rather it is the

quality of the temporaries, the selectivity of the service, the responsiveness to the customer that are the competitive features. And as offices continue to grow in sophistication and complexity, temporary personnel services are following right along. (*Administrative Management*, May 1974, 21)

Charles Sigrist, president of Stivers Lifesavers, confidently observed that his industry had changed qualitatively and had developed a fully normalized industrial niche in American business. He, too, contrasted the quaint practices of the past with the updated, competitive techniques of the industry in the early 1970s.

I believe the client [today] has a complete understanding of the value of a temporary. This, of course, was not so back in 1945 when Clifford L. Stivers founded our firm. At that time, he had to sell the idea of using temporary office help because of cost, etc. Today, it is not a question of convincing the client to use temporary office help, but convincing him to use us rather than our competitors. (*Office*, December 1972, 42)

Even earlier, in the 1960s, that the temporary help industry was modernizing and rationalizing its practices was a cornerstone of the sales pitch. Leaders of the industry went to lengths to announce that they were not simply "body shops" but innovators at the cutting edge of personnel methods and techniques. Among other things, some writers "apologized" for what might look like an inhumane aspect of the "new" temporary employment and took pains to distance the THS industry from an image that seemed self-serving or unfair to workers.

Barron's National Business and Financial Weekly, for example, in an article titled "More Warm Bodies" (December 17, 1962, 3), noted that the growth of contract or temporary work was morphing into a different phenomenon in the 1960s. In discussing the proliferation of this reinvented employment practice, the article tried to downplay the deleterious connotations of widespread temporary employment, admitting that "at first glance, to be sure, dealing in people seems a little barbarous, especially since those in the trade habitually speak of the workers they represent as warm bodies, or even more outrageously, as 'skins'."

To rebut such a view, Tom Graham, vice president of sales for Kelly Girls, was interviewed for the same article as an expert about this possible abuse. Graham's words serve to neutralize the exploitive, warm-body perspective by going to the heart of what it was that the THS industry was selling. The industry was not about exploiting people, according to Graham; it was about developing an excellent new product that was flooding the market like most other goods and services: "Even though we are dealing in human beings, our business essentially is no different from any other with a product to sell.... The outfit which markets the best item for the price will get the business."

Industry practice was not to place bodies randomly, according to the experts, but to eliminate guesswork and fuzziness in the way firms hired temporary workers. Belief in this industry asset had crystallized by the late 1980s, as exemplified in the comments of Mitchell Fromstein, the president of Manpower. For an article about employers' potential anxiety about using THS firms, Fromstein was interviewed about the personnel tests that Manpower commonly used to screen applicants for temporary jobs. His rhetoric represents a blend of the alleged benefits of scientific analysis, the power to control outcomes, and the industry's concern with its high-quality product:

> Before these tests we couldn't tell whether or not a temporary person could fill capsules on a drug-company assembly line or whether the person had the desire to fill capsules.... Yet, ability and desire are the two keys to productivity.... Our objective is to take what is viewed as a commodity (an unskilled worker), bring sophistication to the selection process, and deliver a premium product. In the process we will be able to deliver more value for the cost. (*Industry Week*, March 21, 1988, 20–21)

Throughout these efforts to change its image, authors emphasized that the THS industry had quality control mechanisms in place and that they were not hiring just any old person to work as a temporary. This, too, appeared to distance the industry from the warm-body or mindless stopgap paradigm of temporary employment. Numerous articles focus on these quality-control mechanisms, which included testing (technical, aptitude, and personality), work incentives (such as bonuses and benefits), and training.

Striving to convince the public that the THS industry could rationalize the temporary help employment system, that it was modern and forward looking, and that it was concerned with the quality of its product underpinned a major effort to sell the new paradigm and the new commodity, good temporary help.

Revealing the "True" or "Hidden" Cost of Labor

Aside from making bold and sweeping announcements about industry progress and sophistication, how precisely did the personnel and THS industry go about selling a new product and new paradigm? One way was to uncover and attack the real, the true, and the hidden cost of permanent labor. Permanent workers—those who had a steady employment relationship with a firm, whose jobs were secure, who worked full time and might well work for the same firm for a lifetime—were increasingly framed by proponents of temporary workers as a drag on company efficiency and profits. Writers insinuated that permanent workforces were destined for obsolescence, in general terms as well as for very particular reasons. This element of the new discourse about employment called on American managers to shift their thinking about the "right" size of their workforces, why and when they needed workers, and the consequences of having too many workers on their payrolls when business was slow or demand declined.[4] As Richard Essey, president of the Association of Temporary Personnel Contractors and of the for-profit firm Tempositions, wrote in 1967: "Profits can be siphoned off remarkably fast by having too many people. With availability of temporaries, management can keep the permanent staff under projected requirements, and complement them with temps. As the workload is analyzed, temps can be cut back or permanent staff expanded for good balance between work volume and payroll" (*Office*, January 1967, 173).

In the quest to disparage permanent workers and convince managers that they needed to fine-tune the size of their workforces, writers in personnel magazines—independent business writers and industry leaders alike—developed a full-scale economic analysis of the price tag of large permanent workforces. Breaking down the cost of employment into fine-grained categories, they often used mythical statistics that, in retrospect, seem to defy reasonable calculation. The pages of these magazines provided a micro-accounting of every dimension of company workforces and alerted managers and owners to the costs of labor by stressing (1) the costs of administering the employment relationship, (2) the financial costs of having more people on the payroll than necessary, (3) the burden of having to pay extra-wage compensation (fringe benefits), and (4) the behavioral and attitudinal costs associated with permanent, full-time workers.

First, many articles broke out the administrative costs incurred by the employment relationship itself. Authors routinely reminded readers of the not-always-visible expense of recruiting and advertising, interviewing, hiring, training, monitoring, and terminating regular workers, as well as of the voluminous record keeping required by all these activities. As companies were experiencing fluctuations in demand, trying to adjust to ebbs and flows in their workloads, and simultaneously experiencing a squeeze on their profits, personnel and THS writers were hunting down every source of an expense related to labor, examining it under a microscope, and questioning its dispensability.[5] Elmer Winter, the cofounder of Manpower and its president for many years, provided a precise formula that hinted at the cumbersome aspects and the costliness of hiring regular employees. His day-by-day breakdown strongly justified his commercial efforts to scientize the recruitment, hiring process, and sale of his product, temporary labor. According to Winter, in "The Flexible Work Force: A New Concept for Cost Control," if one took an "X-ray look" at hiring, one would find this:

1st Day: Decision made to hire. Recruiting ad prepared and placed in newspaper.
3rd Day: Initial interviewing of applicants, including administration of tests.

6th Day: References checked.

9th Day: Second round of interviews with applicants.

12th Day: Evaluation of tests and comparison of applicants.

15th Day: Selection of best-qualified applicant.

18th Day: Final interview with applicant and completion of
   paperwork to place applicant on payroll.

21st Day: Applicant begins work.

And, Winter added, "during this three-week period, the employer is subjected to a number of risks": applicant may withdraw from process or in fact turn out to be unsuitable; companies needing work finished now may not have the luxury of waiting three weeks to fill a position (*Best's Review*, September 1972, 96).

In case those complexities were not obvious, other commentators further broke into discrete categories the costs of keeping workers on the company payroll. A variety of articles in the 1960s and 1970s earmarked the following documentation and record keeping deemed necessary to hire and manage a permanent employee: preparation of the initial employment form, keeping earnings records, calculating and preparing paychecks, preparing W-2 forms for the government, completing quarterly government forms, maintaining Social Security and worker's compensation forms, and (perhaps eventually) severance paperwork. Moreover, employers were mandated by law to keep all employee records for six years after an individual left a firm or was terminated, according to an article in *Personnel Journal* (March 1989, 40). Noteworthy here is not that employing people on a permanent basis required so much paperwork—this is a well-known aspect of personnel management—but that authors so frequently singled out each dimension of employment paperwork as a tactical device to delegitimize the permanent employment relationship.

Second, many articles criticized the high cost of carrying an unnecessarily large permanent workforce when business was lax. From the 1960s through the 1980s, personnel writers outlined a model of the lean-and-mean payroll, urging managers to calculate the minimum number of employees needed to get basic work done. Having more than that minimum on the permanent payroll, writers warned, led to a surplus of staff that just cut into company profitability. Too many permanent workers were unpractical and uneconomical, and managers needed to be more conscious of cost control.

As early as 1963, Nathan Picker, the president of Echelons, articulated the incipient core-periphery framework that had become normalized in labor market practices by the 1990s. In making a claim that the THS industry increasingly had to focus on providing quality temporary workers, he explained the institutional explanation underlying this focus.

> The [temporary] jobs will be available...but more than ever before emphasis will be placed on quality of performance. Management is faced with increasing overhead costs and a growing squeeze on profits which demands that they examine every phase of their operations to eliminate deadwood and increase efficiency. This is difficult, because reduction of staff inevitably means that there will be times when permanent employees have more work than they can handle. It is here that temporary help offers the solution. The job gets done without the cost of adding permanent employees. (*Office*, March 1963, 104)

Amplifying this point, "Efficient Use of Temporaries May Be Key to Future Staffing," published in 1972, suggested that having too many permanent workers on payroll contributed to the "real" cost of labor to which managers had heretofore turned a blind eye. Elaborate cost breakdowns, the president of a THS firm believed, would help managers see the real cost of a [permanent] employee and consequently lead them to more finely tune their workforces (*Office*, December 1972, 40).

Industry leaders pointed to the ways in which overstaffing could lead to unanticipated negative consequences. For example, W. Robert Stover, president and founder of Western Temporary Services, argued that when companies had workforces that were too large, they most likely would have to lay off their permanent workers during economic downturns and incur high unemployment benefits costs. He assembled the pieces of this particular puzzle in the following way:

> Temporaries can be used during periods of uncertainty. Overcommitting a company or department to additional permanent

employees when the outlook is unclear may result in high unemployment costs in the event that layoffs have to be made. As
companies become increasingly cost-conscious, policies restricting
additions to the payroll are beginning to appear more and more frequently. When a regular employee leaves, rather than automatically
finding a permanent replacement, the company brings in a temporary employee while a study is made to see whether a replacement
is really necessary. When business is expanding, the same approach
can be used. If new openings are staffed with temporary employees, workloads can be rearranged and other adjustments explored
before a permanent commitment is made to increase the regular
staff. During the process, a close watch can be maintained on earnings and production levels, and reasonable work standards can be
determined. (*Management Review*, December 1974, 22)

Third, across time, industry leaders and personnel industry experts
emphasized employers' increasing burden of paying permanent workers' fringe benefits, including pensions, health benefits, paid vacations,
sick leave, profit-sharing bonuses—even paid breaks and lunch hours.
A number of articles estimated that employers spent 30 to 40 percent
over and above the wages of each permanent worker on "fringes." In
1965 the author of an article called "Renting People Is Good Business" cited the finding of a 1964 survey that the "hidden costs of
labor [fringe benefits] were 33.8% of the base salary" of a regular employee (*Credit and Financial Management*, February 1965, 12).

Business Week, noting the rising cost of "fringes," claimed that
in 1978 the average nonmanufacturing employee earned "nearly
40% on top of wages for fringe benefits" (October 6, 1980, 98). By the
1980s the ballpark figure of 40 percent wavered only slightly from
article to article. A U.S. Chamber of Commerce study cited in *Office Administration and Automation* (August 1984, 49) claimed a
"40–42% hidden cost in every permanent worker's salary" (including the cost of hiring, downtime, benefits, payroll taxes); in another
issue of this journal, "Making the Most of Temporary Help" claimed
that these hidden costs were "37%" precisely (August 1985, 34); *Modern Office Technology* gave a slightly wider range of 30–40 percent
(March 1985, 94). These statistical "facts" led one author to decry

the sobering increase in fringe benefits and assert that "there's little wonder some companies are analyzing their tables of organization, department by department, and planning cutbacks to streamline the permanent workforce wherever they can without impairing operations" (*Industry Week*, January 13, 1975, 43).

Finally, the permanent job itself was assumed by experts to generate significant but usually unexamined costs and risks to the firm by creating attitudes and behaviors that were expensive and counterproductive. Emergent in these articles was what Dobbin et al. (1993, 400) might term a "new managerial conception of worker/individual," which called into question whether any person working a full-time, permanent job could be productive and efficient every working hour. Articles reminiscent of Frederick Taylor's worry that workers had a natural disinclination to work efficiently seemed to say that a person with a permanent job would inevitably experience boredom, lack of challenge, and complacency (all of which would lead to labor inefficiencies), a claim that was asserted as if there were something inherently deadening about all full-time jobs or as if the equation of full-time work with lack of productivity reflected a well-known fact about human nature. Personnel writers argued that there was a predictable amount of downtime for any full-time permanent worker in any job; employers who relied exclusively on such a workforce would pay for a great deal of unproductive labor. They exhorted managers to stop paying a full-time wage to a worker who was in reality working only part time: "Are you paying a full-time salary for a part-time job? There's a good chance that you are. Studies have shown that many companies have employees, mostly clerical workers, who are actually busy only 10 or 12 days a month" (*Purchasing*, March 11, 1963, 119).

One article reported that a "recent study by one of the top 10 CPA firms [the firm is unnamed] suggested that employers were getting only about 50% effective work results from their [regular] employees" (*Office*, January 1975, 82). The prolific Elmer Winter shored up his sales pitch about temporary help by referring to "published surveys" (unspecified) showing "that as much as 80% of the [permanent] American workforce doesn't give a damn about their work." According to Winter, "Tardiness, extended coffee breaks, boredom with repetitive jobs, and declining productivity at the end of the day have cut into work output [for permanent workers] dramatically" (*Best's Review,* August 1974, 82).

Elsewhere, Winter cited a study (conducted by the Serge Brin Co.) which purported to find that regular employees were not much more than 50 percent productive, that they "spent 20 hours at work in a conventional 37.5 hour week." Many companies, he lamented, were "experiencing the 4-day week syndrome unknowingly as the weekend stretches to include a no-work day on either Monday or Friday" (*Administrative Management,* November 1970, 25). Guy Millner, president of NATS and of Norrell Services, supported the spirit of Winter's claim, himself pointing to Bureau of Labor data that purportedly showed that temporary workers were productive "80–90% of the time," whereas full-time workers were productive only "65–70% of the time" (*Management World,* June-August 1987, 8)—two statistics later repeated in *Personnel Journal* (October 1989, 10) and *Office Administration and Automation* (August 1984, 49).

Concerns with the cost of unproductive time appeared in narrative form in one article on "manpower leasing," which identified many different ways that temps could be used. The following scenario nicely captures the precision with which personnel managers were thinking about the tiny increments of time potentially lost when using permanent employees and striving to whittle down the amount of underutilized time to the extent possible. Using an example of one temporary employment arrangement, the author described its successful implementation:

> A payroll problem prompted an auto plant to try manpower leasing. To handle a new three-days-a-week payroll the company figured it needed five full-time girls [*sic*]. Trouble was the girls each had two days of idle time per week when they finished the job. Company policy prohibited hiring part-time workers through regular personnel channels. But leasing the five girls is giving the company competent, precise performance at a fixed cost for the three days. (*Factory,* October 1962, 88)

Permanent employment opened up a number of time sinks, according to THS and personnel industry experts, moments during which managers would not be able to recoup the full value of their employees. When Elmer Winter argued that clients liked temps because "they do not get involved in office politics or gossip around the water cooler" (*Dun's Review and Modern Industry*, October 1966, 51), he was reminding readers of the valuable time lost when regular employees got caught up in the unavoidable informal aspects of organizational life. Low productivity was only one problem; permanent employees often extended their coffee breaks beyond their allotted time, he contended, thus decreasing their output by the end of the workday, had higher rates of absenteeism, were underutilized by their managers, experienced costly "burnout," and were bored. Temporary employees were cast as the solution to this considerable problem. John Fanning, CEO of Uniforce Temporary Services, stressed that temporary workers would not experience the downside of permanent jobs: "Well-trained, qualified data-entry and word-processing temporaries are a 'no-problem' work force for various reasons. Temps can avoid being trapped by burnout by always choosing the type of assignment and length of time they wish to work, whether it is for a day, a week, or for months at a time" (*Office*, September 1984, 102).

The flip side of the temporary's enthusiasm and eagerness for new assignments involved what Fanning called "permanent staff woes" related to tedium, physical problems, and emotional stress. Whenever permanent workers suffered from boredom, burnout, or lack of motivation, employers were paying them for time not worked and work done inefficiently. Fanning went further to posit that making permanent workers work overtime rather than bringing in temps to perform extra work was also a problem because "studies showed" that the productivity of the former during overtime hours was only about 50 percent.

Temporary workers were marketed as being particularly valuable in situations where work was deskilled and unengaging. While regular workers would likely slough off, let their minds wander, and possibly even sabotage work tasks that they found demeaning, temporary workers would be ideal for such positions because their participation would be intermittent enough that the risk of boredom and resistance was low. As W. Robert Stover, president of Western Temporary Services, argued in *Management Review* in 1974: "It has been found that even tedious, unrewarding work routines can be interesting and challenging for a short time while they are new to an employee. Temporary help in such cases increases output and reduces wasteful errors" (December 1974, 21).

His view was echoed by Sharon Bredeson, then president of NATS and of Staff-Plus, a THS firm: "Routine jobs can get so routine that [permanent] employee turnover and recruitment becomes an expensive liability" (*Office*, January 1981, 120). This reasoning—amounting to advice to save the low-skill, repetitive scut work for temporary employees—was an ideological underpinning of the new framework, in which temporaries were viewed as *more* productive, *more* efficient, and *less* risky than workers with permanent employment contracts.

One advertisement seemed to drive the final nail into the coffin of the traditional, casually deployed, Kelly Girl image. The text of this ad for the "Never-Never Girl, invented by Kelly" evoked virtually all the themes discussed here and framed the Kelly Girl not as a stopgap measure but as an ongoing staffing solution to the foibles of human labor power as embodied in the permanent, full-time worker. The ad hyped the following positive attributes for Kelly's new product: .

Never takes a vacation or holiday. Never asks for a raise. Never costs you a dime for slack time. (When the workload drops, you drop her.) Never has a cold, slipped disc or loose tooth. (Not on your time anyway!) Never costs you for unemployment taxes and social security payments. (None of the paperwork, either!) Never costs you for fringe benefits. (They add up to 30% of every payroll dollar.) Never fails to please. (If our Kelly Girl employee doesn't work out, you don't pay. We're that sure of all our girls!) (*Administrative Management*, March 1971, 81; all punctuation in original)

Temps and Templates: Ways of Using Temporary Workers and Agencies

Bringing temporary workers into corporate settings would have been daunting and disruptive had there not been a methodology for doing so. From the early 1960s on, the features of two templates—one for how to use temps and one for finding and interacting with temp agencies—were endlessly discussed in personnel and other industry magazines. The templates varied little over time or from periodical to periodical. The rationale behind them was as follows: company managers who decided to hire temps and bring them into their businesses would defeat themselves if they were not self-conscious about how they proceeded; a temp poorly used was a temp who would pose the same drain on productivity, efficiency, and profitability as a permanent worker. Lack of planning, writers also suggested, would compromise the quality of temporaries' work and of the firm's products. Managing temporaries presented "special problems," and managers who did not plan their use of temps well would essentially sabotage the whole logic behind the new paradigm. These warnings constituted a kind of fearmongering about the potential deleterious consequences of this new employment arrangement, improperly deployed. The emergence of a prespecified template reflected industry goals for the education of managers on the ground: "Thought must be given to the effectiveness of the 'temporary' when *she* reaches your office," argued one writer. "The efficiency of permanent workers varies and, though usually for different reasons, the productivity of a temporary will vary, too" (*Office*, June 1966, 24; emphasis added).

Mythical statistics, sprinkled throughout various articles, bolstered the rationale behind the planning, foresight, and calculation that a template could provide. "The effectiveness of using temporary help [could] vary by at least 25%" if temps were not utilized "properly," according to Elmer Winter of Manpower (*Office*, October 1964, 85, a figure cited also in *Office*, June 1966, 24). An article in *Supervisory Management* (June 1964, 14) estimated the percentage of money wasted on temporaries because they were used inefficiently was 30 percent. According to Guy Millner of Norrell Services, employers could have "ultimate control" over this massive waste by using temporary workers well. Much as Frederick Taylor believed that time-and-motion studies would enable employers to minimize wasted efforts on the part of their workers, personnel and industry leaders believed that the careful and systematic application of the template would enable managers to minimize any waste incurred in the use of workers who were not part of the permanent or regular workforce.

Summarized here are the elements of the detailed template, addressed to managers, culled from a variety of articles:

First, before the temp actually arrives, you need to preplan the work. Know what you will assign to your temps; don't simply wait until they show up for the job and then decide what you would like them to do. Preplanning and prespecification allows you, as a manager, to start the temp off right away. Second, make sure that any equipment that the temp might need is available and functioning. Equipment could range from functioning typewriters to the right types of paper and stationery, writing implements, erasers, staplers, and later, computer stations. Third, once the temp arrives, explain the tasks very carefully. Don't assume that you can point temps to the task and let them loose; they need instructions and guidance. (By the 1970s this point is stated a bit differently: managers should pretrain their temporary workers and/or require them to go through an orientation.) Fourth, be sure to explain the office rules. These might include the formal rules regarding dress, conduct, punctuality, whether one could use the phone for personal reasons or eat at one's desk, and breaks. Fifth, be sure to introduce temporary workers to their permanent coworkers and appoint an office mentor (also referred to variously as "working companion," "helper," "guide," and "buddy") to the temp. Don't leave temps on their own. With a coworker to serve as a mentor, there will always be some degree of supervision over the temp as well as a person the temp can turn to if she or he has a problem. Finally, be sure to explain the presence of temporary workers to your permanent workers. Make sure that they understand that bringing in temps does not threaten their jobs, and above all, strive to maintain the goodwill of your permanent employees about the new arrangement.

These steps—preplanning the work, readying the equipment, explaining the job, laying out the rules, putting the temp under the wing and observation of a regular worker, and assuaging the potential uneasiness of permanent workers—appear repeatedly over time. Articles tried to raise managerial awareness of the differences between temporary and permanent workers, give managers tactics for eliminating waste as workplaces shifted to a new human resource strategy, and provide a model for both rationalizing the new employment system and minimizing its disruptiveness.

Overall, the personnel and THS industry rhetoric emphasized precision, fine-tuning, and adjustment to achieve the perfect outcome for companies incorporating temporaries into their workplaces. Business managers were urged to exercise a microscopic degree of control over their workforces and workload flows. The comment of Allen Sorenson, president of Personnel Pool of America, revealed the belief that managers could control wholesale the integration of temporary workers into the workplace. Cited as an expert on how to manage batch hiring of temporary workers, Sorenson suggested that "when groups of 50, 100, or more temporaries are hired, they should be phased into the workflow at rates of ten a day in order to minimize confusion and lighten the workload on the permanent staff. By 'building up' or 'taking bite sizes,' clients can reduce the confusion that occurs when major projects must be completed within short periods of time" (*Office Administration and Automation*, August 1985, 35).

Emergent in this perspective was a theory of control not only about the efforts of individual workers or the collective labor process but of *workforce* control, the direction and coordination of entire groups of workers.

The second template contained advice to line and human resources managers about how to find and work with temporary help agencies. Regular discussion of how to select and use the "right" agency began only around 1973 but grew louder as years passed. The company-agency interaction, it appeared, contained a hidden land mine of trouble, and business managers were cautioned against a "haphazard approach" to the recruitment of temps (*Personnel Management*, November 1985). Articles taught managers the "Pitfalls to Avoid in Selecting Temporary Help," the title of an article in *Best's Insurance News* (November 1968), which simply explained how agencies work. In fact, a number of articles of this period performed this basic educative task, describing how agencies, selling temporary labor in the new way of using temps, conducted their operations.

Mike Kutka, vice president of Temporaries, a regional THS firm, spoke to managers in "How to Get Your Money's Worth from

Temporary Help Services" (*Management World*, June 1978, 8), warning that even though companies often spent "thousands or hundreds of thousand of dollars every year" on temps, all too often, "very little, if any, care may be given towards how to select a temporary help firm." What factors were managers supposed to take into consideration in making their decisions about agencies?

The experts prodded managers to ask the following critical questions before doing business with an agency.

- How well trained are the agency's staff members?
- Does the agency offer temporaries with a variety of skills?
- Is the agency confident about its recommendations and/or does it offer a guarantee?
- Does the agency carefully screen its temps?
- What is the reputation of the agency?
- Does the agency carry worker's compensation liability insurance and bond its employees?
- What are the turnover and absenteeism rates of an agency's temps?
- How long has the agency been in business?
- Is it well capitalized?
- How does it attract its temps?

In other words, an agency that did not provide quality temps—that is, appropriate and carefully designated temps—could cost the firm in various and substantial ways. Agencies might hire temps whom they had not sufficiently screened. They might send temps who were not suited to the tasks of the job or the company to which they were sent. An agency itself might be in weak financial shape or have a questionable reputation in the temporary-help service industry. In the view of Linda Bain McKinney, president of a firm that specialized in temporary office help and a member of the National Association of Temporary Services, success with temporary help pivoted on whether hiring firms had done their homework on the agencies they selected to supply temps:

The temporary help service business is approaching middle-age maturity. A mere child in the Forties, it has since grown to become an important element of today's business world. As economic pressures come to bear on staffing and productivity levels, managers are increasingly turning to temporary help to relieve workload pressures in an economical manner. As a result, temporary help services have proliferated. . . . [T]he astute business executive needs to determine the quality and value of the services offered by temporary help services in his or her area *before* enlisting assistance. (*Management World*, September 1980b, 9; original emphasis)

Redefining the Labor Pool: Who Is Qualified?

The historically constructed and situated Kelly *Girl*—the so-called typical temporary worker—was a 37.5-year-old woman, with two children, who had had previous labor market experiences and wanted to supplement her income without detriment to her family. This demographic description appeared repeatedly in magazine articles and was supposedly attributable to a Manpower survey conducted in the late 1950s or early 1960s. But "Mrs. Employee," as she was called in an *American Business Magazine* article in July 1958, turns out to have been a fleeting figure, at least in discursive constructions of good temporary workers. Even though the author of an article in *Office* (September 1962, 297) believed that temporaries were mainly "marginal groups such as housewives and mothers of school children," this formulation of the temporary worker steadily dwindled over the next few decades. Maybe Mrs. Employee was actually fleeing from the temporary ghetto. Women statistically remained the substantial majority of temporary workers well into the 1990s, but early on, personnel and THS leaders were increasingly concerned with the shrinking supply of available married women for temp work and with expanding the pool of available labor. In the early 1960s, writers were already mulling over alternative populations of people who could be tapped for temporary employment.[6] We can trace a demographic and social reconceptualization of who would make a good temp.

As one early institutional indicator of this change, Kelly Girls, which had already changed its name to Kelly Girl Service in 1959, adopted the moniker Kelly Services in 1966, a name that has persisted to this day. By the mid-1970s, gendered names for temporary agencies had all but disappeared from personnel management articles. Whereas in the 1960s THS firms still went by such names as Executive Girls, Western Girl, American Girl Service, Dot Girls, and Lé Gals, (even female temps at Manpower were called "White Glove Girls," according to *Dun's Review and Modern Industry* [October 1966]), by the late 1970s and the 1980s they had degendered their names and adopted titles that reflected the emphasis on staffing and job temporality: TemPositions, Staff Builders, Personnel Pool of America, Uniforce Temporary Services, AccounTemps, Staff-Plus, Employment Overload, among others.

Several factors underlay this ongoing social and demographic reconstruction. First, demand for temporary workers increased as the THS industry worked to increase the sales of its product and as American businesses embraced the practice of hiring people on a temporary basis. Second, in the 1970s the effects of the women's movement reverberated throughout personnel analyses, as they did throughout the society and world as a whole. The fact that more women were pursuing higher education and meaningful, regular, full-time employment meant that the population of women who fit the traditional Kelly Girl profile was shrinking—at least, so personnel and THS industry writers believed. (Consistent with this change employers' prohibition of married women from the workplace—the marriage bar—vanished "almost entirely" after 1950, writes Goldin [1990, 174–75]; also see chapter 1, note 7.) Sharon Bredeson, of NATS and the agency Staff-Plus, articulated the issue this way: "The trend toward the two-income family means that those who are available to work in part-time jobs are scarce. The middle-class housewife is no longer sitting at home with time on her hands. This, coupled with the fact that many women are no longer willing to work in typical office jobs, is changing the composition of the temporary work force as well" (*Office*, January 1981, 120).

In the writings of personnel and THS representatives, women were not the only source of potential labor. Offering the national business community a vision of who could populate these new, normalized temporary jobs was an important part of the construction of this labor market. Writers discussed the pros and cons of various groups, often comparing them to the "traditional" temporary employee and sometimes comparing them to the "problematic" permanent employee. In so doing, personnel and THS industry articles provoked new ways of thinking about the temp.

Most notably, articles increasingly appeared which either explicitly or implicitly identified men as potential temporary workers. References in the very early 1960s to "jobbers"—men who worked as temporaries in construction, engineering, and sales—indicate that before the entrenchment of the new paradigm, male temps constituted a category separate from that of traditional temporary workers in the mind of the business community (see *Chemical Week*, March 19, 1960; *Sales Management*, September 16, 1960).

But even though references to jobbers disappeared, later article titles communicated that magazine editors understood that the notion of male temps would jar the hegemonic and heavily gendered association of temporary work with women. The male model of the career worker, in which adult white men were presumed to hold full-time, lifelong jobs prevailed in the early 1960s. In the transitional formulation, temporary work was acceptable for men but it was cast as a secondary preference to permanent jobs.

Men as temps had to be explained and justified, as illustrated in the article, "Why Not Rent Salesmen? Dow Did!"[7] Historically gender-legitimate reasons were evoked to explain why an employer might consider hiring men in these positions or why working men might want them. This article claimed—pointing to experiences at Salespowers, a company that had successfully used temporary salesmen—that these were "men who wish to work merely on a temporary basis. Some are new in the community and have not as yet located a permanent position. Some are between jobs and require an intermediate activity to tide them over. Many are retired or own their own business but find occasional sales activity desirable" (*Sales Management*, September 16, 1960, 80). This description implied that these were "normal" men, dissociating them from the possible image of losers who couldn't find a "real" job. These men were simply in between jobs or had not yet made the necessary connections in a new community.

Over time, however, articles on men as temps began implicitly to criticize the model of permanent, full-time employment, connecting that critique to new ways of thinking about what men wanted from their jobs. The rhetoric in these articles prefigured new ideologies about employment in the late twentieth century, which romanticized continually shifting career patterns. In "Male Temps: Clerks to Controllers" (*Administrative Management*, March 1971), Sam Bellotto tried to explain why more men were taking temporary jobs: "The reasons propelling this sort of men's liberation in this traditionally distaff [authors' note: "distaff" is archaic for women's work] dominated field are many." Among these reasons he cited the opinion of the national director of Western Girl, Inc., that "today's younger men, fresh out of business schools, do not feel the need for the security and identity that made their fathers *real* company men.... [T]hese young men would rather try many jobs at many companies, exactly the sort of opportunity a temporary service can provide" (*Administrative Management*, March 1971, 54; emphasis added).

Additional efforts were made to expand the potential pool of temporary laborers along the lines of social rather than gendered categories. One article on *handicapped* people pointed to the virtues of matching people with disabilities, who might not otherwise be hired, to specific types of temporary positions. "Services of Handicapped Rented" (*Factory*, January 1963) offered a successful example in which Detroit Edison Company employed handicapped people in salvage work and other low-skill, blue-collar temporary positions. The selling points of using this population—people who apparently would follow orders compliantly and be satisfied with simple routines—were manifest, according to the author: "The disabled also strip wire, disassemble components, and recondition transformer assemblies in addition to grading scrap metal and repairing flat irons. The workers' accident rate and absenteeism are below the company average. Besides, they have always been able to do any job assigned to them" (*Factory*, January 1963, 195).

Older and retired workers would also be efficient and careful in temporary jobs, according to several articles. People who had had significant experience in the labor force could bring their experience to bear on temporary positions. Again using an example of a successful model, one article related how Allied Chemical had hired older temporaries from Olsten Temporary Services to help bring its mailroom service up to snuff. Olsten had provided a group of people who had retired, and the contract administrator for Allied bragged that

> the advantages of the temporary help system are obvious. Absenteeism dropped from over 10% to under 2%. Because of increased productivity, we reduced our budgeted staff from 25 to 22. Total spending is running considerably under budget, and service has improved so remarkably that we have changed a pattern of complaints into one of compliments. There are very few problems because the system is a tight and simple one. Moreover, the interest, care and initiative generated by the retired personnel helps us continue to streamline operations. (*Office*, November 1972, 52)

Former company employees could be another high-quality source of temporary labor in that they had experience with the particular company and thus would understand its procedures, rules, and cultures. The suggestion to look more favorably upon "qualified" *minority and underprivileged* workers was introduced into the ongoing discussion of whom industry leaders might turn to and companies might hire for temporary jobs.[8] Finally, *moonlighters* could be ideal because in looking for multiple jobs, they could fit temporary jobs into their work schedules.

Singling out particular groups of workers and carefully inspecting their work ethics, qualifications, histories, and commitments represented an ongoing effort to find new populations who might work in the temporary-help employment sector. By defining groups as suitable for temporary employment because of their social status, experience, or ascriptive characteristics, personnel and THS managers broadened the parameters of this potential supply of labor for temporary jobs.

Stimulating Demand: New Niches for Temporary Workers

The final major theme that emerged from content analysis of articles in the 1960s through 1980s involved efforts to identify new ways that temporary workers could be used and new occupations and industries where they could work. If the industry wanted to stimulate demand, it had to propose novel tasks and spaces for temps. In the traditional and narrower paradigm of temporary employment, temporary employees were truly temporary, and they primarily were office workers: typists, machine operators, general office workers, switchboard operators, file clerks, and receptionists. The Kelly Girl—embodiment of the traditional temp—was a person with weak attachments to the labor market—perhaps a secretary who typed, filed, and answered the phone. Even though in fact temporaries were deployed in other jobs and even though this portrayal of women who worked as temps undoubtedly was a shallow stereotype, the public vision of a temp—the vision from which personnel and THS industry leaders struggled to distance themselves—was the flighty Kelly Girl.[9]

As noted earlier, writers often evoked the traditional image that equated temps with Kelly-Girls-as-secretaries but then moved on to stress that that image had become outdated. Such articles appeared to try to distance the industry from its early days, but beyond that, they increasingly identified occupational niches for temps which were novel to the business world. New occupations included jobs in factories (assemblers, assembly line packaging, welding, machine monitoring, inventory work), sales*men*, product testers, inspectors, insurance industry workers (such as risk managers, account underwriters, and programmers), supervisors, controllers, accountants, advertising workers, traffic management professionals, and, in the 1970s and on, executives, engineers, lawyers, managers, and various stripes of scientists. Throughout the 1980s, discussion of temporary and contract workers in high-tech jobs was widespread, as was discussion about how temporary employment no longer pertained simply to low-level and unskilled work. Many of these articles reflected real trends in the world of labor and employment, and the multiplicity of articles treating each new trend as a noteworthy social problem served to validate and normalize these new ways in which employers were using workers on a temporary basis.

New functions for temporary workers were identified as well. For example, firms were encouraged to use temps as *fill-in workers* if a company had to relocate and couldn't take its workforce along (*Management Review*, September 1978, 32; *Office*, May 1982). They might also use temps as *scabs* (referred to as "replacements" in the article) in the event of a strike on the part of their permanent workers (*Personnel Journal*, April 1986). "*Machinery down-time problems* can also be solved with temporary personnel," according to John Fanning of Uniforce, "since they will work at any hour of the day or night, simply because they wish to" (*Office*, September 1984, 102).

Probably assisting in the definition of new uses for temporary workers were the frequent allusions to workers' preferences to justify the growth of temporary jobs and to normalize temporary work as a labor market experience. Personnel and THS industry leaders increasingly wrote as if to legitimate and elevate the status of temporary work. For one thing, over time the language of "careers" in reference to temporary work seeped into the writings of personnel journals. In coming up with new labels for workers who worked as temporaries on an ongoing basis, personnel and THS industry writers were constructing a new place in the labor market: a career niche, to be staffed by credible workers with labor market attachments on whom employers could rely. The terms "permanent temporaries," "career temporaries," "full-time temporaries," "permanent niches for temps," "permatemp," and "temp-to-perm" entered the discourse in the late 1970s, with writers often asserting that more workers *desired* the change, the flexibility, the opportunity, and the challenge that could arise from not being stuck in one job.

Although our data don't allow us to address this issue from the point of view of people who worked as temps, it seems probable that redefining temporary jobs as careers could have the effect of attracting workers who had not previously viewed temporary jobs as suitable. Daniel Struve's words, for example, seemed pitched to such individuals: Struve, president of a THS firm and of a professional industry association, claimed that the demand for temporary services had "given birth to a new breed of worker: the full-time temporary" (*Office*, September 1985, 141). Likewise, the author of "Need a Pro? Try Temporary Help" pointed to the new trend of the "career temporary," wherein "a person is happy working just as a temp because they can acquire different skills and have flexible hours" (*Office Administration and Automation*, August 1984, 49).

Bredeson explained the emergence of full-time temporaries as a "positive trend...a work-style that has gained acceptance and even a status of its own. This kind of worker finds a challenge and an appeal in not being committed to one company, one desk, or even one job. The variety and flexibility, combined with good pay and handsome benefit packages, is attracting more and more workers to the field" (*Office,* January 1981, 120). Other experts who discussed workers' preferences attached similar attitudinal traits to individuals whom managers might hire as temps, such as workers' desire for control over their work time or for new employment opportunities. In 1989 a leader of an organization that focused on developing quality workplace practices urged managers: "You have to target populations that want this kind of work. There are some workers who want less commitment than regular employment demands or who want more flexibility and control of their work time than a standard 9-to-5 schedule affords" (*Industry Week,* April 1989, 18).

New identity-based (or characterological) conceptions about temps had strong affinity with changing corporate structures. The notion that workers preferred short-tenured jobs, that they enjoyed change and the lifestyle flexibility afforded by this kind of employment, justified the goals of the THS industry to expand the sector of jobs that might draw in greater numbers of people. Of course, these identity-based conceptions of workers also justified other recent labor market phenomena such as "boundaryless careers," shorter job tenure, and career hopping. As was true of the ideational fit between capitalism and religious tenets (Weber 1958), new ideas about careers and claims about workers' need for challenge and change were greatly in sync with transformations in the economic structure, especially in the way corporations, labor markets, and jobs were being organized on a more flexible basis.

The Zero Defect Temp

Analyzing how personnel magazines and business periodicals created a new realm of ideas about the THS industry reveals the professional and ideological scaffolding of "lean-and-mean" that has become so pervasive in the twenty-first century. The way that writers pitched their product shaped a hospitable framework for reorganizing employment relations, a concept with the capacity to seep into and materially change standard business practices. Using the "management media" (personnel magazines), personnel and THS industry writers relied on standard tactics such as pointing out inefficiencies and performance gaps, providing examples of successes, cautioning managers about the risks of not subscribing to new ways of deploying workers, and liberally supporting their cases with mythical statistics. Articles not only encouraged readers to use *more* temps—a quantitative sales pitch—but encouraged readers to use them *differently,* a qualitative pitch to substitute temps for permanent workforces rather than complement them.

Micro-accounting of costs allowed experts to point out that retaining a maximum number of workers on the payroll was inefficient and unprofitable, given the way work unpredictably ebbed and flowed. Moreover, personnel writers marketed temporary workers as good employees whose work quality might surpass that of permanent workers, systematically presenting evidence—albeit evidence of dubious origins—to support their claims. They offered advice for how to construct temps as good workers by developing templates that would maximize their effectiveness. Emergent seeds of a discourse about flexibility took root and grew, with discussions in the 1960s and 1970s of the need for core and peripheral workforces and flexible workforces sounding very much like the full-blown rhetoric of flexibility that had become familiar by the 1990s.

The new model of employment proposed by personnel managers and the THS industry was suggestive of a novel "science" of workforces, much like Frederick Taylor's "science," in an earlier era, of workers' bodies. (In fact, it isn't much of a stretch to view Elmer Winter, cofounder and president of Manpower for several decades, as the Frederick Taylor of the temporary-help services industry.)[10] This was a science of the "zero defect" temporary worker, in the words of Mitchell Fromstein, chairman of Manpower in 1988, who proclaimed:

> With an increased use of temporary workers in assembly plants, we needed to find a way to measure and predict who will best fit into that environment.... Our business is devoted to supplying people,

and our product is made at the point of sale. These tests will help us to drive errors out of the product we sell. It's critical to have zero defects before we deliver our product. (Quoted in *Industry Week*, March 21, 1988, 20)

Manpower's product, of course, was the good temporary worker. Workforce science would allow personnel, human resource, and business managers to adjust and control with precision the size, the flow, and the quality of the employees on their payroll. As they advised managers to collect and analyze data, recommend efficiencies, and recalibrate the ratio of permanent to temporary workers, the tacticians who advocated scientizing and rationalizing workforce policies had an impact on employment relations that has been no less powerful than the effect that scientific management has had on the labor process over time.

In so doing, the THS industry became an active and purposive collaborator in a restructuring of American employment relations that had culminated, by the twenty-first century, in a normalized employment framework that is insecure, remains impermanent across jobs and occupations, and places high degrees of risk on workers. Did these new discourses and ways of framing temporary work *cause* the rise of the temporary-employment system? Obviously not; the story of the rise and entrenchment of temporary employment clearly includes many more strands than those presented here. The THS and personnel industry's discursive efforts are one strand of many. As we know, changes in the global economy were creating structural opportunities for employers, increasing their receptivity to the idea of aggressively attacking labor and imagining new ways of employing workers. In addition, as Gonos (1997, 98–99) notes, in the 1960s organized labor "seems to have underestimated the strength of the trend toward increased use of temporary workers and its consequences for the U.S. workforce," while at the same time, pressure from public interest groups was lacking: all told, the issue "raised remarkably little public concern." The subsequent political vacuum, it seems, gave the THS industry a wide-open deck for promoting its agenda.

This chapter has shown how the temporary help service and personnel industries actively constructed new images of how and where temporary workers could be used, how they could be recruited and incorporated into workplaces, and who they might be. (Integral to this process of market making was a loud attack on permanent labor, an insistent idea that employing large workforces on a permanent and ongoing basis was costly to American business. In denouncing the true cost of permanent labor, personnel managers and THS leaders contributed to an ideological erosion of the permanent employment contract and a fundamental reorientation of management toward labor.)

By the 1990s the new paradigm of temporary employment had taken hold in the U.S. employment landscape. The structural, legal, and ideational accomplishments we have outlined set the global stage for understanding the contours of temporary employment today. The THS industry has endeavored to sell a commodity—the good temp—and worked hard to shape labor market practices. But obviously, an analysis based purely on macro-level forces is partial. It is now time to examine individual agencies and their staff to see how they create and sustain these new employment relations.

Field data from the trenches of one agency allow us to bring the global picture down to local practices. The next three chapters narrate this story in the voices of contemporary observers rather than historical archivists; they show how industry logic and agency representatives' efforts *explain* why temporary employment looks the way it does today. Agencies and agency workers are the purveyors of new employment relations.

Personnel and Business Magazine
Articles Referenced in Chapter 2

Administrative Management. November 1970. Elmer L. Winter, "Program Your Optimum Staff Needs." 31:24–27.

——. March 1971. Sam Bellotto Jr., "Male Temps: Clerks to Controllers." 32:54–55, 79–80.

——. May 1974. Dwayne Meisner, "The New Economics of Temporary Personnel." 35:20–21.

American Business Magazine. July 1958. "Temporary Office Workers: Do They Pay Off? Survey of the Month." 28:23–24.

Barron's National Business and Financial Weekly. December 17, 1962. David A. Loehwing, "More Warm Bodies: Contract Personnel Has Become a Big and Profitable Business." 42:3.

Best's Review, Property/Liability Edition. September 1972. Elmer L. Winter, "The Flexible Work Force—A New Concept for Cost Control." 73:96, 98–100.

——. August 1974. Elmer L. Winter, "Temporary Help—A Permanent Thing." 75:82–85.

Best's Insurance News, Life Edition. November 1968. "Pitfalls to Avoid in Selecting Temporary Help." 69:100–101.

Business Week. October 6, 1980. "Big Boost for the Temps." 98:102.

Chemical Week. March 19, 1960. "Rented Manpower Keeps Jobs on Schedule." 86:65–66.

Credit and Financial Management. February 1965. Marion M. Whalen, "Renting People Is Good Business." 67:12–15.

Dun's Review and Modern Industry. September 1958. "How Temporary Workers Can Fill the Gap." 72:118–119.

——. October 1966. Robert Levy, "Man with the Power." 88:50–52.

Factory. October 1962. "Manpower Leasing." 120:86–89.

——. January 1963. "Services of Handicapped Rented." 121:194–195.

Forbes. October 25, 1982. William Harris, "Kelly Boys." 130:114.

Fortune. October 1968. Irwin Ross, "For Rent: Secretaries, Salesmen, Physicists, and Human Guinea Pigs." 78:164–166, 238, 243–244.

Industry Week. January 13, 1975. "More Temporaries in Industry's Future?" 184:43.

——. March 21, 1988. Brian S. Moskal, "Manpower's Mousetrap: How to Get a More Productive Workforce." 236:20–21.

——. April 3, 1989. Michael A. Verespej, "Part-Time Workers: No Temporary Phenomenon." 238:13, 17–18.

Management Review. December 1974. W. Robert Stover, "Third-Generation Use of Temporary Services." 63:17–22.

———. September 1978. W. Robert Stover, "Easing Relocations with Temporary Workers." 67:32, 34–35.

Management World. June 1978. Mike Kutka, "How to Get Your Money's Worth from Temporary Help Services." 7:8–10.

———. September 1980a. Mike Kutka, "The Temporary—Becoming a Permanent Office Employee." 9:10.

———. September 1980b. Linda Bain McKinney, "What to Look For in a Temporary Help Service." 9:8–9, 11.

———. June–August 1987. Paul Scelsi, "Temp Help: On the Fast Track." 16:8–9.

Modern Office Technology. March 1985. David L. Farkas, "A Temporary Habit." 30:90–94.

Office. September 1962. Harold W. Dickhut, "Temporary Help." 56:296–297.

———. March 1963. "Supplying Tested and Rated Temporary Office Help." 57:104, 108, 110.

———. October 1964. Elmer L. Winter, "Get Maximum Benefits When You Use a Temporary Help Service." 60:85–89.

———. June 1966. "Hiring Temporary Help for Vacation Replacements." 63:24, 26, 28, 33, 37.

———. January 1967. Richard P. Essey, "Second Generation of Instant People." 65:92, 173–174.

———. January 1969. Helga Tarver, "Understanding Temporary Help." 69:94–95.

———. November 1972. "Retired Temporaries Improved Mail Service at Allied Chemical." 76:51–53.

———. December 1972. "Efficient Use of Temporaries May Be Key to Future Office Staffing." 76:39–43.

———. December 1974. Howard W. Scott Jr., "Development of the Temporary Help Industry." 80:20–22.

———. January 1975. Guy W. Millner, "Future Trends in Temporary Help Services." 81:82, 84.

———. January 1981. Sharon N. Bredeson, "The 80s: High Technology and a Changing Work Force." 93:120, 168.

———. May 1982. "A Corporate Move Eased by Temporary Personnel." 95:152.

———. September 1984. John Fanning, "Employee Burnout in the Office Can Be Prevented with Use of Temporaries." 100:102.

Office. September 1985. Daniel C. Struve, "Demand for Temporaries Spurs Opportunities." 102:141–143.

Office Administration and Automation. August 1984. Josephine Fiamingo, "Need a Pro? Try Temporary Help." 45:48–50, 55, 68, 70.

——. August 1985. William Cowan, "Making the Most of Temporary Help." 46:32–35, 64.

Personnel Journal. April 1986. "Replacement Workers during Strikes: Strategic Options for Managers." 65:93–98.

——. January 1987. Betty Southard Murphy, Wayne E. Barlow, and D. Diane Hatch, "NLRB Permits Replacement during Legal Lockout." 66:14, 16.

——. March 1989. Kevin M. Kelly and Ann M. Kelly, "Employment by Trial." 68:40–43.

——. October 1989. "Temporary Services." 68:10.

Personnel Management. November 1985. "Haphazard Approach to Recruitment of Temps." 17:75.

Purchasing. March 11, 1963. "Does It Pay to Use Temporary Help?" 54:119.

Sales Management. September 16, 1960. "Why Not Rent Salesmen? Dow Did." 85:79–80.

Supervisory Management. June 1964. Sylvia Auerbach, "Make the Most of Summer Replacements: Tips on Temporaries." 9:13–20.

Chapter Three

"We're Not Body Pushers"
Constructing a Pool of Good Temps

For a temporary help service agency, attracting, developing, keeping, and controlling good temps is by no means automatic or straightforward. Nor is convincing people who really want permanent jobs that a temporary job is acceptable. Just as the THS industry has had to work over decades to achieve legitimacy for a new type of employment relationship, so, too, do agencies now repeatedly have to build and control their temp workforces. A number of research studies have framed the labor problem facing the industry as a one-dimensional matter of control. Gottfried (1991), Rogers (2000), and Vosko (2000), among others, have argued that agency staff use a variety of methods to control temporary workers (difficult, given that temporaries work at a great distance from the agency office), but what they have left unanalyzed is the way in which agencies have to *construct* good, qualified temps, to *build*, *cultivate*, and *maintain* marketable workforces not only at any individual temp's work site but within the walls of the agency itself.

This chapter describes daily life at Select Labor, then discusses the mechanisms by which the agency endeavored to manufacture a workforce of good temps. What sells in the world of temporary employment is not simply warm bodies; it is good *workers* who are willing to work on a temporary basis. And control of this workforce is embedded in its construction: cultivating good temps very likely will increase their consent, their cooperation, and the likelihood they'll return to Select Labor for placement services. Moving from the lofty reaches of mid-twentieth-century personnel rhetoric to the lived experiences within early twenty-first-century agencies, we now examine how Select Labor tried to succeed in this endeavor.

The Daily Context: What Market Forces Look Like on the Ground

The high pitch of Silicon Valley's economic climate—in 2000, a boom year—was audible in the Select Labor office. SL's phones seemed to be ringing off the hook, and the branch manager and recruitment specialists (also referred to as placement specialists) were both overwhelmed and delighted by the number of job orders coming in from firms. The economy in the Silicon Valley in 2000 was "hot," in the words of staffing industry leaders: dynamic, unpredictable, and turbulent. Even as many companies were inundating Select Labor with requests for temps, other firms were implementing hiring freezes, closing shop, or considering leaving the Silicon Valley. Unemployment was low—a little under 2 percent by December 2000 (Benner 2002, 207, fig. 7.1). Ninety-five percent of SL's revenue came from the placement of temporary workers, payroll services, and temporary-to-permanent placements. The majority of those placements were in light industrial, administrative support, warehouse, and assembly jobs.

At one point the newly formed technical recruiting division had over one hundred job orders from firms looking for personnel, a very large volume of orders for a midsized firm such as Select Labor. At times the staff had trouble keeping up with incoming orders and had to concentrate much of their energy on placing workers rather than drumming up accounts with new clients. On any given day an individual placement specialist could be found conducting an in-take interview with a new job seeker and then entering that person's occupational history into their applicant database. Alternatively, staff members could be found on the telephone calling one of the agency's regular temps to see whether he or she was available for a job opening. Or, staff might be "prequalifying" a temp before sending that person off to talk to a hiring manager about a specific placement.[1]

To meet demand, Select Labor staff occasionally relied on secondary contracting arrangements with other temporary placement agencies to fill an order for workers. For example, one day Lisa, the agency branch manager, received a call from a production manager at Built to Order (BTO), one of SL's largest clients. Built to Order manufactured and assembled customized computers for several large, well-known computer companies and needed sixty temporary assemblers as soon as possible. As soon as Lisa got off the phone with the BTO manager, she called the branch manager at another staffing agency, asking for help in meeting BTO's hiring needs. Her counterpart at the other agency was "more than happy" to help Lisa fill this order. SL staff regularly called other agencies for backup to help meet large job orders when SL didn't have the in-house capability to fill them. In turn, Select Labor served as a secondary provider to other large staffing agencies, a routine action taken in an extended network of providers.

Dealing with boom conditions was only one part of the new economy in the Silicon Valley, however. Concurrent with the high level of demand from many high-tech-related firms, other companies were experiencing contraction, slack, fluctuation, and unpredictability—dynamics that conditioned Select Labor's staff members' task of creating and maintaining a pool of qualified temps. This underbelly of employment, typical of the churning that economists associate with the new economy (Brown, Haltiwanger, and Lane 2006), was as much a part of the Silicon Valley labor market as the phenomenal demand for temps. Routine were telephone calls from individuals who were "desperate" to find a temporary job. Calls came from their current temps when jobs ended, whether the ending was planned or sudden (as in the case of unexpected downsizing). Hiring practices were unpredictable: openings for temps might abruptly close when a company turned around and put hiring freezes in place after advertising for help. Other positions would close when competing agencies placed their temps there first. Sometimes, Select Labor's "regular" temps, as well as temps who showed up at the door, got squeezed out when managers decided, despite initial promises, that they could not convert the temp to a perm. Other temps returned to SL after companies imposed time limits on how long they could stay in one position. These myriad effects of a churning labor market were not always visible to those who emphasized the low unemployment figures.

Adding to the unsettled feel of transactions between agency staff and potential workers was the difficulty of reconciling media news reports and Valley hype with the realities that job seekers were running up against. Everyone—agency staff and job seekers—was experiencing cognitive dissonance about the job market. Throughout the summer of 2000, reports appeared intermittently in the *San Jose Mercury* and *San Francisco Chronicle* about high-tech firms' desperate need for skilled labor. The media were full of heated political debates about the creation of additional H-1 visas that would open up short-term and legal positions for foreign workers in the U.S. labor market. And Po Bronson's widely read book on the riches and possibilities of the Silicon Valley (*Nudist on the Late Shift and Other True Tales of Silicon Valley*, 1999) had captured the imagination of hundreds of thousands of people who relocated to take advantage of the alleged opportunities of this high-tech region.[2]

Some of the people who were part of this mass migration came to Select Labor having taken courses at for-profit vocational schools or at community and state colleges and achieved certification or degrees in computer-related fields. Despite having paid handsome amounts of money for training, however, such individuals were often unable to find relevant work. Some had been told in interviews that they needed job experience in order to get hired, others that employees with a different set of skills were needed. Since for many of the workers with degrees or certification, access to real jobs with clear paths of mobility seemed far from their reach, they turned to SL for help in overcoming their lack of networks into and knowledge about the continually changing labor market.

Other evidence of the mismatch between media stories about prosperity and the realities of corporate restructuring was sobering. For example, one of Select Labor's larger clients, MacroGrowth, had recently relocated its entire manufacturing operation to Texas, retaining only a small corporate office in Silicon Valley. When a Select Labor team visited the company's campus where the agency had previously had an on-site facility to manage the firm's contingent workforce, it was as if they were walking into a ghost town. Building after building was empty, and it was impossible not to wonder grimly what would become of the workers, the buildings, and all the equipment.

Some of these workers, it turned out, were relocating to Texas, but most of the staff had been laid off, and many were now unemployed. In another manifestation of churning, this represented both a defeat and an opportunity for SL. On the one hand, MacroGrowth had been one of its larger accounts, and SL's vendor-on-premise arrangement at this company had generated approximately 25 percent of the branch office's revenues. On the other hand, upon returning to the branch office after collecting SL's belongings, Lisa, the Select Labor branch manager, gave a pep talk at a staff meeting, saying "We can turn this around—these laid-off workers need to be placed. Many of them are our people and they are good. Let's find places for them."

Contraction and expansion, or the threat of either, were ubiquitous and often simultaneous in this area. Agency staff casually shared rumors about clients considering a move to Mexico and other regions with lower operating costs and cheaper labor. Given Silicon Valley's high cost of land, housing, and labor a variety of employers already had moved some or all of their facilities to other areas. Yet shortly after losing the MacroGrowth account, SL opened a new technical recruiting division and expanded the branch office. In addition, SL easily landed a new vendor-on-premise contract at another client firm. The ebb and flow in corporations and placements drove daily life at Select Labor. Confounding the sense of continual motion and change was the work that agency staff had to do to interpret orders from client firms and supply temps for the positions and wages that clients were offering. Table 3.1 provides a snapshot of the ambiguities of orders and the positional complexities that challenged their ability to provide the right kind of temporary worker to hiring companies.

The daily work environment at Select Labor, then, was fast-paced, chaotic, full of interruptions and hustle and bustle. Many of the agency's regular temps were coming in with friends and family members,

TABLE 3.1
Sample Job Orders

Company	Job order	Compensation	Skills and other requirements specified for the job	Positional complexities
BuildPro	Assemblers to build circuit boards	$7–8 per hour	Must have at least limited competency speaking and reading English; must work overtime and on short notice	Low pay, specific language competencies, & scheduling unpredictability make it hard to find willing temps
MicroCircuits Inc.	Testers at a production site	Low wages but precise dollar amount not known	Vague; recruiters saw this as an entry-level position requiring little skill on the part of the temp & offering little on-the-job training	Manager at hiring firm keeps refusing to accept the temps sent over; turns out he wants someone with an Associate Arts degree whom he can train and who will stay for a while
Assembly to Go	Assemblers: placing CD roms into computers & packing them up	$9 per hour	Certain level of physical strength to lift boxes; apparently, no experience needed with tools	Turns out that the job requires use of hand tools; the jobs are really "mechanical assemblers," but when the hiring manager recruits just "assemblers," he can pay lower wages to temps
BackTreks	50 assemblers	$6.25 per hour; $200 bonus if temp stays on the job for 300 hours	No skills or capacities stated by the hiring company	Applicants that respond to an ad in a Spanish-speaking magazine refuse to take these low-level jobs at such low wages; so-called bonus takes too long to earn

including their children. Agency placement specialists could send someone they regarded highly over to a company to speak with a manager about a temporary position; he or she might subsequently be rejected by the hiring or human resources manager for reasons not always clear. Agency staff wanted dependable temporary workers, but often the life circumstances of their "raw material" compromised that goal. For example, some temps failed to show up for scheduled interviews (both in the agency and at hiring companies) because of difficulties with transportation or because of miscommunication; others might submit applications but then be difficult to reach by phone. Many workers had second jobs that made it difficult for them to accept placements; some sought particular hours of work such as graveyard shifts, limiting their placement opportunities; temps occasionally flaked out and didn't show up for an assignment that agency staff had worked hard to get them; there were hassles with negotiating time cards and paychecks for temps. To SL staff, these constant letdowns and mishaps constituted business as usual. One placement specialist commented that all the agency staff were "figuring out" how the labor market worked "as they went along." Theirs was a just-in-time, ad hoc production environment where chaos was routine.

It was also a multicultural mosaic. Every day, women and men of diverse nationalities, races, and ethnicities sought out the services of Select Labor, a demographic sea change from the homogenized white female temporaries of an earlier era. Women and men from many different parts of Asia, the Middle East, Central and Latin America, as well as North America were looking for jobs as temps. Many spoke English, but some not at all. When Select Labor staff visited client firms where they had an on-site office, or visited to check in with temps, they found enclaves of temporary workers who were all the same race or ethnicity, such as Latino, Filipino, and Indian. In the office, three of the staff spoke Spanish proficiently; one spoke Mandarin and Cantonese. Frequently, job seekers' friends or family members had to interpret and translate for them.

The double-edged sword of the new economy in the Valley—the mixed quality and precariousness of supply (of labor) and the ebb and flow of demand (for labor)—created a dilemma for Select Labor. While official unemployment figures were low, they masked a tremendous amount of partial, short-term, and uncertain labor market experience for workers in the Silicon Valley. Orders for temps poured in, but so did people coming in off the street to seek temporary jobs. Demand for temps was high, but so was competition for a piece of the market: SL had to vie for its slice with the nearly 300 other temporary help service firms in the broader Silicon Valley (Benner 2002, 104). Competition was also stiff to attract workers themselves, since SL lacked the name recognition of a company like Manpower and might have appeared riskier, compared with the market stature of that behemoth. Thus, even though demand for temps was high, attracting and supplying *good* temps was essential. Few temporary agencies were in a position to hire warm bodies haphazardly and send them off to a temp job.

And judging from the advertising claims found in material gathered from many agencies in the Valley, the promise of excellent-quality, temporary staffing was the cornerstone of competitive practices. SL's advertising material, much like that of other agencies, communicated promises of good workers, not simply good temps. Their staff, SL literature promised, were "productive," "committed to quality performance," "reliable"; they could "integrate with [the client firm's] staff" and "would make significant contributions to [its] projects." SL also offered "continuous monitoring of employee performance." SL's newsletter, distributed to the temps on its payroll, emphasized that "while experience is certainly important, so-called 'soft,' interpersonal skills are also crucial. In some instances soft skills could be considered even more important than actual experience. Often, employers are willing to compromise on exact experience for attributes such as flexibility, initiative, and the ability to learn, ask good questions, and get along with fellow employees."

The agency backed up these behavioral and attitudinal pledges with a financial promise: Select Labor guaranteed that a client not satisfied with a temporary worker would not be charged for the last eight hours that that temp had worked, a "money-back guarantee" that the industry purportedly has been using for decades (Moore 1965, 566; Peck and Theodore 1998, 659; Rogers 2000, 51). The threat of having to take the hit for a bad temp, plus the goal to gain and build market position, constituted a significant financial incentive for agency staff to develop a workforce of "good" temporary workers.

How Select Labor Constructed Good Temporary Workers

Select Labor staff had developed four mechanisms to enhance their ability to build and maintain a workforce of good temps, laborers prepared to step into diverse, sometimes unclear, variably skilled jobs. They actively recruited rather than exclusively relying on individuals to seek out their services; they screened for the good temps and weeded out the bad; modified and redirected workers' goals so that the agency matched the "right" person with the "right" job (aligning aspirations with opportunities); and built a relational culture of "strategic personalism" (Bickham Mendez 1998) with job seekers. Thus, just as temporary-help agencies have aggressively built markets for their product (by working on client firms to hire temporary workers), so do they aggressively construct and maintain their supply of marketable, temporary labor. They must seek out people who are reasonably compatible with temporary positions.

Selective Recruitment

Like virtually every business in America, Select Labor advertised its services in customary places and ways. Anybody wishing to find employment—whether as a temporary worker or as a temporary who could convert to permanent worker—could find out about SL on its Web site, in the yellow pages of the local telephone directory, in a regional *Employment Guide and Career Source* magazine, and at community colleges and training centers. A fair percentage of people seeking the placement services of Select Labor walked into the office having found it through these impersonal methods of advertising. Other potential candidates were rerouted by client firms for whom SL served as vendor-on-premises or otherwise handled all the firm's temporary placements. But, in addition, SL staff recruited widely and selectively for people who could help secure the firm's claim to supply a high-quality temporary workforce. They did not leave the quality of that labor pool to chance, or passively wait for the right kind of temps.

For one thing, SL staff attended local job fairs when possible. Job fairs are fascinating terrain for anyone studying contemporary employment practices. Visitors can find dozens if not hundreds of employers hawking their products, services, and reputations to potential employees. Large urban fairs in particular attract thousands of the job-seeking unemployed, as well as employed people just curious about what the labor market has to offer. Job fairs encompass a surprising number of employers and industries, including government agencies, goods and service providers, internet companies and other high-tech firms, as well as staffing agencies. Temp agency representatives who sponsored tables at a fair could opportunistically find job seekers who may have been looking for permanent work but were willing to learn about the advantages and disadvantages of temporary jobs or about the "temp-to-perm" concept that was readily bandied about in Silicon Valley.[3]

Reeling in job fair attendees by offering promotional items such as chocolates, pens, calendars, and notepads, agency reps (as do virtually all those who staff the tables at job fairs) collected résumés from attendees and conducted impromptu interviews, taking notes on potential job candidates about their preferred hours of work and desired wages, their availability, and so forth. These conversations gave SL reps an opening to educate job seekers about the dynamics of temporary employment and perhaps to shift their opinions about the potential in temporary positions. SL staff also spoke with managers from other companies who were collecting résumés. These discussions often provided inside knowledge on which SL staff could capitalize to sell their own services.

Select Labor reps also networked with staff members from other agencies in the region, comparing notes about labor supply and demand, updating one another on corporate gossip (about which companies might be leaving the area, for example, or were ramping up or shrinking the size of their temporary workforces), and learning of other challenges facing the staffing industry. Among other things, SL staff took advantage of these opportunities to size up their market: which areas of the occupational spectrum other agencies specialized in, strategies other agency representatives were using to solicit more temporary employees, and prevailing norms about wages and markup rates in the Valley. All such information provided valuable insights that helped them formulate competitive and effective policies for their own temporary workforce.

In fact, interacting with staff from competing agencies at job fairs was one way in which SL staff participated in a broad and informal recruitment network with other agencies. In what one SL staff person called relations of "co-opetition"—a blend of cooperation and competition—employees of various agencies conferred, shared news, referred good temps and blacklisted bad ones, requested and provided secondary contracting arrangements, and, in general, provided an infrastructure of support in the Valley. In this way, agency staff tried to use their counterparts in other agencies as recruiting resources.

This network of relations of both cooperation and competition parallels the networks of professionals, managers, and firms that have been widely noted in other studies of Silicon Valley (Barley and Kunda 2004; Benner 2002; Saxenian 1994, 2000). And as is true of these other networks, the network that connected agencies in the THS industry thrived on an uneasy formula: competition for resources and information, yet assistance and backup that allowed agencies to fill orders for laborers at a moment's notice as well as to maintain a reliable pool of temps. "Co-opetition" both set constraints on and enabled economic action in the temporary labor industry.

SL's staff networks extended beyond staffing agencies and into the larger world of training and education. Staffing specialists tried to recruit competitive and qualified temporary workers by maintaining regular contact with job development specialists in the region. These were specialists who worked for various state agencies (both training and placement), with community colleges, and for for-profit training schools and colleges. One staff member in the SL office, for example, sent off job announcements each week to a group of job specialists in the region with whom he had developed close relations throughout his career in the staffing industry, trusting that they would direct these announcements to appropriate individuals who would be interested in temporary positions. Alex, one very active recruiter at Select Labor, said of his systematic approach,

> Many of these people don't make money by placing people—they either work for the county, the city or the state and it's their job to help people find work. So if I have a job opening, I'll go down my list and start calling these folks and say, "Hey, I need this type of candidate with these skills and so on." I'll ask if they have anyone they can send my way. And every Monday morning I try and type out a spreadsheet with all my job openings. Then I fax this list to over thirty-three agencies, schools, and places like that. I'll follow that up with a phone call or even a visit if I have time. Sometimes I'll go ahead and visit the place and post a flyer with my open job orders and I'll attach an envelope to the flyer with my business cards.

Other staff routinely telephoned their contacts at agencies and schools to find out about new graduates who might be good "material" for temporary positions. Further, the branch manager recommended to staff that they keep their eyes open for media reports about local corporate downsizing plans: if they heard about such plans they could go to the company and make presentations about their services.

Trust is an important ingredient in hiring new workers, and as sociologists and labor economists well know, relying on established networks is a common way in which employers strive to recruit good workers whom they can trust (Granovetter 1995; Holzer 1996; Smith 2005; Waldinger and Lichter 2003; Waters 1999). As Waldinger and Lichter note, social ties between workers, the firms they work for, and the friends or family members they will or won't recommend, can be used to enforce obligations and contracts on all sides, such that "to the extent that a group of workers feels bound by these understandings, the employer can count on its exercise of social control to keep recalcitrant fellows in line" (Waldinger and Lichter 2003, 83).

As if intimately familiar with social science research, Select Labor maximized its chances of recruiting reliable temps by tapping the networks of those already on their payroll. SL had an elaborate and modestly lucrative program that offered bonuses to temporary workers for recommending friends or family members who came to work for SL. The parent company estimated that approximately 50 percent of SL's recruits were referrals from current employees. To maximize the quality of those friends and family members who were referred, SL gave temps the bonus only if the recommended person was able to work in good standing for several weeks of full-time temporary employment. Each occupational category was "worth" a bonus of a certain dollar amount to the original temp.[4]

This material incentive reflected SL's hunch that workers already on their payroll would be reluctant to recommend people who would tarnish their own reputation, thus perfectly reflecting Smith's assertion about the "functional deficiencies" of job networks: that is, "the disinclination of potential job contacts to assist when given the opportunity to do so, not because they (the recommenders) lack information or the ability to influence hires, but because they perceive pervasive untrustworthiness among their job-seeking ties and choose not to assist" (2005, 3). And there were occasions when the SL staff would decline to hire someone recommended by a regular temp who was good enough to be sent out to some jobs but just questionable enough to make Select Labor staff wary of his or her recommendations.

Screening, Weeding Out, and Positive Reinforcement

Developing effective and productive recruitment practices does not guarantee that a temp will succeed on the job. Follow-up measures, once the agency reps persuaded people to visit their office, were critical. Screening applicants by interviewing them, administering skills and aptitude tests, and conducting background checks for evidence of criminal activity are all standard ways of evaluating job candidates. Indeed, the reputation of the entire temporary-help service industry rests in part on its claim to minimize problems and do a quality job of the screening, evaluation, and administration involved in hiring temporary workers.

The primary objective of the interview was the inextricably entwined work of weeding out unacceptable and identifying acceptable candidates. SL recruitment and placement specialists were trained to carefully follow a scripted interview protocol. In addition to finding out about the individual's technical skills,[5] Select Labor staff were to take time to ascertain whether job applicants understood the parameters of temporary employment. Job seekers were given a pamphlet outlining "temporary employment opportunities" (the minimum standards of job participation such as arriving on time for one's assignment, observing all client rules, volunteering for more tasks once on the job, maintaining confidentiality about the client's business) and how payroll was handled. When talking with job applicants, agency staff also covered tips for effective interviews: ways of interacting with hiring managers at firms they might be sent to, and how applicants could improve their "presentation of self."

Agency staff were instructed to use the interview to find out how much the candidate knew about temping. Their training literature exhorted them to consider these questions: "What does the candidate hope we can do for him/her? How flexible is he/she regarding assignments and pay? How realistic is the candidate? Does he/she understand the meaning of 'at will' employment? Set forth Select Labor's expectations, policies regarding communication and commitment, business dress and attendance. Gauge what you emphasize by the strengths/weaknesses/problems you suspect."[6] If a recruitment specialist suspected that applicants' expectations were way out of line, that they were misrepresenting their skills, or that they weren't really serious about taking a temporary position, the recruiter would attempt to discourage them but, more notably, "encourage poor candidates to register at other services."

Agency staff were also provided with informational sheets about good and bad workers and primed to detect behaviors believed to correlate with potentially good and potentially bad applicants. Those who looked promising—that is, likely to be punctual, capable of understanding and willing to follow directions, and interactively competent—purportedly had some combination of these good traits: displayed a positive attitude and seemed responsible, reliable, loyal, energetic, intelligent, honest, and trustworthy; these traits, in turn, were associated with close to 100 examples of "good" behavior. Job applicants who looked questionable—that is, they gave off some hint that they were ambivalent, contentious, or had a questionable work record—purportedly had a set of traits that were the polar opposite of those typical of the promising applicant and were similarly associated with close to 100 "bad" behavioral propensities.

Placement specialists were asked to check off particular traits on a list used during the interview—with categories for grooming, verbal facility, awareness, and behavior. Each category contained a range of characteristics from very desirable to unacceptable. Under "Grooming," for example, job seekers were ranked as to whether they appeared to be management and professional material, business "casual" material, fit for light industrial and manual labor, or were unkempt, unhygienic, "counselable," or unacceptable. Under "Awareness," a job seeker could be interpreted as excellent, with strong understanding of expectations, all the way down to unsatisfactory: "shows total lack of understanding of expectations." And under "Behavior," someone seeking temporary employment could be interpreted as extremely good with a positive attitude, all the way down to "unacceptable, exhibits poor attitude."

One method for weeding out unacceptable temps was active quality control whereby SL staff attempted to keep tabs on their temporary workers after sending them off to job assignments. As is conventional in the business world, these quality-control efforts consisted of collecting and studying data on worker performance, monitoring temps at job sites, and rewarding good temps while sanctioning problematic temps. For example, agency staff sent a survey asking the managers at client companies to evaluate individual temps. The short list of questions gathered information about general aptitudes and behaviors, rather than specific skill sets: "production" and "skill level" (both undefined), attendance, judgment, cooperation, dress/grooming, and accuracy—plus the final telling question "Would you accept his/her return?"[7]

Quality control was exercised in other ways as well. Agency policy called for a staff person to conduct a "quality check" by calling within thirty minutes of the scheduled arrival of a new temp or batch of temps to make sure their transition into the workplace had been successful. Had they arrived on time? Had they been able to understand and follow directions? SL staff always hoped that the new temps would blend into the client company in a relatively seamless way. Further follow-up included unannounced spot checks: visiting different work sites to check in with managers, touching base with the temps they had hired, and observing the work site to make sure that everything was in place. One fear that agency staff had was that they would arrive for a spot check and discover that the temps they had sent were being directed to do something other than the work for which they had been requested; when agency staff found disparities, they would do what they could to correct the situation (see the next chapter). Of course, at companies where they had on-site offices—vendor-on-premises arrangements—staff were easily able to monitor temps on the job.

SL staff let good temps know who they were. By using an employee reward system that set a bar for quality work performance, they communicated what they expected of all their temporary workers. SL's Employee Recognition program awarded bonuses to temps who were deemed of the highest quality, with good temps receiving cash, paid days off, and gift cards. The agency encouraged client firms to have Employee of the Month awards for temporary workers, as well.

On the other hand, agency staff could refuse to rehire or re-place those who proved unsuitable. Agencies are not legally bound to place or re-place applicants they have hired. And on the other side of the employment relationship, hiring firms can easily request that a temp not be sent back to them. Although the word "firing" was rarely heard in everyday office conversations, Select Labor staff had near-complete legal latitude to cast off substandard or "sub-optimal" (Peck and Theodore 1998, 670) temps, delineate who was unsatisfactory, who was making managers at client firms unhappy, and who was unlikely to make it as a temp in the long run. Agency staff occasionally sent a temporary worker off to interview for a position, only to hear later from the company, that the individual never made it to the interview. If the job candidate called the agency begging for a second chance, Select Labor's staff had the option of deactivating that job application. In fact, SL staff did give temps with problems a second chance but usually not a third. Occasionally, the placement staff at SL would tell job seekers, after an infraction such as not showing up for an interview or for work, or failing to meet the minimum standards for job performance, that they weren't able to find another position for them—a passive antiretention strategy. The agency's guarantee that if a temp didn't work out, Select Labor would not charge the hiring company for the final eight hours of his or her employment subtly reminded staff about the financial cost of keeping a bad temp.

Maximizing Fit: Modifying Aspirations
and Decoding the Labor Market

Successful sales in the staffing industry come from knowing how to place the right worker in the right job. Select Labor management continually stressed that the work of agency representatives was not primarily to help workers who wanted the best of all employment opportunities but, rather, to give employers what they wanted. And part and parcel of that goal was to know how to avoid setting up temps for failure, which would of course redound to SL's reputation. Time and again, SL staff would refrain from sending applicants out to jobs in which the individuals were particularly interested but for which they were not qualified. Staff would also work to modify job applicants' aspirations, encouraging them to postpone immediate goals that were unrealistic and adjust their expectations to the realities of existing opportunities. In both cases, Select Labor's goal was to eliminate or at least narrow the mismatch between temporary worker and temporary job, and to increase the success of the former in the latter. A successful placement, with a maximum of fit between job seeker and job, was one where a temp could fulfill the terms of the contract; doing so was an integral element of good temporary performance. Notably, in doing this, SL reps endeavored to minimize the mismatch that Kalleberg (2006) argues can be so injurious to workers in today's economy.

For example, Rowena, a Filipina-American in her late thirties, came to SL to find a job as an assembler, explaining that she had previously worked several years for a photocopy company that was subcontracted through a legal firm. She had experienced some upward mobility there, but she had tired of the job and was looking for change. Her goal was to start working as a circuit board assembler and then, once she had gained on-the-job experience, rise to the ranks of management. But

Lisa, SL's branch manager, cognizant of the lack of bridge jobs between assembly and management positions (not to mention between most temporary positions and the ranks of management), advised Rowena to rethink her strategy for achieving upward mobility. In an SL informational interview, Lisa, who had several years of experience placing people in circuit board assembly and manufacturing jobs with Computers R Us and Built to Order, explained to Rowena,

> From what I've seen in all the years I've been placing people in circuit board assembly-line jobs, it is not easy to rise to a managerial position. At these places, they typically use people up and spit them out. These jobs (assembly) are draining, and they work people very hard and replace them often. Surely people become managers and rise in the ranks, but I've rarely seen that in the whole time I've been placing people.

After looking over Rowena's résumé, Lisa advised Rowena to give it to the SL clerical and administrative recruiters who might be able to place her in a position appropriate to her skills and experience. Rowena had strong word processing skills; she was an excellent communicator; and she was fluent in the Tagalog language. Lisa could easily have placed Rowena in an assembler position, since SL had many job orders for which Rowena would easily have qualified; however, Lisa believed that Rowena would quickly become frustrated with that work and quit (indicating an unsuccessful placement), so she tried to help place Rowena in a job that she thought better suited her skills and background and that provided a more realistic path to management, possibly to the supervision of other white-collar, entry-level workers.

Eventually, Select Labor was able to place Rowena in a temp-to-perm position as a customer service representative in a company that was looking for a bilingual English-Tagalog speaker. The job paid more than assembly-line work and had opportunities for upward mobility.

Rowena's experience is one example of many wherein SL staff—with their knowledge of job markets and career paths—were able to provide job counseling and career advice, a service that many workers claimed they were not able to get from other sources. Rowena's example additionally sheds light on the ways in which an agency's efforts to generate greater profits by matching appropriate workers to appropriate jobs can translate into opportunities for workers. In this situation it was profitable for the agency to challenge the candidate's own requests and then redirect them in a way that benefited both the agency and the candidate.

Some workers came to the agency with recently acquired skills but little or no job experience in those areas. Silicon Valley was and continues to be a land of dream making and dream breaking. Many people hoped to capitalize on the prosperity of the high-tech industry by getting a piece of the action. Legends proliferated of (mostly male) nineteen-year-olds who were landing jobs in high-tech and other start-up firms without even a college degree, earning absurdly high salaries, and becoming overnight millionaires through stock option plans.[8] Consequently, some SL job applicants had paid significant sums of money to undergo training in various areas of the high-tech industry, only to learn that getting a job in their field was extremely difficult without experience and connections.

Further, decoding the myriad types of training, programs, and marketable skills was positively bewildering. Job applicants often invested in training programs with little real understanding of how they could deploy their new-found skills or whether their training programs would link them to actual jobs. SL reps recognized the potential of these applicants but were cognizant also that they were not going to be able to place them until they had gotten a foot in the door of a desirable company, possibly in an entry-level temporary job that had little to do with their newly acquired areas of expertise. Entering a company or a field this way could help the job applicant connect to helpful networks for landing jobs. SL worked on them to modify their goals, to adjust and gradually maneuver their way into new fields, and to maximize their fit to particular job assignments.

Mark, for example, was working on getting an MCSE (Microsoft Certified Systems Engineer) certificate and wanted to know what SL might have for him. Employed at the time as a tester (a fairly low-level position in high-tech firms) Mark inspected hard drives, printers, and hardware but wanted to get into the software industry and had been persuaded by Microsoft's claim that people possessing the MCSE certificate would be very marketable. He wanted a high-paying, better job but was not sure how to find one, so next he had decided to learn UNIX because it seemed to him that lots of companies were looking for people proficient in that operating system. SL staff convinced him that starting with a temporary job as a technician at one of the local personal computer (PC) manufacturing firms would be a good bridge job for him, increasing the chances that he would eventually obtain the position he hoped for.

Craig faced virtually the same circumstances as Mark. He had just become MCSE-certified, having spent over $10,000 in the process, but was unable to find a job. He also had forklift certification and held a job as a warehouse worker, but the company that employed him was on the verge of shutting down. With a wife, two children, and a mortgage, he was hoping to earn $14 an hour at a minimum. But he was quite confused by "how the labor market works," particularly by the mantra he heard repeatedly, that all jobs require a minimum of one or more years on the job. How was he supposed to get his first job in this new field, get his proverbial foot in the door?

For Chris, a white male job candidate in his early forties, coming to Select Labor was a last resort. He had spent thousands of dollars and over a year studying full time to get certified as a computer help-desk technician and network administrator. Previously, he had worked at the same company for many years as a materials handler, earning $12 an hour, but desired a new career and more money. Following the wisdom of the day, Chris explained, he had paid out of pocket for retraining in the computer field. He'd been on the job market actively for over four months, but he claimed that despite his recent training and certifications, he had been treated badly at job interviews and unsuccessful in getting a job in his field. Frustrated and disappointed, he turned to SL.

After the agency's recruiters had spent an unsuccessful month trying to get Chris a job as a network administrator or help-desk technician, SL received a job order from a prominent technical company that was seeking a materials handler. This position was disappointingly lower than the network administrator position on which Chris had set his sights, but the SL branch manager suggested trying to place him in this job: not only would he be highly qualified for it because of his previous work experience, but once he had a foot in the door, he might eventually get the opportunity to transfer to the help-desk department. After being persuaded to consider this, Chris got the materials handler position and an offer of $15 an hour—more than he had ever earned. The hiring manager, in discussions with SL, said that he was impressed by Chris, pleased to have such a bright candidate, and that he'd try to put in a good word for him in the firm's help-desk and network administration departments.

Given that possibility, and since $15 an hour was a higher pay rate than initially discussed with Select Labor, Chris accepted the job, having come to believe that this short-term compromise might have a long-term payoff. Although SL could not help Chris get work in his chosen field or immediately get him a permanent position, the agency had found him a job he liked, and one that was paying him a higher salary. In addition, Chris was excited about the prospect of working at a prominent company and working for a manager who was supportive and aware of his desire for career advancement.

Often, when one of the agency's good temporary workers was seeking a temp job but didn't possess the requisite skills for an advertised position, SL placement staff would go out of their way to find out from the manager at the client firm whether there might be other opportunities for that individual. Good temps were something to retain, and SL went to lengths to do so. In one instance, the agency sent out Navit, a long-term temp, to interview at a company about a technician position. In the course of the interview, the manager determined that Navit was not qualified for the position and communicated this decision to Select Labor. The SL placement specialist, however, impressed by Navit's previous record, still felt that he would be a good fit with this particular company, a firm that assembled computer components, and spent a fair amount of time telephoning other contacts she had in the company to see if anyone else there had a need for a trustworthy, hard-working temp. Navit really wanted a job, and she very much wanted to place him in a position with which he would be satisfied, which was the ultimate outcome of these negotiations.

In these ways, SL placement specialists would try to persuade job seekers to make their occupational goals more realistic. Chris and Mark agreed to accept jobs doing the kinds of work they were trying to move away from. Staff persuaded Jack, a web developer, to accept a temp-to-perm position in spite of his concern about its lack of health insurance benefits and vacation time. Partly, agency staff helped job candidates by encouraging them not to dwell on the fact that these were temporary positions. As SL's branch manager advised her staff, "You need to explain to [applicants] that they are not simply temps; they are emergent employees," as if that euphemism would sufficiently cover up the temporary nature of these positions.

Select Labor also persuaded some job seekers who might not otherwise have wanted to work in a temporary capacity to register with the agency. Although employment through a staffing agency is becoming more common, some job seekers did not look favorably upon SL or staffing agencies in general.[9] The staff often had to grapple with a legitimacy problem, when job seekers didn't know exactly what an agency did. When they *did* understand that SL was a temporary placement agency, they sometimes had low expectations that affected the way they presented themselves to SL staff. Harrison, one of the placement specialists, commented that "people don't really understand what we do and that we place people in jobs that *may* become permanent. They often think we're just temp and they don't consider us a 'real' company. So they may come to the interview late and not dressed professionally or something. They don't get what we do, but I try and explain to them that they can get a permanent job through us." In these situations, SL staff had to encourage reluctant job seekers to use their services, agree to lower salaries than they had planned for, or accept the idea of starting on a temporary basis. This was a delicate dance, obviously: talking an extremely reluctant person into accepting a job as a temp might be self-defeating if he or she walked off the job too soon.[10]

SL regularly tried to define clearly the scope of temporary work in order to sell candidates on the merits of a temporary assignment, so that the agency could make placements and generate profits. During staff meetings and SL training sessions, placement specialists at SL were instructed to convince candidates that it was possible to get a permanent job eventually through SL, and that SL could make a range of opportunities available to them.

There is a lamentable irony here. Luring in reluctant temporary workers with vague promises of a permanent job in itself serves to construct temporary workers as good workers. Dangling the carrot— the claim that a temporary position *might* convert to a permanent position—is one of the ways in which agency staff could secure the consent of temps to the positions to which they were assigned even if, from the workers' point of view, the jobs were not ideal. Many researchers have noted that temporary employees are more likely to work well to increase the odds that they will be chosen as the recipient of a permanent job. As Smith argues in her study of temporary workers at a progressive high-tech company, temps "participated in CompTech's work system because they hoped, against obvious statistical odds, that their situation at CompTech was only temporarily temporary, that the job was merely a rung on the ladder to permanent employment with a good employer" (2001a, 117). When temps feel that they have some chance of being hired on in a permanent capacity, they are more willing to display the good worker traits— cooperation, productivity, initiative, punctuality—that make up desirable worker performance.[11]

Strategic Personalism: Developing Caring Relations

Temps' commitment to continue with Select Labor and their willingness to work on a stable, dependable basis was often based on the interpersonal relationships in the office. Although agency staff might distance themselves from problematic temps by refusing to rehire and place them, they extended support and attention to those who were in good standing with the agency. Staff engaged in what Bickham Mendez calls strategic personalism, a mechanism by which employers (in her study, private agency employers of household domestic workers) "engage in emotional labor and create a homelike work environment in order to ensure workers' complicity with management authority and to increase productivity" (1998, 132). Some employers, Bickham Mendez argues, adopt a calculated stance of nurture and compassion toward employees in order to heighten their loyalty to the agency, combat the high turnover that is endemic in the field of private household services and low-wage jobs, and, importantly, disguise exploitation, hierarchy, and demeaning work conditions. Strategic personalism parallels the "highly personalized relationship" of control identified by Rogers (2000, 59–60), a form of interaction that takes staff and temps down a two-way street: it allows agency staff to "gain compliance from the temporary worker," and it allows temps to secure better assignments from the agency.

SL staff engaged in four distinct types of strategic personalism: visiting temps at their jobs; doing emotion work with temps; going "over the top" in providing simple services on an ad hoc basis; and favoring good temps by honoring their requests to work with family members. These methods heightened Select Labor's chances of eliciting the work behaviors of a good temporary employee.

SL staff would visit sites where their employees were working to see how they were doing. As mentioned earlier, they were persistently concerned that once temps went to the job they not be assigned to tasks for which they had not been hired. Such a mismatch would reduce the likelihood that the placement would succeed. In Neuwirth's time at SL she did not observe any instances of "bait and switch" incongruity between the advertised job description and what people were doing when she visited. Notably, however, temps responded warmly to her interest and the interest of other agency reps; their visits were a sign to temps of how much the agency cared about their welfare. The flip side of these visits was that SL staff were monitoring the workers, verifying that there were no obvious problems and ensuring a reasonable level of work performance. Yet monitoring was conducted within a framework of interest in workers' experiences. SL staff also personally delivered paychecks and picked up temps' time cards when they visited the work sites—visible displays of attention to and personal engagement with their temporary workforce.

Inside the agency, and occasionally at work sites, Select Labor staff were the consummate emotion workers (Hochschild 1983). In the broadest terms, agency staff would calm and empathize with their regular, core temporary workers who confided in staff their anxiety, misgivings, and frustrations. It is difficult to convey the degree of personal and familial problems that came across SL staff's desks. To be sure, many of SL's temps who were circulating in and out of temp jobs on a regular basis were not experiencing a personal crisis because of it; nevertheless, many others were. When job applicants had depleted or nearly depleted their financial resources, agency staff had to deal with temps in tears, frustrated with their blocked job searches and anxious about their inability to understand what was happening to them on the job market. Many job seekers who had families for whom they were responsible were reaching the end of their ropes because of their inability to find a job with a steady and livable wage and benefits. A fair number who had recently moved to the Silicon Valley area, hoping to take advantage of the purported opportunities there, were hopelessly disillusioned.

In fact, the "Silicon Valley fever" of excitement and hope that Judith Stacey (1990) had found in 1984, in her study of postindustrial families, was running equally high in the boom of 2000. This fever was fueled by an image of prosperity and mobility, an image that carried with it a downside of uncertainty, wage and occupational inequality, toxicity, and crime. Many of those who came to Select Labor were sucked into the "hydraulic" of these contrasting sides of the Valley.

And unfortunately, much as in the fluid dynamics of a hydraulic (a dangerous river condition in which kayakers and rafters can get pushed down and stuck in the circulating water; escape comes by swimming one's way to the bottom of this vortex, and people almost never escape by swimming directly to the top), many people were going to go down before they could surface to a desirable position. Multiple candidates who had done what they thought were all the right things to gain a foothold in the labor market—earned new credentials and certifications, attended school, quit work in dead-end jobs—were not only disillusioned but angry and depressed as well.

In addition, paychecks occasionally were misplaced, or not issued because time cards were lost or never submitted, leading temps to bring their fear as well as their wrath down upon the heads of the SL staff. Given the extraordinary degree of administrative complexities and hierarchies in the industry, with layer upon layer of subcontracting being the norm, it was surprising that temps' tempers flared as infrequently as they did during Neuwirth's fieldwork. Agency staff tried to anticipate and preempt emotional outbursts when possible. The branch manager, for example, personally withdrew some $300 from her automatic teller machine in order to make a cash advance to a regular temp whose paycheck had not come through; another agency rep drove a temp to her job when the individual arrived at the SL office but had no way to get to a client firm for her shift. When one valued temp, a woman who had contracted for several jobs through Select Labor and had been working in a clerical position for nine months, exhaustedly asked for an additional day off over a long weekend so that she could spend it with her young child, agency staff found a temp to fill her place for that short time—a temp filling in for a temp. These and other incidences of temps' resource-deficient and emotional lives, conditioned by the "hot" economy of the Valley, colored interpersonal interactions at SL day in and day out. Placement representatives spent significant time walking temps through their problems, pointing out silver linings, sharing their anger and demoralization, and brainstorming about solutions.

Finally, in numerous situations, temporary workers on SL's payroll brought members of their extended families into the office, hoping to get their relatives placed with them. Such requests were inevitable, given Select Labor's bonus system for personal referrals, but honoring them was tricky because some managers at client firms felt that having family-based work groups on the shop floor was an impediment rather than an asset to productivity. Families could conceivably bond against management and fellow workers, or might work in accordance with their own small-group norms rather than with the norms of a more impersonal, nonfamilial work group. Yet SL staff cooperated with these requests when they were able to, especially when the person making the request was a valued temp. In addition to building up goodwill with their temporary workers, accommodating family requests such as these expanded the network of trusted temps that SL was explicitly dedicated to building.

As might be predicted, there was a payoff to SL for these caring relations. Taking care of job applicants enhanced workers' sense that the agency's priority was to put applicants' needs first and hiring firms' needs second—despite the fact that SL's explicit business policy was the opposite. Seeing temps through their crises elicited loyalty and deepened the workers' sense of obligation to perform their jobs well. Ironically, in an era in which many observers lament the decline in attachment of many workers toward their employers—as well as a decline in "durable purpose," as Sennett (1998) puts it—the temporary-placement agency was striving to increase the attachment that temps felt to the agency itself. One indication that strategic personalism was at least somewhat effective can be found in a simple observation. Although we lack a definitive figure, it was clear from Neuwirth's four-month position at Select Labor that a sizable number of temps on its payroll had worked for SL for two years or more.

Evidence of Select Labor's success in maintaining a pool of loyal temporary workers was part of daily office experience. One temp who had been pleased with her placements came in with a large platter of freshly baked cookies for the SL staff. A small group of women who were friends, and who worked together at one site, delivered an entire meal of Mexican food to the office. Select Labor staff, on these occasions, reaped the rewards of strategic personalism, to be sure, but these small acts of reciprocity and friendship were vivid reminders of the larger fact that many temps were invested in maintaining good relations with SL office staff and that SL had succeeded in maintaining a core workforce of reliable, good temps.

In contrast to passively waiting to place people who came to their office looking for temporary jobs, Select Labor reps actively constructed a marketable temporary workforce by selectively recruiting qualified temps to the degree possible. In the words of one corporate trainer, "We're not body pushers in this company. In this job market we may do a bit of that, but for the most part, that's not our policy or practice....Integrity is our motto."[12] In point of fact she was right: SL staff endeavored to be much more than just "body pushers." In saying so, the agency trainer echoed the rhetoric of industry leaders in the 1960s and 1970s, when they cultivated an image of integrity and denied that all they were doing was dumping warm bodies on the market. We argue, however, that although the personal integrity of individual staff members *might* add up to a collective organizational integrity, it is not sufficient to explain the

processes and dynamics set forth in this chapter. The logic driving
the anti-body-pusher approach to the market was a logic of capital,
accumulated by selling (or striving to sell) and profiting from good
temporary workers. For this reason staff concerns with reliability,
cooperativeness, and the right person for the right job were threaded
throughout their recruitment, selecting and weeding out, job counseling, and strategic personalism.

These practices did not allow for perfect quality control. Staff
made mistakes in assessing temps' work potential, as evidenced when
they sent out job candidates who never showed up at their assigned
work site, or when a temp became a problem on the job and agency
staff would no longer place him or her. Placement specialists were
sometimes forced to compromise when the urgency of some orders
forced them to send out people about whom they were ambivalent—
knowing them to be far less than good temps. Moreover, SL staff could
not control the quality of temps who came from their secondary contractors, although we would assume that, extending the argument
about the importance of good temps to the broader industry, SL made
every effort to contract with agencies who likewise wanted to maintain a good reputation for the quality of their own temps.

On the whole, the agency attempted to set a bar, achieve a standard, pursue and optimize its chances for building the best temporary
workforce possible. This workforce was the agency's cutting edge, its
competitive commodity, and staff devoted an enormous amount of
their work to its manufacture. In so doing, they continually had to
balance ambiguity in demand (unpredictable and often unclear job
orders) with the vicissitudes of supply (the predictable messiness in
the lives of people who would frequently seek low-wage temporary
employment in a churning economy). Although the industry at large
may have succeeded in establishing a normative framework for the
greater use of temporary workers, enacting the temporary employment relationship requires the active participation and collaboration
of those people who work in agencies day in and day out.

In real ways, in the midst of striving to construct a good workforce, SL staff also advanced the conditions of the lives of many
people seeking temporary employment. Placing job candidates was
the minimal service provided by Select Labor, but in the process,

staff also helped many temps interpret and navigate a confusing labor market, gave them advice about interviewing and presentation of self, helped them improve their résumés, and, in some cases, literally helped them survive by making sure they had money or transportation. In other words, SL provided a number of services that contemporary observers see as critical for workers in an economy that is based on risk and unpredictability.

These processes point to another significant issue for the success of the agency and of the industry as a whole: the issue of retention. Much of the worker-agency relationship described in this chapter has the effect of retaining good temps. On the other side of the equation, how can the temporary *jobs* be constructed such that temps will agree to stay in them, or to stay in temporary employment, with only a sliver of hope for a "real" or "permanent" job? Insofar as agency staff tend to their bottom line, they spend a considerable amount of time improving the terms of temporary work and the temporary employment relationship—another important piece of the puzzle of creating and maintaining good temporary workers.

Chapter Four

Softening "Rough and Tough Managers"

Creating "Good Enough" Jobs for Temps

Select Labor was founded with the idea of offering employment to those seeking work of an interim nature and, at the same time, providing the business community with highly competent employees.... We are glad you came to Select Labor and have been qualified to join our staff.... We look forward to providing you, as a Select Labor employee, with many meaningful and profitable work assignments.

Pamphlet distributed to applicants for temporary jobs at Select Labor, n.d.

Temporary help service agencies have a considerable investment in producing a pool of workers who will accept the terms of temporary employment and work in a reliable, effective fashion. Precarious as their acceptance may be, it is the foundation for participation in a system of contingent employment. Chapter 3 showed how one agency's staff worked with one group of its customers, job seekers who used the services of Select Labor to find temporary positions. It is time to turn to Select Labor's other customers—the hiring firms—and look at how agency staff intervened at two different levels to build a market and protect their investment. Specifically, they worked to stabilize

the corporate demand side of the temporary employment relationship both at the point of production and at the point of higher-level
policymakers. This chapter focuses on the former to show how the
agency staff built new employment relationships on the shop floor
and in the office.

As Gonos, Ofstead, and Peck have shown, and as we found in analyzing business publications, the THS industry went all out in its
market-making efforts to convince employers that temporary employees could be acceptable, relatively trustworthy, and dependable
workers. But scholarly studies and media accounts were silent on the
issue of how a system of temporary jobs would be built, coordinated,
and maintained, once hiring companies had laid out the welcome mat
for temps. Not only must there be jobs for temps; there must be particular types of jobs. If temporary help placement firms hope to stabilize
their product—good temporary workers—they must minimally stabilize and guarantee the quality of jobs in which they can place them.

In the late twentieth century advertising decent temporary jobs
was a marketing pitch: for example, while the sales literature circulated to client firms highlighted the quality of its temporary laborers,
the literature for job applicants (quoted in the epigraph above) lauded
the "meaningful and profitable work assignments" that awaited them
if they used SL's services. Agencies, to remain competitive, have to
minimize the risks their employees will face when they report for
work in diverse companies. They need to be attentive to abusive conditions or legal complications that might lead temporary workers to
sue agencies and client firms.[1] We suggest that, ironically, temporary
employment, a precarious employment relationship, is built on efforts of agencies to eliminate risk and capriciousness on shop and
office floors.[2] Without such intervention, temps might refuse their
consent and cooperation with their hiring managers.

To be precise, agency staff broker relations between the temporary
workforce and the hiring companies. They must heed the practices
of the hiring companies and the ways in which those practices potentially can compromise the quality and output of temporary workers.
Agency staff have to interpret hiring companies' distinct cultures,
markets, and philosophies and learn how to work with and around
them. Then they must teach managers in client firms how to use

temps effectively and gain their compliance. We saw how, in the middle of the twentieth century, personnel and THS industry writers directed their pitch to managers inside hiring companies about ways to use temps efficiently and responsibly. Our field research shows that now, agencies have taken up much of the responsibility of integrating temps into hiring companies and minimizing any disruptiveness that might take place when line managers have to supervise workers who are not part of their regular workforce.

If agency staff place temps at companies with bad work conditions— work sites that are unsafe or are managed by supervisors who resent the addition of temps to their units, who act "rough and tough," as one agency staff member put it, or blatantly exploit temps—they must deal with an increasing volume of complaints and labor turnover.

Given the demise of the fee-splitting arrangement and the advent of the per-hour markup as a source of revenue (Gonos 2001; see chapter 1), agencies do not profit from the turnover of temporary workers. To the contrary, in the era of widespread and long-term use of temporary workers, agencies lose if turnover is too high. In much the same way as when companies hire permanent workers, invest in their training, and pay a cost if they quit prematurely, so do temporary-placement agencies invest in their temps and pay a cost if temps walk off the job without completing the assignment, refuse to return to an assignment, or fail to re-use the agency's services.[3] A continual need to develop new temps becomes a burden to the agency—a cost underestimated in previous studies which insinuate that low-level temporary workers are interchangeable, almost disposable. On the contrary, every new job applicant must be administratively processed: tested, screened, and interviewed for a job. Agency staff must nurture their social relationships with temps. These relations build momentum and endurance; to lose them means that the agency has to begin all over again with new "raw material." Having to deal with a hiring company where bad management practices lead temps to quit their assignments poses a distinct challenge for a placement firm that wishes to maintain a steady and reliable supply of temporary workers. An exploitive and stingy client, in the eyes of Select Labor staff, was as undesirable as a bad temp.[4]

The negotiations, relationships, and complexities involved in constructing and rationalizing a management paradigm for working with temps involves also the efforts of agency staff to upgrade work conditions for temps. "Good enough" temporary jobs emerge in the nexus of give and take (conflict, cooperation, skepticism, and discontent) among agency staff, line managers, and human resources personnel. Examining these processes illuminates the surprising side of contemporary contingent work: that in order to manufacture its product profitably, THS staff must guard the conditions under which temps work.

Recalibrating Abusive and Inept Managers

Caricatures abound of supervisors and managers and the way they deal with temporary employees. The pervasive stereotype of the incompetent, counterproductive, and coercive manager parallels the stereotypes of incompetent and counterproductive temps discussed in chapter 1. Researchers have blamed managers for degrading temporary employees' work, for subjecting temps to toxic and hazardous conditions (McAllister 1998; Parker 1994, chap. 5), for sexual harassment (Rogers and Henson 1997) and homophobia (Henson 1996, chap. 3), among other things. This portrayal of managers, although partial (Smith 2001b), has a kernel of truth: one of the major factors shaping the work experiences of Select Labor's temps was the attitude, interpersonal style, or management philosophy of the person for whom the temp worked. Whether the temp was integrated into a workforce of regular employees or was one of an enclave of temporary workers, on-site supervisors and managers gave directions, kept an eye on the pace at which temps worked, commented on the products they turned out, reprimanded or praised them for the quality of their work, and even timed their breaks.[5]

Select Labor staff had to moderate and rationalize—recalibrate— the behavior of on-site managers who were abusive, despotic, or confused when carrying out their normal oversight functions under trying and opaque conditions. In some cases, managers and supervisors on the shop floor were statistical discriminators, acting as though temporary workers on the whole were untrustworthy, no matter the laudable qualities or attributes of any individual temp. Occasionally, managers baldly revealed their contempt for temps and attacked their vulnerable status. The comments of one hiring manager, as reported by a disgruntled applicant upon returning from an interview, revealed the humiliation that at least some managers were willing to heap upon the temp: "I told Steve [the hiring manager] that I hoped to earn $10 an hour. Steve laughed at me and said, 'With your lack of skills and knowledge of computers, you should just be happy with the salary I'm offering and just be happy to have the job.'"

In other cases, the individual manager was disrespectful and injurious to all subordinates, permanent and temporary workers alike. Morale at firms could be severely affected when there was a sense of unfair or capricious treatment or when workers perceived that management did not care about their complaints. Demoralization registered strongly in the agency when temps' complaints about a particular boss added up. As study after study of work has shown, despotic or coercive managers can create significant organizational costs (to productivity, efficiency, quality) and can lead to high turnover, resistance, and even sabotage (Burawoy 1979; Edwards 1979; Hodson 2001; Jacoby 1985). Supervisors of temporary workers are no exception to this rule: they can incur obvious and concealed costs when they act out their contempt for temps.

SL staff had heard numerous complaints from temps at Computers R Us (CRU) regarding Rina, one of the production supervisors. One day Lisa, SL's branch manager, got a phone call from the senior human resources manager at CRU inviting her to sit in on a special staff meeting that had been called to review Rina's performance. Lisa was already well aware that Rina, who supervised both temporary and permanent workers, was causing problems. Temporary workers at Computers R Us had told of the routine humiliation that Rina handed out: she was rude to them on the shop floor, snapped at them on a regular basis, and had even yelled at them. Some refused to return to CRU. And yet Lisa, in talking about the problem with SL staff, defended Rina, arguing that she, like other production supervisors working at computer manufacturing facilities at this time, was under tremendous pressure to keep pace with intense production schedules.

Lisa thus expressed concern for her two equally pressing constituencies: "her workers" (Select Labor's temps), and the client firm. The human resources manager at Computers R Us told Lisa that she needed her help, that she wanted her to give Rina the feedback from temporary workers and also to strategize with HR staff about how to rectify the situation. Subsequent to a meeting between Lisa and Rina, Rina's behavior appeared to improve; in the weeks that followed, SL had far fewer complaints from the workers she supervised.

Rina's actions had had a destabilizing impact on the ability of Computers R Us to hold on to its temporary workers, and SL willingly stepped in to help ameliorate the problem. In so doing, SL took on aspects of the traditional HR function, participating in performance appraisal, representing employees' grievances, and helping to manage tensions between the temporary and permanent workforce.

SL was asked on another occasion to help manage a problematic supervisor at Computers R Us and again assist HR in communicating employee grievances to him. Alex, a Select Labor placement specialist, was brought in to deal with Steve, the facilities management supervisor at CRU who, like Rina, evoked many complaints from temporary workers. The HR person in charge of temporary workers at CRU had not wanted to confront Steve about his attitude but finally felt there was no alternative: Steve's actions were negatively affecting morale and retention of temporary workers. Alex explained:

> Steve's a rough and tough guy. I haven't met him but I've placed a few janitors with him, and he takes a lot of workers. But he gets people and spits them out. Like, he waits to sign time cards and then sends them in after they are due. He also talks rough with his workers—so people don't want to stay working for him for ten bucks an hour and get that kind of treatment. Laura [a human resources manager at Computers R Us] wants me to talk with Steve about these issues—she wants me to handle these things and keep her out of having these kinds of talks with managers. She's relying on me to have these talks. I'm not sure what to do, but I'll have a talk with him. Maybe I'll take him out to lunch.

Alex's solution was to address Steve outside the workplace and to "socialize" him about the issues facing temporary workers, to educate Steve about the fact that the SL temps were usually very willing to work hard and comply with orders if they were treated respectfully. A significant goal of these one-on-one interventions was to eliminate capriciousness in the handling of temps.

In yet another client company, Lisa had a series of conversations with a line manager, criticizing his harsh attitude and actions toward Select Labor temps. Lisa had heard from a number of temporary workers, as well as from SL office staff, that this particular manager was intimidating temps when he interviewed them. And once they started the job, he often required them to work very long shifts on short notice. When Lisa found this manager unresponsive to her concerns, she decided to go over his head to the manager of the company's HR department. In light of his conversation with Lisa, this senior-level HR manager reprimanded the abusive line manager, leading Lisa to feel that she had succeeded in communicating to both of them that rude and thuggish behavior toward temporary workers would not be tolerated.

Agency staff were also concerned to correct misperceptions, ignorance, and possibly malfeasance with respect to using temporary workers, usually with an eye to minimizing agency liability. Some agency staff voiced the belief that certain line managers hoped to exploit temps (even if they didn't consciously label their actions as exploitation), to get the most out of temps on the cheap without being accountable. At one training session, Katie, a member of Select Labor's corporate staff, pointed out to seminar participants that

> clients sometimes use us as a liability [*sic*], and they think they can use practices they normally wouldn't because they are going through us to hire these people [temps]. But we are [not the sole but] the "joint" employers of these temps, so the corporations— our clients—are also liable. We need to get detailed job descriptions from the clients and make sure they don't go outside the bounds of those job descriptions.

This procedure was especially pertinent to avoiding accusations of discrimination. Agency staff had good reason to feel concerned, because temporary workers can sue the agencies that hire them if they feel an agency is discriminating against them or is aiding and abetting discrimination on the part of line managers in hiring companies (Stone 2006). Katie went on: "Clients may think they can use us to exploit or discriminate against workers but that's not the case, and we go into this partnership with the companies, so if we discriminate, they can get in trouble too. We shouldn't let companies think they can use us to discriminate, because they can't. We are bound by the same laws as they are."

As would be expected, agency staff could not always succeed in improving bad workplaces among those where they placed their temps. The financial power of a client could limit the agency's ability to battle that firm's damaging management practices. Facing a client company that was a significant source of revenue, or one that tried to conceal its shop floor practices, the agency could only try to contain the resultant disgruntlement and turmoil. For example, Select Labor had placed a number of workers in warehouse positions in one firm, packaging computers. Although SL staff had visited the job site and determined that its quality and the health and safety standards were acceptable, over time it emerged that some African American men and women temps felt they were being discriminated against by the line manager. SL staff had wondered why many of their workers came back requesting new placements; a good handful had walked off the job and returned to SL with complaints so vague that the staff had trouble pinning down the precise problem.

It took several weeks of investigation and inquiry to get a handle on this particular line manager's racism: he had publicly stated, SL staff discovered, that he favored male Vietnamese workers and was perceived as treating unfairly all the women workers and any men who came from a different racial or ethnic background. Workers of the "wrong" gender and ethnicity told Rosa, at SL, that the foreman yelled at them, pressured them to work harder, and gave them tasks they claimed were "dirty" or "demeaning." Select Labor staff met with upper management at the firm and complained about the line manager's actions. Nevertheless, that manager retained his position, and SL continued to place workers at this job site: the hiring firm was taking on so many of its temps that SL feared the loss of the considerable revenue.

Socializing Managers and Building
Temporary Employment Relationships

Agency staff did not limit themselves to trying to recalibrate "bad" managers who made it difficult for their temps to succeed or who made the company vulnerable to lawsuits. Their larger goal was to socialize managers across the board, including all those who were unfamiliar with the administrative logistics of temporary employment. Placement specialists would "teach" hiring managers how to use temporary workers and how to use staffing services in general. Partly, doing so entailed building an infrastructure in which agency staff could support line managers on the shop floor. Many managers lacked any regular experience with this different set of employment arrangements. While acquainting them with the unique aspects and virtues of working with temps, SL staff were trying to rationalize and standardize the way the latter were deployed.

The experiences of one Select Labor staff person, Jill, who managed a vendor-on-premises unit at Technology Pathways (TP or TechPath), highlights this process. Jill's desk was situated among the desks of other administrative staff so that to a regular employee who was not in the know, she seemed indistinguishable from other permanent company employees. When not attending to daily paperwork and administrative tasks at her desk, however, Jill walked around the TP "campus," visiting with managers and informally "training" them on how to use SL's services. Jill explained

> when people come off the street to Technology Pathways to apply for temporary jobs, they go on our payroll if they are to start as a temp, but TechPath doesn't yet understand that they can send the person directly to me and I'll handle that paperwork. Now they are putting the person into their system and making a lot of work for themselves. I'll have to teach them and explain the options and possibilities for me to help them out. We can handle all that and save them time. I'm not sure why they are doing all that themselves.

In her first few weeks, Jill spent a great deal of time with managers, getting to know them and learning about their hiring needs, advising them on how SL could save them time by searching for and interviewing potential employees. Working on site, Jill also attended regular HR meetings to gain insight into and shape personnel practices at the company. SL had a vested economic interest in teaching managers how to use temps, at TP and at all their work sites. The following example sheds further light on this interest.

When SL first started its vendor-on-premises (VOP) program at Technology Pathways, there were approximately six temporary workers at the company. Three months later there was a total of seventy-six temps working at TP (thirty-five of whom had been recruited by Select Labor). Jill explained that "even though some of these temps were not recruited by us, we make money on all of them because we have a primary vendor contract with Technology Pathways, so we have a subcontracting relationship with the other agencies—they are subcontracting with us to have temps at Technology Pathways." These multiple layers of subcontracting were common with VOP arrangements, and Jill's presence on site facilitated both the growth of TechPath's contingent workforce and Select Labor's share of this growth. Simply put, the larger the workforce of temps at Technology Pathways, the larger the flow of revenue to Select Labor.

Jill also advised managers on how to enlist SL's help in getting, quickly and efficiently, the kinds of workers they needed. She wrote and designed job descriptions after discussions with managers about their labor force needs. Jill conducted the orientation for temporary employees, helping them with necessary paperwork, giving them a tour of the facility, and training them in matters related to safety and the grievance process. She oversaw performance appraisals and reviews for contingent workers, conducted ergonomic evaluations of workstations, and made recommendations to managers when improvements were necessary. She had regular access to managers through meetings and informal encounters, and often these interactions afforded Jill a significant impact on the direction of HR management at the firm. She even negotiated on behalf of temporary and temp-to-perm workers for higher wages when hiring managers offered pay rates that she thought were too low, given prevailing market wages for temps—something she did with other firms as well. As Jill explained, about another company where SL had a VOP account: "I'm shocked at how low the pay rates are [at Company X]. They don't realize the current pay rates in the Valley now and how competitive things are and how much more people are making these days....I'll try and negotiate with them, and I know I'll have to advocate for some candidates."

Negotiating higher pay for temps was not an uncommon practice for SL staff. Elsewhere, they had been cultivating an account with Building Blocks, working as consultants with BB management when the company relocated from the west side to the east side of the San Francisco Bay. Managers at Building Blocks initially insisted that they intended to pay temporary workers the minimum wage. The SL salesperson told them there would be trouble if they paid only minimum wage; she stated bluntly that no one competent or reliable would come to work for them. After lengthy negotiations the BB managers agreed to start temps at two dollars above minimum wage—still low pay, to be sure, but high enough to increase the chance of filling positions.

When managers were authorized to hire temporary workers to help get unexpected orders out, they were occasionally uncertain as to how they should deploy these workers. As Jill's experiences at Technology Pathways demonstrate, agency staff were often called upon to assess unanticipated work orders, predict employers' needs, and then prepare job descriptions for hiring companies. For all intents and purposes, agency staff were production engineers and organizational consultants, trained to size up jobs, workforce head counts, labor processes, and production procedures and to figure out what was necessary for achieving outcomes in optimally efficient ways. If managers did not request the right types or numbers of temps, the ensuing mismatch between workers and positions could undermine the likelihood of a successful temporary placement, and SL staff had a strong commitment to avoiding failure on this score. Some companies' hiring managers relied on SL staff for this service.

One manager who called from Computer Driven (CD), for example, needed some temps who could work as testers, but she had not prepared a description for the position. She requested that Alex write up a job description and let her review it, after which she planned to authorize SL to recruit people for the position. The Computer Driven manager wanted Alex—in addition to specifying the production schedule and the length of the job, the tasks and the minimal skills required—to benchmark this position by comparing prevailing wages for testers, information for CD to consider. Alex used job descriptions that were on file in the agency as a template for CD's positions. Computer Driven was thus able to rely on the signaling from Select Labor about what constituted a reasonable job, reasonable job expectations, and prevailing wages. In turn, Alex was able to transmit to CD a normative model for a temporary placement.

Assessing Workplace Safety

Occasionally, temps found themselves working in sites where they faced genuine risks to their bodily well-being. Being denied appropriate tools or laboring in workplaces where physical arrangements were dangerously configured had the potential to inflict meaningful damage on workers. Here, as in other cases, avoidance of legal and economic complications, as well as the concern to develop decent work sites for temps, drove agency staff's efforts to minimize injury and harm.

Temporary-placement agencies wish to be recognized as employers of record, and taking the lead in controlling workplace risk and injury is an important criterion for passing the economic reality test (see Appendix II) that is used in courts to determine the identity of the employer. According to this test, the employer sets the working conditions and exercises control over the work process.

In the case of injury and hazard there is an additional incentive for the agency to establish that it, not the client firm, is the employer. Nearly all states prohibit injured workers who receive workers' compensation from suing their employer, even though every state assures that workers injured on the job are compensated for injuries and time lost from work. Thus, agencies try to make it clear that they are the employers, in order to take advantage of this "workers' compensation shield" (Stone 2006, 267).

Agency staff were advised to "hire safe workers," "give all temps safety training," and "make sure clients have safe workplaces and good supervision." They were instructed to ask themselves these questions: Were they providing appropriate safety training? What office procedures did they have in place for responding to accidents? Did they know for sure that the work sites where they were sending temps were safe? Were they "sending temps with proper experience, skill, strength, and attitude?" The agency also had a "return-to-work" policy, which called for staff to find modified, less demanding positions for injured temporary workers until they were able to return to regular temporary employment. Temps themselves would complain of dangerous work settings, and some refused to return to these jobs. These combined factors led agency staff to go to lengths to ensure that risk was minimized and safety maximized.

On several occasions, agency staff refused to open accounts with companies that were reputed to be negligent about work conditions, or they let go of accounts with companies that didn't comply with Select Labor's requests for improvement. Sales staff increasingly tried to avoid accounts with firms we might think of as the "Satanic mills" of the high-tech industry. "Boardhouses"—work sites where temps assembled and soldered circuit boards—exemplified this exploitive type of workplace. Boardhouses had extremely labor-intensive production processes, with stressful jobs. Reportedly, workers found it hard to get breaks even to go to the bathroom in some boardhouses. In short, a boardhouse was a paradigmatically oppressive and relentless factory setting. Computers R Us, discussed earlier in reference to its despotic supervisors, was a boardhouse, and much discussion percolated in the Select Labor office about avoiding similar types of accounts and work sites. CRU was its own "ideal-type" of bad employment practices, a company from which SL staff learned about what they didn't want to do.[6]

About another exploitive hiring company, McTech, temps repeatedly told agency staff that it was a "bad" place to work, and SL was managing out the account, slowly shrinking the number of placements there. Similarly, agency staff were in the process of phasing out another company that routinely ignored requests to improve safety conditions. Select Labor staff also simply dropped a client firm that refused to correct a situation where heavy boxes kept falling on temporary workers.

Select Labor believed that the best way it could keep tabs on what its temps were walking into was to conduct a thorough evaluation of each work site. When possible, recruitment specialists would inspect the sites when they set up new accounts with hiring companies and perhaps make recommendations for improvements. Then, by routine spot checks (described in chapter 3), they were able to monitor ongoing work conditions without advance notice. And where they had vendor-on-premises setups, they could continue to scope out potential risks to their temps. As a company vice president warned participants at a corporate training session,

> you have to make sure that you are eyeballing the job sites where you are sending people. Think to yourself, would I want to work here? Don't just send people to a site you know nothing about. It helps to do on-site visits when possible and see as many places as you can. Yes, we are the legal employer of temps but we have dual—joint—employment so companies can't totally clean their hands of bad practices. As placement specialists, you should be getting detailed job descriptions when possible and remind the client about their joint employment responsibilities. Do as much quality control as possible. Visit clients when possible and develop a rapport with them.

Temp-to-Perm Programs and Job Ladders

By alerting managers to the advantages of converting temps into permanent workers, SL staff encouraged client firms to create regularized, even if infrequent, mobility paths for temps. Soon after Neuwirth began working at Select Labor, one of the regional managers explained the "pitch" she and others in the office should use if she felt someone at a client firm might be interested in temp-to-perm arrangements.

> I want you all to be checking with clients to see how the relationship is going. Is it working out, do they like the person? And if so, might they consider bringing the person onto their staff? Our fees

for conversion are now higher, so it's worth it for us to do this type of transferring and to advocate for it. You should tell the client that good workers are hard to find in this economy, and if they like the temp, they should consider hiring the person permanently. We make a lot when you can negotiate a conversion. Plus, we make the client happy and we make the candidate happy. After the person is on the job for, say, about two to three weeks, you should talk to the client and say, "You may want to lock in as perm because it's hard to find good candidates. And if you lock them in now, you can secure them." You should be forcing the perm issue with clients and encourage that a lot more often these days.

In actuality, adopting temp-to-perm programs is a higher-level, human resources decision, but managers at the point of production needed to be encouraged to use such temps. To the degree that they promoted temp-to-perm replacements, SL staff were building job ladders for their temps that straddled the boundaries of two organizations. Helping client firms formalize their temp-to-perm programs—in which managers observe temps during a trial run to consider whether he or she might be a good permanent worker—was one way the agency consolidated and regularized its position within companies. This may seem contradictory, given our argument that placement agencies want to maintain an on-call pool of good temp workers, but THS agencies do have an investment in promoting temp-to-perm placements.

The most obvious reason for converting a temporary to a permanent worker is monetary, as the "pitch" cited earlier would suggest. SL earned a hefty commission from a conversion, a percentage of which went to individual salespeople in the agency. But the full answer is not that simple. The niche for temp-to-perm employees is a market niche all its own that SL and other agencies hoped to enter. To an increasing degree, temp-to-perm programs are another market-making response to a significant shift in hiring practices inside client firms (Autor 2003). Temporary-help placement agencies respond to companies' demand for workers who will work well enough as temps that client companies will be willing to hire them on as permanent workers. Houseman (2001) and Houseman, Kalleberg, and Erickcek (2003), in fact, note that a major reason employers cite for using the services of THS agencies is to allow them to screen potential workers and help save costs in the long run. In trying to lower the costs and risks involved when a company hires a permanent employee who turns out to be a poor performer, a thief, or simply incompatible with the practices and culture of a firm, businesses are in effect placing potential employees on probation by having them work as a temporary employee. And as David Autor (2003) points out, many companies have turned to the temp-to-perm approach because it enables them to weed out "bad temporary" employees and thus avoid the lawsuits that might be filed if they had to terminate "bad permanent" employees who had been placed on their payrolls without adequate screening. The temp-to-perm market is distinct, in crucial ways, from the market for temporary workers.

Select Labor staff found that managers often were responsive to their pitches for temp-to-perm workers. Some managers wanted workers they could train and were loath to see good workers leave after a short temp stint.[7] Even if they were authorized to hire permanent workers, though, many managers were under pressure from HR to avoid hiring workers without "testing" them first: observing them on a probationary period without any legal complications or obligations. SL staff emphasized what they could do for managers on this score, explaining that unlike the temp agency of old that would simply fill positions with "warm bodies," they could help managers find trainable workers with a good work ethic who might become a permanent part of their workforce. For example, Jill encouraged managers at Technology Pathways to "try out" SL temps, to let Select Labor "do the leg work" for them in recruiting and screening candidates who might prove suitable for permanent employment. Her position inside the hiring company gave SL the ability not only to expand the actual number of temporary workers at that particular site but also to transform TP's managers' ideas about staffing agencies and TP's contingent workforce.

Finally, placing some temp workers in permanent positions was crucial to the agency's sales strategy for enticing new temps to its pool. Staff continually worked to recruit new temps *and* to secure permanent placement for ongoing temps. Part of maintaining a good reputation with job seekers was the agency's ability to back up its claim that temporary workers might be converted to regular workers. As noted in chapter 3, agency staff routinely recruited potential temporary workers by talking up the possibilities of a temporary position turning into a permanent job. Even though very few temps transitioned to permanent positions during the time of Neuwirth's fieldwork, talk of temp-to-perm possibilities figured prominently in discussions with job applicants. From the line managers' point of view, the efficiencies and conveniences of temp-to-perm programs were clear, as we learned from interviews with company managers. Mary, a branch manager at a title company, explained that staffing services played a significant role in her style of management. Mary felt that hiring office personnel through staffing agencies made her job a lot easier. She appreciated having a trial period for new employees; if she hired new permanent employees on her own and they did not work out, she might have to let them go in the first few weeks. She hated that part of her job. With the staffing service, she could just call the agency and tell them to reassign an unsuitable employee. Mary's explanation emphasized the psychoemotional benefits of being able to start a new employee on a temporary basis:

> The real reason why I use temp agencies is because I hate to lay anyone off. And, our business is so cyclical...you know it's going to drop off, and that means laying people off or redistributing them to other branches. Somebody put the idea into my head that, okay, you are this busy and you know it's going to go away, so maybe a temp agency would be the way to go because then you can pick and choose. And then if you want to keep them, if they work out, then you can, and if not, then get rid of them and there's no heartbreak involved. I just feel that if the person is going to work out, and if they want a job, then it would be temp-to-perm.

Mary claimed that she exclusively used staffing services when she wanted to recruit and hire new personnel, saying that she rarely had to let any of her temporary employees go and had even hired some on as permanent employees. Mary had incorporated use of these agencies into her routine management strategy, and she said that she had been encouraging other branch managers to follow her lead.

Another manager explained that screening and hiring workers through staffing agencies made her job a lot easier because she didn't have to do the employment paperwork for an employee hired through an agency until the firm was certain that the person would be retained on a permanent basis. Susan, the hiring manager at a small company that manufactured medical equipment devices, emphasized the administrative advantages to using temporaries:

> The biggest advantage of using staffing agencies is not having to go through the horrendous paperwork to hire someone and then find out it's not going to work out. It's nice to have someone come in and basically you don't have to do official paperwork and then if you like them you can do all the paperwork. It's nice not to have to do it until you have the right person and you like them. The disadvantages? I can't really think of anything that's negative about hiring temps. We have our core people that will always be there, and we look for temps when we get new projects and are not sure about business flow. Business flow is key to how long temps stay here and whether or not they become perm.

George, a hiring manager at a multinational company that refurbished and distributed large semiconductor equipment, explained that even if he knew he needed a permanent worker, he might hire a temporary one so that he could get quicker human resource approval for the hire. Once the temp was on the job, he'd go through the paperwork to make that employee a permanent offer. Expediency was foremost in George's mind:

> Usually the temp approval process is a lot quicker than a regular position. You know you need somebody. You're going to say to your HR manager, here's what I gotta have, can I get a temp in here for a couple weeks? You start moving into that category and getting all your ducks in a row to justify that position while this temp is in place. There's a number of ways of doing this. You could have a

regular req [requisition order], but if you know that you need that person right away, you ask for a temp.

For George and other managers, hiring through staffing agencies helped them get employees quickly because they could bypass elaborate HR protocol for hiring permanent workers (see chapter 5). Managers like George were turning to staffing agencies to hire temporaries even if they knew they needed permanent workers in the long term. For workers, knowledge that sometimes temps *did* move to permanent positions signaled that they might gain access, in the long run, to permanent jobs they would not otherwise have been able to find. The temporary job was the bottom of a unique type of job ladder from temp agency to hiring company.

Cultivating Networks

Select Labor staff also worked to elicit managerial consent to agency goals by developing "strategic alliances" with managers from client firms. Strategic alliances had a similar cast to strategic personalism (chapter 3): both were instrumental relations heavily laden with elements of friendship and affect. In our view, the strategic alliance is horizontal—both parties have more or less equal amounts of power—whereas strategic personalism is a relation of inequality, with one party possessing considerably more power than the other.

SL staff traveled and partied, visited, and cultivated strong ties with hiring managers, to the point that the boundaries between personal friendship and business relationship were nearly nonexistent. Select Labor staff were invited to holiday parties and potlucks at hiring companies. Conversely, SL headquarters sponsored a wine and cheese open house for managers from their client companies. Staff in the agency regularly discussed effective ways to insinuate themselves into managers' good graces, and the logic of this was captured in Lisa's comments to Jane:

> You need to get to really know these people—the managers and staff at a place where you are making placements. You need to be

their friend and not just be there for business. That's how you really develop strong ties with a company, and that's how you develop a strong relationship with a client. It's not all about the business end of things....I like a lot of clients that I work with, and I like to network with them and have friendships with them.

Developing strong, personalized relations with managers in client firms increased SL reps' range of influence over work conditions for temporary employees. Combatting abuse, teaching managers how to use temps, formalizing temp-to-perm programs, and developing networks and relations of trust with company managers all pushed SL closer to achieving a stable and regularized way of running systems of temporary employment at different sites.

Toning down vituperative managers while supporting those who took a constructive stance; stabilizing work conditions in disparate production units; streamlining transactions and procedures—all these measures enhanced the ability of Select Labor representatives to build and buffer systems of temporary employment in client firms. To the degree possible, they reshaped existing managerial practices and introduced new guidelines for the "consumption" of their product: decent temporary workers. While they tried to weed out unreliable and nonmarketable workers, and to build a good pool of temporary workers (using the varied methods outlined in chapter 3), the staff simultaneously worked to build a niche of decent jobs and managerial practices for their temps. Because every site had a different culture, different production settings, and different management policies, it was not possible to achieve complete regularity and stability. But the system Select Labor staff were working out was far from unstructured, chaotic, and random.

Their activities constituted another moment of THS market-making activities. Historically, the THS and personnel industries had carved out a growing market for temporary workers by disseminating new beliefs about employment relations in the news media. As the industry grew and the number of agencies proliferated, it became the job of agency staff—the human embodiment of the industry—to expand this market by recruiting and cultivating temporary workers who could turn in reliable, reasonably competent work performances on a regular basis (a phase of market-making analyzed in chapter 3). This chapter explored yet a third moment: the ways in which agency staff worked directly with the line managers who held power over temps, to change their attitudes, modify their negative stereotypes, reign in their tempers and hostilities, and, in general, create an acceptable work environment for temporary employees.

There is a relevant analogy here to the way the rough edges of management had to be smoothed over during succeeding stages of the early factory system in the United States. Jacoby's (1985) work on the rise of formalized personnel practices documents this particular historical change. Throughout much of the nineteenth century, he argues, production was decentralized, taking place in the small workshops of artisans who managed their own work. By the late 1800s, however, a massive shift occurred: the rise of more centralized production in factory settings. Foremen came to exercise almost complete control over personnel matters, managing factory labor through a direct and exploitive method known as the "drive system." At that historical moment, foremen had the power to set wages and to hire, fire, and promote workers. Much of this was arbitrary; there were few formal rules or regulations governing the factory setting. Jacoby's work portrays the foreman as despot, one who made and interpreted employment policy as he saw fit (see also Edwards 1979 for an account of direct management).

Around 1910 the modern personnel movement challenged the foreman's authority to control labor. Personnel departments were conceived as a third force in the firm, one that could mediate between workers and management on the shop floor (Jacoby 1985, 130). Disparate groups both external and internal to the firm—vocational guidance and education counselors in schools, welfare workers, production managers—influenced notions about how workers should be treated, emphasizing the long-run benefits of a dedicated workforce. These varied groups found common ground in the cause of personnel management. Later, in the post–World War II era, firms began building internal labor markets, providing workers with greater stability, impersonal rule-bound procedures, benefits, career ladders, and job security in exchange for their commitment and loyalty.

The key outcome of the shift from the drive system to a bureaucratic system of employment relations was that the contact between workers and managers at the point of production was no longer unmediated and despotic. Rather, new employment relations were actively brokered by personnel (now human resources) professionals and departments (Jacoby 1985). In our current historical era much labor has been externalized, and temporary-placement agencies help iron out the jagged and ill-fitting intersection of temporary labor with company managers and their practices. In the nineteenth century, internal personnel departments gained control over supervisors' practices. In the late twentieth and early twenty-first centuries, externalized personnel units are gaining control not only over shop floor managers' practices but over corporations' human resources practices as well. These two events represent different waves in the reconfiguration of American management in general and human resources management in particular.

Regularizing a system of temporary employment, building it from the ground up, contributes greatly to the normalization of temporary work. It is a slow, incremental process, in some ways ad hoc. Agency staff become attuned to unique types of problems with temps (by working with individuals looking for temporary jobs, by networking with other human resources and staffing professionals in the area, and by drawing on experiences in firms with whom they have accounts). They take advantage of openings and opportunities to share their expert knowledge with the line managers of hiring firms. As they impart their knowledge about how to use temps effectively, how to interact with temps in ways that don't undermine their motivation, productivity, and goodwill, agency staff contribute to a production environment in which temporary employment, rather than being an aberration in the way client firms staff their ranks, becomes part and parcel of the accomplishment of work, of the production of goods and services.

Lest we think that agencies are solely responsible for improving the work conditions for temporary workers, we need to acknowledge that line managers as well can have a strong interest in creating good enough jobs for temps. Their reactions to and attitudes about temporary workers in their midst are best investigated by fieldwork that looks at these arrangements primarily from their perspective, a perspective for which this research project provides only limited evidence. Smith's (2001b) previous research on temporary workers in a high-tech firm, however, suggests that from the point of view of line managers, the implementation of temporary employment systems can have mixed effects. Using temps on a large scale may *seem* economical and prudent to corporate management, but for line managers it may represent a deep challenge to their ability to get things done.

In her study of CompTech, Smith (2001b) discovered that proactive line managers worked to change agency practices when they felt that the agencies were not paying high enough wages to the temps. She encountered numerous examples in which shop floor managers approached temp agency staff, either insisting that temps' wages had to be raised or pressuring agencies to offer social events and outings for temp workers. At CompTech, a company with strong paternalistic employment practices and a positive corporate culture, line managers were acutely aware that if they didn't find ways to make temporary workers feel valued and included in team processes, the quality of the work for which temps were responsible could suffer. Managers also feared that CompTech's permanent workers would grow resentful of a two-tier system in which temps were second-class citizens. In this context, then, line managers had significant incentive to try to create positive experiences for temps, and they did so by creating "parallel paternalism," a way of treating temps well that was comparable to the way CompTech treated its regular workers; otherwise, they ran the risk of failing to meet their production objectives. Clearly, establishing a niche of good enough temporary jobs occurs as the result of negotiation and contestation between line managers and agency staff.

In examining how temporary-help agency staff adjudicate between temporary workers and their immediate managers in hiring firms, we have uncovered the lowest organizational level of governance in the firm. Climbing the ladder of the organization to a higher level of governance, the next chapter reaches the final moment of market-making of this study: the interactions in which agency staff engage with human resources managers. Line managers' behavior and the organization of the labor process in diverse production sites is important for stabilizing and regularizing temporary employment relationships, but line managers' room to maneuver, the space they have to sustain good enough temporary jobs, is controlled by the human resources managers above them. As the temporary-help staffing industry produces and strives to profit from its product, the good temp, how does it affect and how is it affected by human resources managers' policymaking?

Chapter Five

Shaping and Stabilizing the Personnel Policy Environment

The elephant in the room thus far is the human resources manager. In the previous chapter, HR managers appeared on stage as important actors in the construction of new employment relations: adversaries of some shop floor managers, novitiates who enlisted Select Labor's help on occasion, and begrudging recipients of agency staff's brokering activities. They had bit parts, as objects that agency staff needed to contend with and manipulate in order to construct new workforce practices and a new type of worker, the good temp. These cameo appearances invite a deeper inspection. The narrative about the increase and normalization of temporary employment is intertwined with the narrative about the historical reconfiguration of human resources management. When companies outsource work to temporary labor, they're also outsourcing some of their human resources activities. And as firms try to better control the conditions of work for their temps on the shop floor, they are compelled to reach into and control a higher level of governance: the human resources staff, who have the power to shape line managers' actions. More to the point, human resources managers are the personnel policymakers in the firm, a higher level of management that sets the terms on which line managers below them maneuver.

Select Labor representatives, then, directed their second set of interventions at human resources managers. If HR practices could not be modified to fit the new employment system, the foundation for temporary workers would be too fragile, a threat to the success of agency product-building and market-making goals. Select Labor representatives recruited, interviewed, placed, trained, and evaluated temporary employees, sometimes tipping the balance of power away from traditional human resources or personnel managers and sometimes assisting them. After discussing the historical significance of changes in the corporate human resources function, we zoom in closely and look at this shifting power. Select Labor staff's work reconfigured corporate hierarchies (especially rules about accountability and authorization), blurred the boundaries between internal and external HR management, and stabilized the larger policy environment governing the use of temporary workers, all toward the goal of building good enough temporary jobs.

Origins of HR Management

It would not be an overstatement to say that the work of human resources managers throughout the twentieth century made American economic growth possible. HR personnel have been responsible for a number of interrelated management processes that have been critical to corporate profitmaking and to workers' livelihoods (Table 5.1).

As Jacoby (1985, 1997, 2005) has noted, human resources departments (earlier known as personnel offices) emerged in the United States as a significant institutional force that rationalized and regulated relations between workers and employers. Corporations built HR departments because they needed to professionalize personnel procedures—such as hiring, evaluating, and promoting—and to stabilize and smooth out the rough edges of wage relations under capitalism. HR departments set personnel policies and shaped labor-management relations in the firm. For example, they played a major role historically in depoliticizing relations between capital and labor (specifically, staving off unions, termed "union substitution" by labor economists) and were responsible for creating the model for a whole

TABLE 5.1
Traditional Human Resources Practices

Process	Job description of the traditional human resources manager
Staffing	Assigning workers to positions in the organization. This process includes a range of functions such as attracting, selecting, hiring, and retaining qualified employees
Performance appraisal and review	Evaluating individual and group contributions to the organization and communicating those evaluations to the persons involved. This process can include making judgments about the need for discipline
Organization improvement	Improving the organization's effectiveness by developing systems and strategies that increase cooperation, teamwork, and performance
Employee protection and representation	Formally and informally protecting employees from arbitrary and unfair treatment, physical danger, and health hazards can be divided into three subcategories: (1) *accommodation*—listening and responding to the needs, wants, and complaints of employees; (2) *collective bargaining*—coming to formal agreements between workers and management in a unionized setting (includes the negotiation and administration of the labor-management contract); (3) *health and safety management*—protecting employees from illness and physical danger
Human resources planning	Assessing the organization's human resources needs in light of organizational goals and changing conditions, and making plans to ensure that a competent, motivated workforce is employed
Job and work design	Determining which tasks are performed by employees and the working conditions under which employees perform these tasks
Compensation and reward	Determining employee compensation structures: wages, salaries, benefits, and incentives (including nonfinancial rewards such as recognition and privileges)

Source: Adapted from French (1998).

breed of workplace and industrial relations: those of the paternalistic, "good" employer (Baron, Dobbin, and Jennings 1986; Dobbin and Sutton 1998; Fiorito 2001; Foulkes 1980; Jacoby 1997). Their practices gave birth to the search for "good" workers who would be committed to working hard for one firm, toward the goal of furthering corporate growth and prosperity (Heckscher 1995, chap. 2; Noble 1977, chap. 10).[1] In other words, HR managers in the mid-twentieth century were the midwives of the once-normative good, permanent, full-time worker.

Human resources personnel similarly built up governance structures inside corporations which gave employees the right to due process. The adoption of due process governance, comprising bureaucratically protected grievance procedures and a system of rights for nonunion employees, was influenced both by greater governmental attention to fairness in the workplace and by "the employment relations professionals" whose ranks grew so significantly throughout the twentieth century (Sutton et al. 1994, 966). Due process was important for stabilizing relations between employees and their managers because it placed limits on managerial authority; moreover, it institutionalized a channel through which employees could voice their interests, complaints, and suggestions for reform (Edelman 1990). This infrastructure of rights and protections, even if imperfectly implemented, underpinned commitment, loyalty, and hard work on the part of corporate employees.

These factors fueled American economic hegemony and stability. Over the course of the twentieth century the field of human resources management, tasked with nothing less than nurturing the human effort and commitment that would grease the machinery of monopoly capitalism, experienced greater and lesser periods of legitimacy and prosperity, ebbing and flowing with shifts in macroeconomic conditions, changes in employment legislation, and variations in corporate governance structures and managerial philosophies (Jacoby 2005, chap. 4). Nevertheless, until the latter part of the twentieth century, human resources management remained a relatively stable functional area in U.S. corporations.

Three Trends: Outsourcing, Downsizing, and Flexibilization

Three trends in recent decades have weakened and reshaped the traditional bureaucratic human resources unit.[2] First, faced with the necessity of adapting to shifting market demand and global competition, firms reached outside the ranks of their "permanent" workers and hired workers who could be used temporarily on a just-in-time basis. When they did so, corporate managers invited external agencies— temporary-placement or headhunting agencies—to work with traditional, in-house human resources managers to recruit, interview, evaluate, and monitor their temporary labor forces. External agencies developed an expertise in temporary employment, achieving economies of scale and insights into workforce management which human resources personnel could not.

As shown in previous chapters, pressures to use temporary workers to meet fluctuating demands emanated both from within firms— corporate managers experimented with new ways of maximizing their bottom line—and from without: leaders of the temporary-help industry developed and pushed its commodity, good temporary laborers. Consequently, human resources managers were forced into a "partnership" with the staffing industry which partially eroded the authority and power of the former and also represented a dramatic shift in the management of labor and employment relations. As the THS industry became involved in the ideological work of "proving" the benefits of temporary workers, it was also rolling back the privileged role of HR management in preserving the secure employment model.

A second trend reshaped the mission of traditional human resources management: since 1980, corporate leaders have both downsized their core labor forces by the millions (under the mantle of reengineering, right-sizing, and restructuring) and compressed their overly hierarchical organizations (Capelli 2000; Uchitelle 2006). In doing so, they not only decreased the size of their permanent workforces but eliminated job security for remaining workers.

Jacoby (2005) argues that this trend alone had three nested consequences for HR management. First, downsizing, mergers and acquisitions, and the subsequent threat to secure employment eroded the paternalistic frameworks of which HR managers were the architects and keepers. Downsizing was not simply a quantitative phenomenon: while entailing a reduction in the numbers of employees, it also entailed a withering of promises, expectations, and corporate loyalty. The scores of support programs, benefits, amenities, and training opportunities that were at the center of paternalism and of the good permanent worker model, and the need for human resources personnel to design, coordinate, and manage them, took on a vastly different complexion (Jacoby 2005, chap. 4). Downsizing and corporate compression also meant the erosion of internal labor markets (ILMs), once central to expectations of mobility and security.[3] Whereas sustaining paternalistic programs and internal labor markets was the bread and butter of human resources personnel, the "draconian contraction" (Jacoby 2005, 92) of their domain has transformed their work and their profession. Heckscher (2001, 268) argues that contemporary HR managers' resolution to these pressures seems to be to "divide the workforce into 'first-class' and 'second-class' employees with very different expectations." In present times HR managers more typically must manage the psychological fallout from layoffs and downsizing, and dispel workers' expectations for loyalty or attachment from the companies they work for rather than try to encourage it (Andrews 2003; Marks 2003; "Revamping" 2003; Smith 1999, 136; Uchitelle 2006, chap. 5). Greengard (2003) also notes that human resources units themselves are often downsized and centralized after a merger.

A second consequence of downsizing was that it indirectly diminished the resources and influence that HR specialists could garner for their projects, since in corporate budget calculations their share of resources depends on the specific head count in their departments and divisions. Their budgets declined as their head counts declined, as did the size of their policymaking terrain.

In the third of Jacoby's nested consequences, downsizing rendered human resources personnel vulnerable because HR is a notorious "soft" budget item, often the first to be axed when companies streamline, tighten their belts, and struggle to remain competitive.

HR professionals have not been immune to their own unique form of outsourcing. Aside from the fact that firms are outsourcing work to their temporary labor, they are also outsourcing human resources work—notorious for the fact that it is "non-revenue-generating" (Bates 2002)—across the board. A new market niche has arisen for companies (such as Exult, Inc.) that perform human resources

tasks—such as training, recruitment, and benefits management—
for the core workforces of other companies; they develop expertise
and economies of scale in the area of HR in the same way that temporary help agencies do in the specific area of staffing (see Bates
2002; Shelgren 2001; Shuit 2003; and Tyler 2004 for a few examples). Headhunting firms, for example, occupy part of this market
niche.[4]

The third trend gave rise to organizational practices that would
bypass traditional human resources managers: increasing numbers of
American firms developed the organizational capacity to align their
production processes with fluctuations in market forces.[5] Line managers who, as Jacoby comments, have been "closer to market signals"
(2005, 93), gained greater authority to make decisions and policies
about hiring and other issues as they received orders and developed
relations with their customers. A market signal, for example, might
be an unanticipated order for 100 customized servers, information
about an emergent product niche that a firm hopes to enter quickly,
or a technological innovation that requires new or different skills
than an existing workforce possesses. Some companies have authorized their line managers to contact temporary-help agencies or other
staffing firms directly to place orders for workers, thus bypassing
the traditional mandate to consult first with their human resources
managers.

These three, not mutually exclusive, trends have compromised
the position of HR managers over several decades. Outsourcing; com-
pressing bureaucratic organizations and dismantling internal labor
markets; dashing expectations of permanent employment: all these
have wrought a new regime of employment relationships. Squeezed
by shrinking budgets, functional vulnerability, eroding political influence, and declining organizational capital, human resources managers have played a role in reshaping employment relations, to be
sure, but in critical ways they have also been reshaped by them.

Human resources managers' work is increasingly constrained
and made more complex by changing legal and technological environments, as well, some of which dovetail with changes being
brought on by the rise in temporary workforces. In addition to
needing expertise in traditional employment law, they now must

familiarize themselves with newer employment regulations related to, for example, temporary workers, contracted agencies, and changes in retirement, benefits, and privacy legislation (Hirschman 2003, 2004; Leonard 2002). Human resources managers are under considerable pressure to engage in "risk mitigation" to make sure that they are not misclassifying their temporary workers (see Appendix II). Recent years have been a time of extensive automation and reengineering of HR work: software packages retrieve, organize, manipulate, analyze, and distribute relevant HR data, including data about contingent workforces; web-based screening programs accept job applications and evaluate them; and online information systems with which HR staff can coordinate their work (for example, IQ Navigator can be used to send standardized job requests to specific staffing firms, remind HR staff when contracts expire and when payment is due, and produce staffing reports [Klaff 2003]) (Dineen, Noe, and Wang 2004; Hempel 2004; Robb 2003; Shrivastava and Shaw 2003; Shuit 2003).[6] Given all these pressures, human resources managers often experience high levels of burnout (Andrews 2003) as their autonomy and purview of decision-making has contracted.

These changes have been amply documented in business, personnel, and human resources publications. One survey shows that 91 percent of 100 large companies (representing two million employees) are outsourcing or planning to outsource various HR functions (Ketter 2007). A 2002 survey of 500 chief financial officers at very large companies found that two-thirds of these companies were outsourcing five or more HR functions, most commonly the management of health and group benefits and defined contribution plans, payroll, staffing/recruiting, training, and employee relations (Hewitt Associates 2002). In other words, firms now reconfigure and outsource many functions once considered to be at the core of HR.[7] Given these macro-level trends, what are the precise organizational interactions that knit together THS agency representatives and in-house HR management? What is the basis of agency representatives' leverage over corporate HR managers, enabling them to challenge HR's expertise and influence the ways line managers and supervisors use temporary workers? Looking at the experiences of Select Labor gives us a fine-grained understanding of how the temporary-help industry, in its quest to extend a market for its product and to shape the conditions under which temporary workers are brought into client firms, plays a role in changing traditional human resources management.

The Incorporation of External Agencies: Blurred Boundaries

Select Labor *was* a human resources unit. The agency recruited, interviewed, and hired workers; it collected data, devised programs to elicit consent to the agency, managed and oversaw the implementation of temporary-help systems in diverse companies. As the previous chapter showed, they did not engage in these activities in isolation from the managers, the human resources specialists, or the practices and cultures of the firms where they placed temps; rather, agency staff strove to establish relationships—entering into partnerships, acting as advocates in some cases and as adversaries in others—with various groups in those firms. Select Labor representatives staked out their turf in hiring companies and brought human resources staff into their organizational purview by brokering with, bypassing, and entirely taking over some tasks of HR personnel. In particular, SL reps worked to change corporate policies that left too much decision-making about the use of temporary workers in HR's hands and not enough within the grasp of the agency.

With special attention to what all this means for human resources managers, we first describe Select Labor's HR work at Global Connections. We provide a thick description of the bundle of practices in which agency staff engaged, then break down each type of intervention in some detail. Seemingly small here, seemingly tangential there, these interventions and tactics allowed SL representatives to chip away, work site by work site and company by company, at traditional HR practices while constructing new ones. Thick description of activities and social relations best exposes the dynamism of these processes, the collaboration over employment policies; it reveals the murky boundaries being pushed in one direction and another, as agency staff became involved with the HR staff in their client firms.

It also shows how a new system of employment relations is built and sustained—sometimes over the heads of line managers, at other times with their stubborn and persistent engagement.

Partnering up at Global Connections

Select Labor had developed a long-standing relationship with Global Connections (GC), providing this Silicon Valley facility with a range of temporary workers including assemblers and technicians. Global Connections had several facilities throughout the United States and abroad, and although it used several agencies to staff its Silicon Valley facility, SL was its largest supplier of temps. In the summer of 2000, Global Connections was one of the oldest and biggest clients at the Silicon Valley branch office, accounting for approximately 25 percent of the branch's business. The largest group of workers SL provided to Global Connections was made up of temps who soldered and assembled circuit boards.

The SL/GC partnership exemplifies how staffing agencies become crucial to the successful integration of temporary workers and take the lead in internal HR processes by embedding themselves in their client firms. In the mid-1990s, GC had begun to acknowledge that it was having problems retaining temporary workers in various production departments. GC human resources managers invited Lisa (the SL branch manager) and the Select Labor regional manager to meet to discuss strategies for reducing temporary-employee turnover. One outcome of this initial meeting was that Lisa was invited and agreed to spend one day a week working out of the Global Connections facility—interviewing and screening temporary workers, and assisting in-house GC managers with their immediate hiring needs. (This arrangement lessened the distance between the agency and Global Connections, although it fell short of a full-time vendor-on-premises setup.) Lisa used her weekly visits to observe the practices in the production department, which in turn enabled her to provide strategic advice to the HR team and production managers about the kinds of temps they needed. Throughout this time, Lisa and other Select Labor employees helped the human resources staff with planning and organizational improvement.

Over time, SL staff took on more and more HR tasks, obtaining direct access to information about how to meet the needs of line managers and tailoring SL's procedures to the company's needs as a whole. Their work encompassed activities starting at the front end of Global Connection's operations. SL's own office, located just a few miles away, was the location for recruiting, testing, and screening potential temporaries when Lisa was not doing this work at GC. SL reps dipped into their pool of regular temps, reviewed résumés of new applicants, carried out face-to-face interviews, and gauged candidates' technical skills and competency in basic math and English. Setting up a soldering iron in the testing room at their office, SL placement specialists evaluated candidates' soldering abilities, using GC's own production materials. This allowed SL to observe job applicants under conditions that simulated the specific conditions of production they would face at Global Connections. Qualified workers, after leaving the Select Labor office with test scores, a brief training session in health and safety matters, and SL certification in hand, were usually quickly approved for temporary employment at Global Connections. Typically, they began work there after only a very brief interview with a line manager.

SL staff nurtured trusting and close professional relationships with GC human resources staff and production managers. By 2000, managers at Global Connections routinely consulted with Lisa and others in the SL office about their organizational processes so that they could get the most appropriate temporary personnel and help with retaining them. When line managers picked up "market signals," they were able to get Lisa's help interpreting them and translating them into an order for temporary workers, such as how many to request or what skill sets they needed. Although Lisa primarily advised GC staff about the recruitment and retention of temporary and temp-to-perm candidates, she occasionally leveraged her close-knit ties to gain early access to information about other staffing needs, enabling her to recruit and place higher-level employees as well. For example, her insider knowledge allowed her to find out when HR managers were leaving the company for other opportunities, thus leaving open positions in their wake which SL might fill.

Lisa occasionally bypassed HR to improve conditions for temporary workers. For example, one temporary candidate was offered a job at GC only after Lisa made a special call to recommend him to a senior production manager with whom she had developed a personal friendship. Initially, the candidate had been interviewed and turned down by a more junior manager who said he lacked the appropriate experience. After going over the junior manager's head to the senior manager, Lisa received authorization to hire the candidate. When a Select Labor agency employee called Lisa's HR liaison at Global Connections to verify this hire, the latter was not even aware that the production manager had been looking for a new temp. Thus, although technically operating as an "outside agency," SL knew more about some details of hiring than the internal HR staff. In this instance and others, SL staff leveraged either personal or professional relationships to affect hiring decisions in a way that benefited temporary workers, aside from benefiting SL's own bottom line.

Select Labor staff, invited to a company holiday party at Global Connections, sat with the human resources group and were handed badges allowing them free access to all parts of the facility. One of the production team leaders gave them a guided tour, explaining the different jobs throughout the production department. The SL reps were encouraged to wander around and ask the workers questions. For all intents and purposes, agency staff were treated as if they were part of the internal HR management team, and were given the opportunity to build relations of trust with temporaries on the job. Through these close relationships—relationships observed at other hiring companies—SL gained a position of structural oversight with respect to many aspects of human resources management.

Beyond Global Connections: Challenging Hierarchical HR

Select Labor representatives often found themselves defending line managers from bureaucratically insistent and turf-protecting HR managers. The dilemma of one line manager at the firm Built to Order (BTO) highlights how they did so and how the efforts of Select Labor staff ultimately enabled line managers to bypass or do an end run around their human resources managers.

Built to Order's account with Select Labor generated approximately $1.5 million in revenue for SL's branch office in 1999 alone

from placements of warehouse workers, assemblers, and receptionists and other clerical workers. Built to Order manufactured and
assembled customized computers for several large, well-known computer companies. The economic boom in the region meant that BTO
had more work than ever, and management was under tremendous
pressure to meet the intense production deadlines imposed by their
clients. The company's HR managers explained to Select Labor staff
on numerous occasions that their production department had a high
demand for temporary workers and a very short turnaround time for
their products.

Prior to Lisa's intervention, managers had to go through their
central HR department before any arrangements were made with
any staffing agency. Line managers vociferously complained about
this bureaucratic hassle. Not only did it mean that they had to
go through an additional layer of approval to meet their labor needs;
they also had to compete with other units to get HR's attention—
that is, their request entered the queue behind the requests of others. BTO's human resources vice president invited several Select
Labor staff to advise them on how to work through this impasse
and on other issues related to the company's temporary workforce.
When they met, the Select Labor branch manager advocated higher
wages for workers, better working conditions (including training
for unskilled personnel), and more flexible hours to attract an even
more diverse workforce. It was here that Lisa also advised BTO's
management to streamline the temporary-worker hiring process.
She told them that they should authorize line managers to skip HR
and go directly to SL: "Let us send people directly to the production
department—we can prequalify these folks and help get them on
board much faster. We're already doing this with some of our other
clients." In the immediate wake of this meeting, the HR department simply agreed to raise pay rates for temporary workers on a
case-by-case basis.

It took a full-on confrontation for things to change more radically.
Fernando, a production manager for one of the largest and busiest
departments at Built to Order, continually found himself confronting
intense production quotas and was regularly at odds with the human
resources department over his hiring needs. Fernando was frustrated

at having to direct all his requests through the HR office, believing that HR was not sending him people fast enough and not sending appropriately qualified people because their pay rates for temps were too low. In brief, Fernando felt that HR was tying his hands. The human resources department at Built to Order had been downsized considerably—as was true in several of the hiring companies, so that HR managers often felt under the gun, pressured on many fronts to respond to different and urgent needs.[8] Different departments throughout the BTO plant required immediate attention, and HR staff simply could not meet everyone's needs on a timely basis. In addition, senior managers continued to direct HR to limit pay increases as much as possible because of what they claimed were decreasing profit margins on their products.

The HR team sought Select Labor's assistance in managing internal political conflicts with Fernando, just when Fernando turned to SL to help him work out his disagreements with the HR staff. The HR staff viewed Fernando as a thorn in their side because he persistently pressured them to meet his department's hiring needs. Yet, quite reasonably, Fernando said that he did not want simply to fill positions with "warm bodies" or to waste time with completely unskilled workers. Instead, he wanted good temps whom he could train and start off on a temporary basis but possibly move them to a more permanent status over time—and he wanted them quickly. HR characterized Fernando as "too picky," asserting that his complaints lacked legitimacy and that Fernando was undermining himself by being too choosy.

The Select Labor representative intervened, brokering one outcome that allowed Fernando to exercise his judgment and authority against the HR people. Fernando wanted to hire Peter, a temp whom SL had sent to apply for one of the technician positions in Fernando's department. But Peter would take the job only if it paid $15 an hour, more than the standard rate for technicians that BTO management had authorized. Fernando told the SL staff about his dilemma. He needed a competent technician, but the HR department was not giving him the authority to hire Peter at the wage he wanted.

Advocating for Fernando, SL was able to persuade Built to Order's HR department to raise Peter's hourly salary. But the more significant outcome of this ongoing conflict was a policy change that gave managers greater discretion in hiring temporary workers and cut the HR department out of the loop. Shortly after the Fernando–human resources conflagration, one Built to Order senior-level HR manager sent out a memo to Select Labor and other agencies that BTO used, proclaiming the following:

> Hello Everyone! Due to the high demand for temps, and the very short turn around time we have, I have changed the process so the hiring managers can now call the agencies directly, without having to go through the Temp Hotline! This should make the process easier for all involved! By calling you directly, all qualifications and expectations can be discussed first hand [with staffing agency personnel], eliminating placements that are not a position match. The price table listed below should help eliminate any problems, in addition to maybe speeding up the process for filling our open positions! If a rate requested [hourly pay rate for an employee] is different from those listed below (an increase), please have the manager call me to discuss prior to filling. Managers now have the responsibility of knowing if the right names are on the invoices, as well as the right pay rate. And we will no longer be the ones in charge of the payment cycle, they will! [All original punctuation.]

As the memo indicates, giving line managers the go-ahead to contact staffing agencies on their own simultaneously gave them more power and allowed SL reps direct access to information about open job orders. Importantly, this new policy meant that Select Labor did not have to depend on the HR office's interpretations of what line managers needed.

When line managers and staffing agency reps were directly linked, the former could bypass a layer of HR bureaucracy, and both groups were situated more closely to market signals. These practices in turn gave staffing agencies such as SL more opportunity to control the supply of and demand for workers. On the supply side, SL staff could keep their eyes open for the specific kinds of temporaries that line managers were looking for and locate temps appropriate for these jobs. On the demand side, agency staff might use their proximity to line managers to scope out where the use of temps could be expanded, thus increasing the number of opportunities for their temps.

Occasionally, linking line managers to staffing agencies had the effect of keeping human resources managers utterly in the dark about hiring practices in their own units. Clarissa (an HR manager at Flexitron) gave Megan, the Select Labor placement specialist, a sophisticated flowchart that outlined the temporary-worker hiring process that she wanted SL placement specialists to follow. Megan presented the flowchart to Lisa at SL, who laughed, stating that "no one follows that process, and I'm certain that none of the agencies work with Flexitron like that."

The flowchart detailed a cumbersome protocol for both hiring managers and staffing agencies which integrated HR at multiple decision-making points throughout a four-step process: (1) to initiate the temporary-worker hiring procedure, the line manager needed to forward a requisition form to the HR department for approval; (2) HR staff, using their determination of a manager's need, would then request résumés from THS agencies; (3) HR staff were to screen and review the résumés and then (4) send the appropriate ones to the hiring manager.

In reality, Select Labor employees usually handled all four steps, contacting HR personnel at Flexitron only when a line manager actually needed approval to hire a temp—which was rare, because higher-level management had, without informing HR, approved allowing line managers to contact the temp agency directly. In this way, SL's work at a hiring firm had streamlined the human resources process and made things easier for line managers by cutting out bureaucratic layers of HR intervention. Not surprisingly, Clarissa expressed substantial frustration when she discovered that line managers were doing end runs around her unit. Select Labor specialists routinely spent time on the telephone with both line and HR managers, smoothing out conflicts and misunderstandings and just as routinely complained of the "gap in communication" they had to fill between line and HR managers.

When they saw the opportunity, Select Labor staff did what they could to bypass human resources managers in client firms, sometimes with the relieved consent of the latter. Experimental Labs had contracted with Select Labor for a batch order of temps, sight unseen: forty people to work as packers for $7.00 an hour. Experimental Labs, in the words of one SL rep, was "allowing us (SL) to just walk people on to the job—they're not even interviewing these people. They are giving us full power to screen and just send people to the job site." In this case, the streamlining was welcome, not resisted by company HR.

Larry, a regionally based Select Labor manager, hoped to institutionalize this streamlined approach and implement it on a wider scale. As he told everyone at one branch staff meeting, "We have to compete and do things faster and better than our competitors." His idea was to increase the speed at which they could place clerical and administrative temps. Larry's confidence in his agency's better temps—not to mention his confidence in the cost-effectiveness of his plan—was high enough that he wanted to strike a deal with HR managers: SL would no longer be obligated to submit résumés to client firms for whom the agency supplied clerical workers. Instead, Larry proposed, SL would guarantee eight free hours of the temp's time if the hiring company would simply allow SL staff to use their own judgment about who would be a suitable temp. This proposal had not been implemented by the time the fieldwork for this project was completed, but it speaks to the capacity and the desire on the part of a higher-ranking Select Labor manager to eliminate one part of the traditional human resources manager's job.

As they had done at Global Connections, Select Labor staff attended social events at other client firms as well. At Built to Order, they joined temporary and other workers for an "honor-the-company" ceremony, for which all employees provided a lavish feast of chicken, roast pig, salmon, vegetables, salads, and desserts. Both temps and regular workers received awards at this celebration. One of the lead temporary workers, a southeast Asian woman in her mid-thirties, took the SL reps on a tour of her production area, giving them a chance to closely examine sites where so many of their temps worked. The reps were able to see how jobs such as "touch up and rework," "pinning," "bonding," and "testing" looked at BTO. Mingling with the HR staff who were responsible for contracting for their services and labor, Select Labor staff were, again, just part of the Built to Order human resources staff.

Vendor-on-Premises: Agency Staff Moving into Their Client Firms

When agency staff were physically located in the hiring firm in vendor-on-premises arrangements, their involvement in human resources work was all the more deeply entrenched. Offering the service of a vendor-on-premises arrangement is one way that temporary-placement agencies have marketed themselves to companies and tried to garner a greater share of the temporary market. But aside from being a source of profitability to agencies, this spatial arrangement also allowed agency staff to monitor and comment on prevailing human resources practices, to help HR specialists fine-tune those practices in alignment with the exigencies of temporary-employment systems, and to observe directly the work of their temps. For example, Rosa, a placement specialist at SL, was working on a new account with AutoMate in a city south of the Silicon Valley. This company, fairly new to the region, specialized in producing information and communications components, measuring instruments, and industrial equipment. Rosa had contracted for and was organizing a vendor-on-premises unit with AutoMate. In the process, she commented:

> The AutoMate managers are pretty new to on-site vendors; they don't quite understand all that we can do for them. So we need to explain to them a lot and help them realize our potential. I'm going to their HR meetings and making myself known to the managers there. Many of them say, "I need this" or "I need that," and they don't have a clue how unreasonable some of their requests are, especially because they're paying such low rates. They have to learn the hard way. I'll try and negotiate with them, but I know we'll lose a bunch of employees [temps] until the managers realize they have to raise the rates. I'll have to be an advocate for some of the candidates [the temps]—I'm OK with that, but those managers are going to be really hard to deal with.

Select Labor's vendor-on-premises setups accounted for approximately 25 percent of the firm's revenue.[9] When they worked on the premises, SL staff performed traditional human resources tasks: greeting incoming temps with an orientation packet, discussing their particular needs, making sure their time cards were available, and answering any questions that individual temporary workers had about their assignments. On-premise agency reps also transmitted information from hiring company managers and HR personnel back to the agency's office, acting as a conduit for hiring- and production-relevant information. The on-site staff "processed" temps, working to integrate them into the firm. The core HR work—informing new workers about company practices, compensation and payroll administration, safety, and schedules; listening to complaints and grievances, and smoothing over disturbances—was completely shifted from the in-house HR group to the on-site agency.[10] Agency staff smoothed the transition of temps into various workplaces and minimized disruptions associated with blending temporary and permanent workforces.

Managing Other Subcontractors

Select Labor workers took on no less than the function of managing the outsourcing process per se. Conventional wisdom has it that outsourcing is coordinated by in-house human resources staff, but the expertise for doing so often rested in the hands of this agency. Specifically, SL subcontracted with additional staffing agencies to meet their clients' labor demands. For example, when Lisa received a call from a production manager at BTO who needed sixty temporary assemblers as soon as possible, she immediately called the branch manager at another staffing agency, asking for help in meeting BTO's hiring needs. Georgina, the branch manager at the competing staffing agency, was more than happy to help Lisa out. Lisa often called other agencies for backup to help meet large job orders that SL did not have the in-house capability to fill. These agencies, in turn, would call SL to provide backup for *their* job orders. And backup was sought not just when staffing agencies needed large job orders filled; sometimes other agencies called for help in recruiting specific workers such as engineers and HR personnel because Lisa had developed strong networks in these fields.

This was the practice Lisa called "co-opetition," the combination of cooperation and competition. She had learned this word at an industry conference, and for her it captured the new phenomenon of staffing agency partnerships in the region. Lisa was told that the success of the industry as a whole was increasingly predicated upon the viability of partnerships between individual agencies, and the term enabled her to articulate her view of other staffing agencies as both resources and competitors.

Built to Order human resources managers rarely got involved in the secondary subcontracting relationships, and they were often not aware when backup was called for; once SL collected payment from the client firm (BTO, in this case) for all the temporary workers, it would pay the secondary vendor. These multiple layers of subcontracting, commonly observed, improved managers' flexibility because they could access the pooled labor of multiple agencies to find workers quickly. But these practices also led to the "hidden hierarchies" that are created with the growth of externalized employment relations (Pfeffer and Baron 1988; Smith 1994) and, as Smith has argued, can lead to new sources of workplace tension and conflict. Temporary workers were often confused about whom to consult when they had grievances, needed to arrange time off, or wanted to negotiate for improved conditions of employment.

Whether or not Select Labor was directly managing subcontractors, SL staff occasionally got caught up in helping HR managers with the complexities of a workforce composed of temps from multiple agencies. For example, multiple currents of complexity rose to the surface in one company that hired a particularly large number of temporary workers. Laura was a human resources manager at BackTreks, a company that used many temporary assemblers. Laura sought the help of SL staff in order to get some control over the information about temporary workers in several of the units for which she was responsible. She was having trouble staying on top of administrative matters such as which agency had sent a particular temporary worker for an interview, which agency employed a given temporary worker, the total head count for temporary workers from any given staffing agency, which expenses were related to which agency, and which temporary workers had or had not completed the proper administrative forms for employment.

Her difficulty first came to the attention of SL staff when she called to complain about a temp who, she had heard, was performing poorly on the job. It turned out that the temp under scrutiny was not one of Select Labor's but had been sent by one of the other agencies servicing Laura's company. The discussion that followed resulted in Laura's admitting that she could use some assistance in coordinating the temporary-help system in her firm. SL staff were glad to help her sort through these complexities because her confusion—in particular, her (unfounded, as it turned out) complaint against a temp who she believed to be from SL—had the potential to affect their temps negatively. To the degree that Laura couldn't keep track of who was doing what in her unit, there was more risk that she or a line manager would unjustly accuse a temporary worker to his or her face, or alienate temporary workers if she seemed to deny them their individuality by forgetting who they were. The agency staff worked with Laura to develop a database that she could use to track and monitor this workforce.

Hidden and irregular levels of administrative hierarchy were facts of life in many firms, like Laura's, with which SL had accounts and were exacerbated by the use of multiple agencies and secondary contracting arrangements.[11]

Through the foregoing activities and relationships, Select Labor staff became high-level policy negotiators in hiring companies. Table 5.1 shows that a number of tasks that fall under the purview of the traditional human resources manager have been transferred, wholly or in part, into the hands of temporary-placement agency staff. Select Labor staff engaged in the full range of recruitment, hiring, screening, and placement activities. They communicated information to temporary workers about their performance and gave or withheld rewards accordingly, in the form of decent temporary jobs and, occasionally, bonuses or paid days off. SL staff were setting the terms on which line managers would work with temporaries on the shop floor: they contributed to organizational development by studying individual work sites, collecting data about them, writing up new job descriptions, and making recommendations about how to improve organizational effectiveness. For temporary workers, they served as sounding board and grievance agent, and they advocated for worker safety. Select Labor staff helped hiring company line and human resources managers plan their HR needs, determining how many and what kinds of temporary workers they needed, and they intervened in the wage-setting process. Finally, in their own office, Select Labor staff coached temps, provided information to them about many aspects of the job search process, and directed people seeking temporary employment to appropriate job opportunities.

This list makes clear that Select Labor staff performed many of the traditional human resources tasks both for the temps in their employ and for HR managers at their client companies. The agency was a fully functioning human resources unit that had the added advantage of being part of a broad network of labor market intermediaries in Silicon Valley (including other for-profit agencies, community colleges, and government-sponsored training organizations). Furthermore, its staff routinely participated in training opportunities sponsored by their parent company to update their skill sets about temporary workforce management.

Temporary help staffing agencies have very concrete market-making strategies that enable them to shape firms' outsourcing processes and, consequently, their human resources departments (Gonos 1997; Peck and Theodore 2002). What appear to be purely market-mediated employment relationships are constructed in the negotiations and occasional struggles between HR staff, line managers, and personnel from labor market intermediaries. In specific and small ways that cumulatively built a new social system, Select Labor representatives worked with human resources managers in various firms to direct them, advise them, and even take them out of the loop of employment transactions. And, the Select Labor case corroborates another point made by economic sociologists: today, the lines between infrastructures that are internal and those that are external to firms are becoming blurred (DiMaggio 2001; Powell 2001).

It is useful to return to Cynthia Ofstead's research to appreciate and corroborate the significance of these points about agencies' market-making efforts. Ofstead showed how, in the second half of the twentieth century, staffing agencies worked on business managers to create demand for their product. Acting entrepreneurially to change managers' minds about the pros and cons of using temporary workers, and to offer new services to meet their clients' needs (not to mention defining and creating new needs in the business world), temporary-help agencies "actively promote[d] their own growth, intervening in labor markets to forge a role for themselves as employment intermediaries and gatekeepers to permanent jobs." These agencies, Ofstead explained, played a highly proactive role in shaping local labor markets, creating demand where it had not otherwise been present. She also explained that some clients used these agencies like external personnel departments and empowered the agencies by allowing them to make hiring decisions (Ofstead 1999, 273, 288–90). Likewise, Vosko found that temporary-help agencies contributed to the outsourcing and downsizing of human resource functions by acting as extensions to firms' internal HR departments (2000, 117–18, 141–52).

These studies show how THS industry staff both convinced managers in private industry to open their doors to temporary workers and changed managers' mind-sets from thinking of temps as stopgap, marginal workers to thinking of temps as reliable workforces. Our research shows that once the door has been opened and the use of temps is pervasive, staffing agency representatives take over a range of traditional HR functions, creating a deeper basis for the institutionalization of temporary-employment systems. Agency practices shape labor markets at the micro-level through everyday interactions between agency staff and managers—line and human resources—at their client firms and through the staffing agency's relatively new internalized role inside firms. Ironically, although it was initially brought in because of its clients' outsourcing strategies (specifically, to externalize the management of temporary workers), SL became a core institutionalized feature and a critical resource within several of its largest client-firms. Although some of the hiring managers that Select Labor representatives met with and interviewed were initially unfamiliar with the expanded scope of staffing services, by developing close-knit ties with managers and HR staff, SL was able to market its services, "teaching" clients how to outsource; recruiting, interviewing, and prescreening temporary workers; showing line managers how to manage temps effectively and how to use the staffing agency to streamline their HR-related organizational processes.

If, in past times, personnel professionals were addressing their advice to line and human resources managers of corporations, providing guidelines for finding temporary workers and successfully bringing them into their firms—as chapter 2 shows that they did—the more pertinent advice today would be different.[12] More likely, personnel management experts would advise human resources managers nearly exclusively about how to work with agencies. For many organizational and practical reasons, in-house human resources managers are comparatively disconnected from temporary workforces and have become almost auxiliaries of THS agencies, which in turn have become human resources units in their own right. Since it is agency staff who recruit temps and integrate them into varied work sites, in-house human resources managers might be given tips on how to negotiate with agency staff or how to hold their ground—especially with the advent of vendor-on-premises arrangements, whereby agencies establish their own organizational units and their own capacities for intervention in human resources practice, directly at the point of production.

We argue that agencies have significant leverage over human resources managers because the latter have no choice but to take seriously ways to obtain quality temps, to process and retain them. As temporary work has become normalized (cemented by the fact that managers and supervisors often are authorized to hire temporary but not permanent workers or can get authorization fairly quickly to hire temps), both line and HR managers increasingly are dependent on the expertise of agency staff and on temporary workers. HR managers lack the time and resources to manage temporary workforces and must depend on agency representatives to help them do it.

This new employment relationship, ostensibly developed over time to cut costs and create efficiencies, ironically has led to a remarkable depth and pervasiveness of hidden hierarchies and complexities. Turn to any single actor in this relationship for confirmation of this fact. The temporary worker must contend with agency staff, line managers, and temporary and permanent coworkers. The temp must also decipher the identity of his or her employer: the agency or the line manager at the hiring firm. The line manager now finds him- or herself either having to go to in-house HR managers for approval to hire temps or having to maneuver out from under the HR manager, who often has hierarchical notions about appropriate channels for communication and for recruitment procedures. The HR manager may feel threatened both on procedural grounds (line managers are subverting HR authority if they go directly to agency reps) and on personal or professional grounds (line managers and agency reps are making it clear that HR expertise is superfluous and its influence is waning). Communications have become more multilayered, and accountability is not necessarily or exclusively hierarchical but may be both hierarchical and lateral. Our data show that while a line manager is negotiating with an agency rep to hire a temp, an HR manager may remain oblivious of the fact that the line manager needed a temp in the first place.

The labor market landscape has steadily changed as staffing agencies have become embedded in their client firms' HR practices, and an increasing number of workers—temporary and contract—have been placed on the payroll of staffing agencies. Staffing agencies are not passively responding to market demands or to the needs of their client firms; indeed, agency staff are defining those needs. And yet, although SL was embedded in its client firms and was able to influence practices at these firms—to different degrees, depending upon the nature of its relationship with individual companies—this process was not seamless. Partnerships between SL and its clients required cooperation but created confusion and turf wars. The examples in this chapter, then, suggest that the labor market for temporary employment is socially constructed and mediated at the organizational level by multiple actors.

Activity by activity, temporary-agency representatives have built a new system of employment relations by usurping or redefining many aspects of traditional HR work and by setting forth new ideas about how to use temporary workers. Discussions in personnel and management journals about the fate of HR management tend to worry that the combination of the many forces discussed in this chapter are leading to substantial shrinking or even disappearance of the human resources function; article titles such as "HR Needs to Be Wary of Losing Its Role Altogether" (Dempsey 2006) or "Why HR Management Will Never Be the Same Again" (Tyson 2007) have been a dime a dozen in recent years. Our data do not enable us to generalize about whether HR is quantitatively shrinking or disappearing (although we are skeptical about the latter). Analyzing the activities of labor market intermediaries such as Select Labor, however, does show the reconfiguration of HR management; specifically, its expertise, authority, and influence have been transformed by the rise of temporary-employment relations. Our data suggest that this transformation has by and large had positive implications for temporary workers themselves.

Chapter Six

Do Good Enough Temporary Jobs Make Good Enough Temporary Employment?

The Case for Transitional Mobility

Select Labor shaped and sustained the labor market for temporary workers in a variety of ways. Its staff extended many genuine forms of assistance and guidance to people seeking temporary jobs. They tried to select people who showed promise of being good, quality temporary workers and, once hiring them, tried to further construct and maintain them as such. They provided what they saw as realistic guidance about how to enter the labor market, advocated for higher wages for temps, championed individual temps in landing decent jobs, and, in a larger context of insecurity and precariousness, provided emotional support to the temps whom they favored and wished to keep on their payroll. Agency staff monitored the work sites of hiring companies to make sure that there was a fit between job orders that line and human resources managers had submitted and the actual conditions of work that temps would walk into. Their goal was to maintain good enough temporary jobs, jobs where the conditions of work were risk-free to the extent possible. Agency staff intervened to subdue supervisors and managers who were rude, angry, or discriminatory.

Importantly, however, agency staff constructed this market because they were primarily concerned to meet the needs and expectations of

the hiring companies. In order to compete for a share of the lucrati
temporary help service market, Select Labor had to create and se.
good temps: the idea, if not the reality, of the reliable and minimally
qualified temporary worker who could supply reasonably productive
labor within various firms. SL was able to profit to the degree that
hiring companies would choose them either as a source of temporary
workers or as a source of administrative and human resource expertise. Fundamentally, SL was an outsourcing organization, benefiting
from a huge shift (as have other agencies over recent decades) in the
way companies do their business, hire their workers, withdraw their
commitments to permanent workers, and make it more incumbent
on workers across the board to bear the burden of employment risk.

We have argued that temporary help agencies that compete to
maintain a strong share of their market must insulate their temps
from the worst effects of temporary employment. To bring job applicants in the door and to keep valued temps on its payroll, Select
Labor needed to develop practices to enhance its reputation as a
desirable agency to work for. We would not expect this to be true
of small, unstable operations, of agencies that supply day laborers
only, or of contractors who pick up vulnerable day laborers on street
corners to work in fields, clean houses, construct buildings, or mow
lawns. But for stable, mainstream agencies that must compete for
a share of the market, sending temporary employees into abusive,
overtly unpleasant, harmful, or illegal work settings would be counterproductive to their profitmaking goals. As the case of Select Labor
shows, agency representatives strove to avoid setting up accounts
with hiring companies that matched the profile of the bad employer,
as the reps construed it. Furthermore, since wages in this niche of the
labor market were low, agency staff frequently pressured managers in
hiring companies to increase the hourly wages for temps.

From the point of view of the agency, sending temps into risky
work sites and subjecting them to the lowest pay inevitably caused
high turnover, which in turn jeopardized the quality of their temporary workforce and its value to hiring companies. With temporary employment so securely institutionalized, agencies have a
stake in minimizing turnover much as other employers do. Temporary-help agencies invest in their temps, even if their investment

is lower than the investment that firms make in their permanent workforces. In addition to the administrative costs of hiring a temp (recruiting, advertising, processing the paperwork, interviewing, and testing skill levels), other costs must be considered. Agency staff must educate people about the temporary employment relationship (what it is; what you can and can't expect; what rights you have and don't have), advise temps about basic interviewing procedures and how to demonstrate an appropriate work ethic once they get a job. If a person works for an agency for a long period of time as a temp, the agency may benefit from his or her trust and goodwill. It would be impossible to quantify the advantage here, but trust and loyalty clearly benefit the agency: when a temp is committed and loyal to the agency, he or she more likely will turn in the performance of the good temp. And any loss of that reservoir of trust and goodwill is immeasurable.

Transitional Mobility: What Temporary Employment Can Offer Job Seekers

The Good Temp, like other studies, points to the fact that we cannot view temporary employment as unequivocally negative, even for someone in a low niche of the spectrum of contingent employment. Indeed, from the point of view of improving the lives of working people and developing policies to assist workers across the board, it does not make sense to take the one-dimensional view that all temporary employment is bad. Such a view misses the complexities, the nuances, the very real desires and aspirations that people have, and their restricted labor market alternatives, all related to their social location: education, gender, race, class, age, community, and occupational history. This type of employment and these agencies can provide important "transitional mobility" opportunities to job seekers today, even if they are constrained opportunities and if, given the choice, people would prefer permanent jobs. Agencies can link people to jobs when they otherwise might not be able to make labor market connections, serve as a bridge to employment by providing information, direction, and resources to those who need them.

Many factors enter into one's calculations of the costs and benefits of a temporary job. Temporary positions may offer a much-needed bridge into the world of employment to certain populations of workers. For example, Addison and Surfield show that unemployed workers who became reemployed were more likely to have found work in alternative arrangements such as temporary work than in regular or permanent jobs. They found that unemployed workers' reference point was unemployment: in other words, comparing temporary jobs with the experience of unemployment, they saw the former as preferable, a pathway or stepping-stone out of their unemployed status in the labor market. Addison and Surfield found that this held for all unemployed groups, regardless of the cause of their unemployment (2006, 159). Taking a subgroup of the unemployed, Farber (1999, 2000) looked specifically at people who had been displaced by plant closings or slack work. Temporary employment allowed these displaced workers to maintain employment continuity, Farber argues. Keeping a foot in the labor force and avoiding employment gaps in their work histories is significant because periods of prolonged labor market inactivity (signified by a gap on one's résumé) can be held against workers who are searching for jobs. According to Farber, as well as Addison and Surfield, these unemployed workers used temporary employment as a transition to permanent employment (1999, S157).

Other researchers have noted that finding temporary jobs through placement agencies can be a boon to individuals who might, in the eyes of employers, appear to be high-risk hires. Temporary employment can offer people with difficult personal and workforce histories an opportunity to gain work experience and possibly reinvent themselves as workers with good employment records. Job seekers who have histories of criminal activity or weak labor force attachment, for example, may find agencies particularly useful. Agencies obviously screen and shoulder the cost of hiring and firing these temps, and

> by lowering compensation and firing costs, temporary help agencies made it more attractive for companies to try out workers with criminal records, poor work histories, or otherwise "risky" characteristics. Because many of these workers might not otherwise have had the opportunity to audition for a permanent position, they

potentially benefitted from the temporary employment arrangement. (Houseman and Erickcek 2002, 3)

As Erickcek, Houseman, and Kalleberg point out, "temporary agencies may provide an important linkage for these [high-risk] workers
to full-time jobs with benefits" (2003, 398). And temporary employment may be a valuable backup option for workers who experience
racial discrimination in the labor market (Bernasek and Kinnear
1999). Given that Hispanics are overrepresented in the contingent
workforce, as are African Americans (although to a lesser degree),
this hypothesis is compelling (Bureau of Labor Statistics 2005a,
table 2).

The same screening and auditioning function may improve the
employment opportunities for other populations of people who might
be viewed by hiring companies as high-risk unemployables. Analyzing a representative sample of women welfare recipients, Heinrich
established that temporary employment was an accessible employment route for them and that they were satisfied with their wages
and work conditions (indeed, she found that for the most part, the
wages of these women were quite close to the wages of women who
were employed in regular jobs—a comment on the low-wage job
market in general, we would speculate). In addition, these women
cited various benefits they acquired from their temporary jobs:
79 percent stated that they had received formal or informal employer-
provided training in such areas as occupational safety, basic skills
(math, writing, reading, and language), and occupationally specific
skills (clerical, customer service, and so forth). Seventy-one percent
believed their temporary positions might lead to future employment
advancement, and 69 percent reported that employer-provided training helped them stay current with new technology and regulations
(2005, 343).

For people who are at risk of going on public assistance (individuals who had either received public assistance or had had a family
income below 150 percent of the poverty line in the previous year),
working as a temporary employee through an agency produced only
"slightly worse outcomes relative to traditional employment"; again,
for them, temporary employment was better than unemployment

(Lane et al. 2003, 585, 593). The latter finding seems obvious but requires pointing out when assessing the implications of temporary work for people with limited alternatives in the job market.[1]

Finegold, Levenson, and Van Buren corroborate these findings, noting, in their study of low-wage temporary workers, that many temps who worked for more than two weeks with any given agency experienced wage progression and skill development or found a permanent job. They also note, however, that many factors come into play in determining such outcomes, such as employers' motivations and strategies for using temps, the work setting, the local labor market, and the autonomy of managers who supervise temporary workers (2003, 344–45; Levenson and Finegold 2001). Putting a slightly different spin on the issue of the advantages of temporary employment to low-wage workers, Andersson, Holzer, and Lane (2005) found that agency employment improved long-term earnings outcomes for this population and, moreover, that employment accessed through temporary placement agencies increased the likelihood that they could escape poverty and low-wage work.

Disadvantaged job seekers often find that their lack of social capital and connectedness hinders their ability to find permanent jobs and therefore turn to labor market intermediaries (LMIs) that substitute for and build social networks. Benner, Leete, and Pastor's comprehensive study of a range of labor market intermediaries in Silicon Valley and Milwaukee is centrally concerned with which LMIs most help socially and economically disadvantaged job seekers to improve their incomes, opportunities, and mobility. Comparing how nonprofit, government, and for-profit staffing agencies serve disadvantaged populations, they found that nonprofit and government organizations tended to provide more services, improve labor market outcomes, and in general assist people to a greater degree. Yet even private-sector agencies, they argue, serve an important function when "those with lower levels of social connectedness...find that their networks are inadequate and hence turn to a formal institution as a substitute" (Benner, Leete, and Pastor 2007, 190). In their study, people who were less socially connected used LMIs more than did job seekers with higher levels of social connections (2007, 177, fig. 6.1). Across the board, they argue, labor market intermediaries play a crucial role in shaping the quantity and quality of jobs for low-income individuals.

The temporary workers in Smith's (2001a) study (who performed assembly work at CompTech, a reputable high-tech firm) valued their temporary positions for several reasons. A temporary job in a "good" company was superior to many of the jobs they had held before, which were mostly regular (but for all intents and purposes, insecure) jobs in the secondary labor market. They had worked in fast food, nursing homes, home health care, and the like, where they had experienced high turnover and had been subjected to despotic employment practices. Many of the temps at CompTech hoped to segue into a permanent job with that company or believed that gaining work experience in a good company would help them land a good job elsewhere. Some reveled in their "status by association," the higher regard accorded a worker who was able to hold down a job, even a temporary one, in a reputable company.[2] Many of the temps Smith interviewed were people of color from working-class backgrounds who had not had access to higher educational opportunities and were pleased to have gained a foot in the door of a good company. (Along these lines, Morris and Vekker argue that young people with low educational attainment, who come from minority backgrounds or lack citizenship, are most likely to be found in temporary positions: they lack "superior employment opportunities" [2001, 384]; see also Bureau of Labor Statistics 2005a.)

At Select Labor, a number of temporary workers who regularly sought its services did so because they were confident that SL would place them in a decent temporary position, whereas on their own they were looking at insecure and poorly paid jobs. Some of the individuals who came into the office had turned down offers of so-called permanent jobs because they didn't match up to the good enough temporary positions these applicants were obtaining through SL.

Lautsch's research on the way companies organize their temporary-employment systems gets at the complicated calculus surrounding temporary jobs. She proposes a minimum of four paradigmatic contingent-employment systems, characterized by differing social relations, technology, market position, and corporate cultures. Her fourfold typology is useful for grasping the multiple possibilities, the subsequent complexities and tensions that result from the way temporary workers are deployed. As she notes, temporary-work systems are negotiated work forms, and contingent jobs are "complex social relationships," not "simple wage contracts" (2002, 41). Understanding that temporary-employment systems vary, according to the culture, management styles, and production imperatives of different firms, makes it clear that the construction of good enough temporary jobs is not a foregone conclusion, even though it is an underlying logic for the THS industry. It also makes clear that there is no simple way of evaluating how workers might feel about or benefit from temporary employment.

But a preponderance of evidence strongly suggests that temporary-help placement agencies are vehicles of "transitional mobility": at certain moments in the labor force trajectories of some groups of people, an agency can help them get past racial barriers or other forms of social discrimination; can place workers in positions that might enable them to segue into good jobs; can help workers develop skills (minimal training in word processing and soldering, in how to write and improve résumés, in how to decipher the labor market, prepare for an interview, and so forth); and can provide workers an opportunity to sustain their labor market participation, even if in temporary jobs, thus avoiding gaps in their employment records. In an era of continual change in occupational and industrial structures and of upheavals in economic cycles, agencies that provide transitional opportunity are undeniably valuable to many.

Utilizing the services of a temporary-help placement agency can be a rational labor market strategy for many people seeking a "real"—that is, permanent—job today. In early 2006, 53 percent of temps who remained in the workforce after having taken a temporary position reported that they had been able to move on to permanent positions.[3] People often take temporary jobs in the belief that doing so will enable them to move eventually into a permanent position, make them more employable in the future, and provide opportunities for training, skill development, and experience-building. And workers are increasingly likely to stay in any given temporary job for substantial periods of time. In 1995 about 24 percent of temporary agency workers had been employed for one year or more in a single position; this percentage had reached nearly 34 percent by 2005.[4] Nevertheless, it is necessary to go beyond job placement and work conditions to reflect on the whole system of temporary employment and ask about its fundamental limitations and drawbacks.

The True Cost to Workers of Temporary Labor

Even though agencies such as Select Labor can do their best to carve out decent work and employment conditions for workers; even though some people may prefer temporary positions at different stages of their lives; and even though some temporary jobs may be superior to some permanent jobs—temporary employment of the sort we have analyzed in this book, even when good enough, is inherently problematic. Temporary placement agencies that try to do right by their temps still leave the temporary employment framework intact. THS firms and the agencies that do their work on the ground perpetuate and reinforce a system of employment relationships that disadvantage workers structurally, financially, and normatively. Whatever agencies do to protect the workers who seek their assistance, they are not challenging the fact that the American system of work and employment has evolved in a way that leaves huge numbers of people on the margins and nearly all people uncertain about their future employment opportunities. Let us make these claims more concrete.

The Problems of Wages and Health Care

First, on average, from any study of temporary workers we learn that their wages are lower than those earned by their noncontingent counterparts, even when they perform the same work. Second, virtually no temporary jobs in the tier that we have been discussing—low-paid positions for people who lack extensive educational backgrounds or specialized skill sets—enable workers to access health plans or other benefits. That in the United States the majority of people who do have health benefits get them through their jobs is, in itself, one of the greatest gaps in our social safety net. Linking benefits to good jobs penalizes all people who lack jobs. It also penalizes those who have jobs but work for an employer who offers no health coverage, and those who earn too little to buy coverage on the open market but enough that they are ineligible for state health programs. This coupling of good jobs and health coverage leaves many people on the edge of crisis. Since the late 1990s there has been a notable decline in the number of American workers who are covered by employer-sponsored medical care programs (Wiatrowski 2004). Lack of health benefits is a major source of job anxiety today; it makes people fearful to leave jobs with benefits, and compels people to accept work with employers and organizations where their job satisfaction may be low.

There is a growing body of literature on "job lock": the belief that workers who hold employer-provided health insurance suffer reduced job mobility. Usually, they are reluctant to take other jobs because they are afraid to leave positions where they have benefits (Wiatrowski 1995, 42). If a worker has a preexisting health condition that might make it difficult to switch plans, or is nervous about making it without coverage through a waiting period (i.e., employment in a new job for a specified number of months before going on the new employer's health plan), his or her reluctance may be even greater. Job lock is an important social problem because workers are discouraged from finding jobs with better wages and working conditions and from seeking opportunities for mobility.[5] It is also an important organizational problem because when workplaces are staffed by people who are unhappy in their jobs but afraid to leave, the quality of organizational processes and social relations inevitably will suffer. Across the board, this is one of the most pressing policy issues in the United States today, and many social-change groups and legislators are proposing plans to change this essential inequity.

And when we shift our gaze to low-level temporary workers, the picture is even more grim. To work as a temp is not just to live on the edge; it is potentially to be in the abyss with respect to health coverage. Hiring companies do not extend health coverage to the typical temporary worker. Bureau of Labor Statistics data indicate that four-fifths of contingent workers lack employer-sponsored health care, compared with slightly more than half of noncontingent workers (Bureau of Labor Statistics 2005a). Does this mean that temporary workers lack access to health benefits altogether? No: nearly 60 percent of contingent workers, broadly defined, actually do have health insurance from some source (Bureau of Labor Statistics 2005a, table 9). The most likely explanation, according to the BLS, is that many of these contingent workers are covered by the health benefits of spouses. The drawback, of course, is that just as our current system of health benefits creates workers' dependencies on a job, having to rely on a spouse or domestic partner for health coverage may create dependencies and strains on traditional family structures and relations. Whereas staying in a job for fear that moving might mean loss of health benefits (job lock), people might also stay in a marriage for fear of losing access to benefits: marriage lock.

Second, a surprising fact about many temporary firms today is that they often *can* give their temps access to health programs. But since temporary placement agencies do not pay a portion of temps' health packages as in many employer-sponsored benefits programs, the cost of the benefits is borne exclusively by the temps—and, as many are well aware, the premiums on such packages are usually unaffordable to people who earn low wages, whether they work as a temp or full time at poverty-level wages. Commonly today, temporary placement firms will call attention to the availability of health coverage, publicizing it as an advantage they can give people who use their services. Yet this is an illusory advantage; in 2005, less than one-fifth (18 percent) of contingent workers were covered by employer-sponsored health care (Bureau of Labor Statistics 2005a); the cost of purchasing it is usually out of reach of the low-wage temp.

The Problem of Insecurity

The fact that nearly all low-level temporary jobs lack health care coverage leaves the vast majority of low-wage temporary workers extremely vulnerable. Temporary employment also leaves them extremely insecure, since the inescapable element of the temporary job is that it is unpredictable. Even if a temp is sent to a job for three weeks, nothing guarantees that the hiring company will keep her or him for the full time. Any number of incidents could create a mismatch between the temp and the client firm, despite the efforts of agency workers to achieve the best match possible. If a temp does not click with a manager; if temps argue with other temps or with permanent workers about what they are supposed to be doing; if a temporary worker develops a physical condition that makes him or her unable to keep doing the work; or if a company decides to cut the size of its workforces, permanent and temporary alike—any of these events could lead to an abrupt termination of the temporary position. No advance warning for termination is required, and no guarantees are made for the length of the job.

The very nature of the temporary employment relationship, then, means that uncertainty and open-endedness are ever present. Occupational unpredictability is not unique to temporary workers today, obviously; pervasive job layoffs, a widespread sense of instability in jobs and careers, and economic turmoil affect workers across the occupational and industrial spectrum. Numerous social commentators and theorists have detailed the way this precariousness affects individual American workers and our collective life.[6] But even though these perceptions and anxieties are pervasive, it is one thing to worry about the future when you have a so-called permanent job and can expect, at a minimum, two weeks notice (with pay) and possibly severance pay if your employer lays you off. It is another if you have a temporary job and desperately want to reach a career ladder in a company and stay there, but when you look around, all the ladders seem to be disintegrating. For temporary workers, this double risk factor—lacking a sense of the *possibility* of finding a regular job and lacking the basic security net that one has with health benefits—is a major disadvantage in our culture.

Focusing on the "unemployed, underemployed, and anxiously employed," Ehrenreich and Draut note that the insecurity and instability of professional and other middle-class jobs has remained invisible, compared with the national discussion about the working poor and low-paid temporary workers. Downwardly mobile middle-class people sometimes have well-paid "permanent" jobs but then face bouts of unemployment or low-wage employment. They suffer from income volatility, are squeezed by layoffs, disappearing pensions, and health benefits, and fall back on contingent work when they can't find anything else. This middle-class insecurity constitutes a "quiet" erosion of middle-class workers in the United States, according to Ehrenreich and Draut (2006, 3), in which temporary employment is playing a significant role.

The Problem of Voice

Lower-than-average wages, lack of health benefits, and job insecurity are three primary sources of disadvantage and marginalization for temps. Yet a fourth source of disadvantage is the lack of voice and low sense of empowerment. At this time it is difficult to envision the conditions which might enhance the political efficacy of this "fractured" group of workers (Smith 1998). Researchers have found a number of structural obstacles within work sites which make the conditions of powerlessness and inequality for temps murky and difficult to confront. In Rogers's (2000) terms, a "powerful yet incomplete web of controls," a multivalent control structure, masks the nature of exploitation and inequality in the experiences of many temporary workers.

Most notably, temporary workers often lack a clear sense of who is in control, one of the surest sources of the galvanization of workers to protest the conditions of their work. That is, temps frequently don't understand exactly who their employer is, or even who the boss is. Although they may understand that their paychecks are issued by a temporary-placement agency, they may believe that the hiring company where they work is their real employer, and the line manager there the only boss who matters. After all, they report to the client's work site every day and often receive orders from a line manager. More complicated, if they work in a company where teamwork is valued, they may actually work side by side with permanent workers who collaboratively monitor what they do. In some cases, temporary workers may even be appointed lead workers on a team, creating an impression that they, the temps, are in charge (Smith 2001a).

Working under a paternalistic manager can lead temps to overlook the structural exploitation inherent in the temporary employment relationship, as well (Smith 2001b), as can devices that temporary-help firms use to celebrate and honor temps: employee recognition programs and rewards, or social events (Gottfried 1991; Rogers 2000;

Smith 2001b). Extra layers of subcontracting dilute the sense of a center of power even more. Some of Select Labor's temporary workers were sent out to back up the temps hired by another agency; in other words, a separate agency would contract for SL's temps, who would then be sent to a wholly separate work site—layers of subcontracting arrangements observed in other settings and a phenomenon Smith also observed in her earlier study of CompTech (2001a, 2001b).

Finally, some optimists might hope that permanent workers would take up the cause of the temporary workers in their midst, seeing temps as a group with whom to align to fight off management's efforts to attack labor. Study after study, however, highlights the very great difficulty of pulling off such a mobilizing feat. Most case studies report that permanent workers view temporary workers as a threat to their own job security, not as a group with whom they share occupational interests (see Graham 1995, 135–36). Despite the exhortations of personnel writers in the 1960s and 1970s (recall that one element of the template for the successful use of temps was that managers should always make sure their regular workers were apprised of the benefits of using temps so that permanent workers would not see temps as rate busters or job stealers but as help mates), workers in the late twentieth and the early twenty-first century are more likely to view temps as a frightening projection of their own futures and therefore fight to keep temporary jobs from growing and encroaching on their own terrain.

And it is perhaps this last observation that is key to understanding the fundamental problem with living in a society in which people across the board understand that temporary employment is pervasive and possible. Even if a temporary job is good enough, what it represents to people more broadly is that employment today is tenuous and unreliable. The growth of temporary work has occurred because many good permanent jobs, jobs that once offered benefits and better wages and security, have been bulldozed aside, replaced by insecure and less-well-paid jobs. Having access to a series of temporary jobs may allow people to put food on their tables, but an institutionalized system of temporary employment makes it hard to live beyond the day-to-day, to plan for their own future and for the future of their families.

Ameliorating the Downside of Temporary Employment

What are some viable strategies for improving the situations of the millions of people who work as temporaries but would prefer and need permanent, full-time jobs? What might bridge the gap between good enough temporary jobs and a good enough system in which people could work on a temporary basis but not be continually on the margins and at risk?

This is a complex issue. Low wages, lack of health coverage and other benefits, job insecurity, and the fractured nature of the workforce are not problems for temporary workers alone. Indeed, these employment-related conditions hurt workers across the entire occupational and industrial spectrum. Millions of people have jobs that are full time and allegedly permanent but that pay poverty-level wages, don't provide benefits, and can be eliminated in an instant (Appelbaum, Bernhardt, and Murnane 2003; Ehrenreich 2001; Hayes 2003; Shipley 2004). Others have comparatively well-paid jobs but face the "intense insecurity" of an ethos in which workers are expendable and where even college-educated workers fear losing those good jobs (Hacker 2006). This is a societal problem of enormous magnitude which people across the country—policymakers, legislators, academics, community activists, and others concerned with progressive social change—are tackling day in and day out. In struggles to raise the federal minimum wage, campaign for living wages (Gertner 2006; Luce 2004, 2005), develop workforce development strategies that create career ladders for low-wage workers (Fitzgerald 2006), mobilize support for legislation that will ensure access to health care for all citizens, and make corporations more socially responsible to their workers and the communities where they do business, people are striving to create conditions that will guarantee everyone certain basic social and economic rights (Sirianni and Friedland 2001; Osterman 2002).

But specifically, there are many efforts taking place across the nation to improve conditions for temporary workers and turn up the volume of their political voice. In the spirit of progressively remedying the labor market inopportunity associated with temporary work, we identify four approaches—building membership associations that are geared specifically to developing health and human services for contingent workers; reforming labor law; establishing labor- and community-based organizations that place contingent workers in jobs; and pressuring for-profit agencies to develop a set of best practices around the use and placement of contingent workers.

Employment Associations

Paul Osterman notes, "There is unlikely to be any single union model [for organizing contingent workers] that makes sense in all circumstances" (1999, 172). Reflecting this fact, a variety of associations have been established to meet the needs of "nontraditional" or contingent workers, including temps, contract workers, and freelancers. These membership associations advocate for temporary workers in much the same way that traditional labor unions have advocated for regular, permanent workers. But whereas traditional labor unions typically cover workers in a single occupation or industry, organizations for contingent workers strive to cover people who work in a variety of occupations as they move in and out of jobs. Several strategies have emerged from their efforts, one being to create associations through which contingent workers can gain access to benefits and insurance.

Working Today, for example, is a membership organization that was founded in 1995 to serve the needs of the New York City community of "independent" workers. Working Today developed a portable benefits network that allows contingent workers to buy health insurance at a group rate, obtain it outside the employment relationship, and take it with them as they move from employer to employer. Because they can get a group rate for their premiums, Working Today claims that their independent workers can get health insurance at less than one-third the average market price. This portable benefits system, named the Freelancers Union in 2001 (a national nonprofit), now provides contingent workers benefits such as health, life, and disability insurance and serves as a resource and advocacy agent for contingent workers. Boasting a membership of 14,000 in New York City, Working Today has also entered into partnership with other intermediary organizations all together allowing it to reach 45,000 workers. It is currently working to develop accessible retirement plans, and legal, financial, and tax services for its members.[7]

Other associations have replicated this model, which provides access to benefits, legal advice, information about the job market, and other resources. United Professionals, for example, is a membership-based organization that specifically addresses the deleterious consequences of contingent employment for college-educated workers. Its goal, like the goal of the National Employment Lawyers Association (http://www.nela.org), is to "offer services and advocacy to millions that can cover them through periods of unemployment and occupational change" (Ehrenreich and Draut 2006, 3; see also http://www.unitedprofessionals.org). Seeing their dilemmas as part of larger structural problems that affect not just contingent but all workers, these organizations also engage in activism at the national level, such as working toward the creation of a universal health plan, an improved unemployment insurance system, living wage policies, and other socioeconomic policies to support American people.

Primarily serving the national population of contingent workers, some associations disseminate information about the costs and benefits of temporary employment and strive to raise temporary workers' awareness in order to minimize their marginalization and exploitation. The Temp Workers Alliance of New Jersey, for example, produces a lengthy *Consumer Guide* for people who are looking to be or are employed as temps and for contract workers. It lists agencies in the region that use "best practices" toward their temps and provides data on the realities of working as a temp: statistics about the likelihood of moving from a temporary to a permanent position; information about how companies have restructured their workforces to protect core workers and profit from temporary ones; facts about relevant employment law, including the meaning of at-will employment; and tips about how to avoid being exploited by hiring companies (Temp Workers Alliance 2003).

Similarly, the National Alliance for Fair Employment, a conglomeration of organizations, works to provide information, advice, and resources to contingent workers; it comprises working groups that address specific problems related to temporary employment and to serving different constituencies (http://datacenter.org/programs/naffe-fol.htm). The highly visible union WashTech/CWA (which assisted contract workers in the Microsoft lawsuit, Van Jaarsveld 2004) addresses, among other issues, the problems that high-tech, often well-paid contract workers face (http://www.washtech.org). Some activists have even tried to establish nonprofit temporary coopera-tives (http://boston.indymedia.org/feature/display/198106). Finally, outside the domain of temporary-agency workers, a number of occupation-specific groups of day laborers, health-care and home-care workers, domestic workers, and landscapers are developing worker centers or cooperatives to train, place, provide benefits, and assure fair-labor practices for contingent workers (Fine 2006).

The obstacles to using a more traditional union model to organize temps are legion, as are the obstacles to organizing any workers in the twenty-first-century United States. Union organizing is problem-atic and difficult even with regular workers, and rates of unioniza-tion have declined for all workers over four decades. The conditions of work for temps—"structural ambiguity," as Chun (2005) calls it—make this project even more problematic. Temps move from as-signment to assignment, from work site to work site; their mobil-ity makes it difficult for them to develop a sense of community and shared perspective with other people in the same situation. Temps rarely want to identify with and remain temps; typically, anyone in-voluntarily working as a temp hopes to move beyond temporary sta-tus, into the ranks of the regularly employed. The self-image that one is only temporarily a temp means that the identity basis for unity is fleeting and transient—another roadblock to mobilizing temporary workers into an effective organization or social movement. Never-theless, some leading public sociologists and labor activists continue to strategize and theorize about how to organize in an economy where many workers are employed on a contingent basis and many workers work in sectors that traditionally have not been unionized.[8]

Changing Labor Law

Many labor activists and legal scholars have struggled to enact new policies that might improve the work conditions for and favor the employment status of temporary employees. Among other things, labor organizers have tried to challenge the legal status of temporary workers and improve their access to union representation and collective bargaining rights. Recent court rulings have twisted back and forth with respect to temporary workers—"permatemps" in particular, who are employed in long-term temporary positions (DuRivage 2001).

In the case of M. B. Sturgis, Inc. and Jeffboat Division, for example, the National Labor Relations Board ruled that temporary workers who were jointly employed (by a staffing agency and a hiring company) could not be excluded from a bargaining unit if temps worked in that unit and performed the same tasks as permanent employees. The NLRB thus extended to temps the right to be covered by the same regulations, working conditions, and benefits as regular workers. This ruling was viewed by many as a promising basis for aggressively combatting companies that tried to substitute low-paid temporary workers without benefits for more highly paid permanent workers with benefits. It was also regarded with a fair amount of alarm by the THS industry. The NLRB overturned that ruling in 2004, this time using the fact of joint employment *against* temporaries to specify that workers who are supplied to a hiring company by a staffing company are employees of both and therefore need the consent of both before they can be included in a bargaining unit (Freeman and Gonos 2005; Hely 2003).

Striving to win temporary and contract workers' right to organize and participate in collective bargaining units remains a key goal of labor and legal activists (Befort 2003; Kennedy 2005). Katherine Stone (2006, 283) argues that it is also essential to develop labor law allowing legal organizational units (encompassing all "atypical" workers, including temporary and part-time workers, independent contractors, and even the unemployed) to be given formal representation inside particular workplaces. Freeman and Gonos believe that temp agencies should be reclassified and subjected to the "regime of regulation and structural transparency similar to that which governs union hiring halls"; a piece of legal reform that would give temporary workers parity with other categories of workers (2005, 294–95). Others have advocated legislation that would require equal pay for temporaries who do work that is equal to that of regular employees (Vockrodt 2005). Working through the courts to improve labor law clearly is an important pillar of reform and progress for all employees who, as Stone (2006) refers to them, are "atypical" in that they lack an employer and are not embedded in a permanent employment relationship.[9]

Alternative Community and Staffing Organizations

A third strategy for addressing the problem of temporary employment has been to build community- and labor-based organizations that might improve and advance the lives of workers on the edge. One effort has been the creation of community partnerships, in which various workforce development organizations come together to provide social support services, advice, training opportunities, and sometimes child care and transportation for disadvantaged workers. As Fine (2006) argues, because many traditional community institutions—such as trade unions, political parties, and mutual aid societies—have been dramatically weakened in recent years, new institutional forms are desirable to fill this gap and meet the needs of new constituencies in the reconfigured economy. Fine focuses on worker centers around the United States, organizations that take a holistic approach to poverty and low-wage employment. Worker centers try to meet the needs of low-wage workers, especially undocumented immigrants, providing access to social services, advocacy in human and civil rights issues, and neighborhood and public school improvement. Organizations within these larger partnerships may specialize in training, in negotiating with employers for better work or compensation, in job search assistance, or in brokering between job seekers and employers, matching the former to the latter (Rosenfeld 2006).

Giloth's (2003) volume of essays describes such workforce development organizations and intermediaries, focusing especially on collaborative efforts among unions, community colleges, economic development organizations, and governmental organizations such as One-Stop Career Centers (although for a pessimistic assessment of One-Stop Centers, see Smith, Flynn, and Isler 2006). Fitzgerald

(2006) argues that employers might develop career ladders for low-wage workers; she, too, highlights the importance of labor market intermediaries such as unions, community colleges, and other community-based organizations. Her proposal is provocative because it suggests thatlow-wageworkdoesn'tnecessarilyhavetobedead-endworkandthat companies and workforce development specialists can target the multitude of low-wage jobs as sites of advancement for workers who lack many employment options. One difficulty with Fitzgerald's proposal, however, is that it relies on a high degree of "buy in" on the part of employers who may have no interest in restructuring low-wage jobs.

We find another type of prefigurative practice in nonprofit temporary-placement agencies that are pro-worker rather than pro-business. The majority of these alternative staffing agencies provide services to improve the labor market experience of low-wage, disadvantaged, temporary workers and mitigate barriers to more equitable workplace participation for the contingent labor force (Carré et al. 2001, 2003). Alternative staffing agencies' goals include placing workers in jobs that meet living-wage standards, providing comprehensive training and benefits programs (health insurance, paid holidays, vacations, and sick leaves) to temps, and placing them in jobs that have a high probability of converting to permanent employment.

Significant structural barriers, however, limit alternative organizations' ability to become robust labor market intermediaries that can advocate for temporary workers and get them into permanent jobs. Becoming a self-sustaining staffing service while putting workers' needs first can create insurmountable contradictions, as case studies have shown (Neuwirth 2006). Alternative staffing agencies face significant pressure to conform to the hegemonic model of temporary-placement agencies. Competing for a share of the temporary-help service market can end up shaping the activity of alternative organizations nearly as much as of for-profit agencies such as Select Labor; the difference between them is a matter of degree, not of type, and the work of promoting mobility for individual temporary workers can conflict with the work of promoting empowerment for labor as a collectivity.

Best Practices for Agencies

Putting all these elements together gives us a powerful understanding of why temporary employment is problematic for so many people. In light of the relative precariousness, disadvantage, lack of power, and sense of constricted opportunity, we can give temporary help agencies only so much credit for making temporary jobs decent ones. And were it not for the bottom-line profitmaking strategies of temporary-help placement firms—to sell reputable, reliable, marketable temporary workers; to make themselves the agency of choice to hiring companies and temps—very likely we would not even be able to give them that limited credit. But it is possible that something can be done to sway temporary-placement agencies to do more to improve the experiences of temporary workers, even if only to help maximize the quality of a period of transitional opportunity. Herein rests a fourth approach to ameliorating conditions for temporary workers, the "best practices" approach. If agencies knew that they could recruit greater numbers of job seekers offering "best practices" to workers looking for temporary jobs, they might find that doing so adds enough to their bottom line that it would pay to make it part of their marketing strategy.

Barley and Kunda argue that well-paid contractors *and* hiring contractors in the Silicon Valley cared so much about the quality of staffing agencies that they routinely visited Web sites dedicated to sharing information about good and bad agencies. Both contractors and hiring companies used this information to decide which agencies to approach and which to avoid. From the point of view of hiring companies, according to Barley and Kunda, a good agency was one that provided contractors who did quality work and that invested in training in order to upgrade their skills (2004, 90–91). These agencies were widely viewed as being careful about selecting and screening contractors, as well as professional and reliable.

Contractors themselves viewed investment in training as evidence of a good agency. They also defined good agencies as those with employees who were helpful, maintained contact with their contractors, and set up accounts with hiring companies that contractors viewed as desirable places to work. Good agencies also offered benefits and sometimes even stock options. All these factors combined led contractors to feel that a good agency did not take advantage of them. Agencies viewed as bad by both hiring companies and contractors, on the other hand, "skimped on service to cut costs and maximize profits," and their staff were considered to be uncooperative and unprofessional (Barley and Kunda 2004, 91).

These observations reflect the point of view of highly paid contractors and the companies that hire them. What might a good agency look like from the point of view of temps located at the lower end of the wage and occupational perspective? Not surprisingly, many of the services provided by good agencies for contract workers would pertain also to agencies that place low-level temps. When agencies invest in a modicum of skills training that can prepare workers for existing jobs; when they purposely develop accounts with hiring companies that have reasonable employment practices and avoid setting up accounts with hiring companies where managers are abusive or expose temps to risk; when they provide job search assistance such as résumé and interview preparation; if they make the acquisition of health benefits more transparent to temps and endeavor to create less expensive group plans for their temps—all these services would be part of a package of best practices that would both attract good temps and make temporary-placement agencies even more effective vehicles for transitional mobility. Furthermore, agencies that are known for placing permatemps could make even greater effort to make affordable health-care packages available to people who tend to work as temps on a long-term basis.

The *Consumer Guide* of the Temp Workers Alliance (2003) provides a blueprint of best practices for temp agencies. The agencies that made their list train temps to use cutting-edge software packages and prepare them for positions for which there is high demand in the local area; provide "post-placement" follow-up support services; have special counseling staff for temps; supply guidance for moving from temporary to permanent positions; schedule mentoring, stress management, and professional growth workshops; and sometimes offer assistance with child care and transportation to jobs. Best practices agencies often provide holiday pay for their temporary workers, paid vacation days, incentive programs, 401K programs, portable health and dental plans, and bonuses. Some agencies expressly espouse social commitments to improving workers' long-term outcomes; Newsource Staffing, for example, dedicates itself to "helping entry-level workers gain a foothold into the employment market so that they can begin to earn good wages and improve the quality of their lives" (Temp Workers Alliance 2003, 5; also see http://www.newcommunity.org/whatwedo.htm). Conversion policies such as those of GoodTemps, located in New York, might also find its way onto a list of best practices for temporary workers. GoodTemps claims to be chiefly "concerned with keeping their temporary staff employed and motivated" (and to be "people-oriented, not profit-driven"), and it charges no conversion fee, thus increasing incentive to hiring companies to convert temporary workers to permanent status (http://www.goodtemps.org/).

If best practices were fully articulated and publicly disseminated, people seeking temporary jobs would have a yardstick against which agencies could be measured and thus find those that come close to measuring up. Benner, Leete, and Pastor (2007, chap. 7) also point out that knowing which types of labor market intermediaries deliver the best practices would enable temporary workers to make informed decisions about the whole population of for-profit, nonprofit, and governmental agencies that place temporary workers (a list about which their overview of LMIs provides). Community organizations might approach local hiring companies and educate them about the benefits of hiring temps from best practices agencies, especially highlighting the likelihood that temps from these agencies have the potential to be more motivated and committed and to turn in a quality work performance.

Temporary-placement agencies could compete for the business of temporary workers by making these services available. In many cases, they already have (simply read the Web sites of many of the leading THS companies), but the problem is that doing so is not systematic and most likely not enough. Temporary-help agencies could take a much larger role in workforce development in the United States by publicizing to a greater degree the opportunities they offer for training workers and by creating more online training opportunities for those who need it (Finegold, Levenson, and Van Buren 2003, 357). If individual job seekers and social change activists and organizations developed a concerted and widespread campaign to get THS firms to adopt a set of best practices, we might move away from the patch-work system of temporary jobs that maximize insecurity to a more coherent, good enough employment system with support services and resources that would minimize the risk and insecurity that seem to be inevitable in our present economy. Doing all this would not elimi-nate the profit-seeking basis for the production of good temps, but it might help push these profitmaking activities in a way that softens the harsher and more frightening aspects of insecure employment. As Benner, Leete, and Pastor argue, "encouraging 'best practice' [on the part of temporary-help service agencies] to become common practice could yield significant social benefits" (2007, 236).

Our study points to several directions for research on the topic of temporary employment and of employment relations more broadly. Clearly, collecting comparative data on agencies is important. Re-search that investigates a greater number and variety of agencies could show the degree to which Select Labor was typical or unusual, and could specify more precisely the conditions under which agen-cies cultivate good temporary workers. Looking at agencies that mar-ket themselves to different industrial sectors (manufacturing, health care, service, high technology, and so forth) or that are located in different regions (geographical regions, regions with tighter or looser labor markets, or areas that are primarily manufacturing-based versus high-technology based) could help us understand how and whether the definition of good or desirable temporary workers and jobs varies, as does the process of producing and marketing temporary workers.

An important study parallel to ours might look at the issues we raise from the viewpoint of people who regularly work on a tem-porary basis. Such a study—which would allow us to discover how temps themselves judge the efforts of agencies to cultivate and market good temps—could either interview or survey workers and attempt to answer the following questions about labor market be-haviors and decisions. How do people decide which agency they want to use? What influences their decision to continue to use an agency or to continue working on a temporary basis? How would they rank their use of an agency or agencies against their use of other job search techniques? What qualities do people look for in an agency: the most extensive training? the highest wages? placements in the best companies? respect? decent treatment by agency employees? Do temps think that agencies are "good"? What is their identity as temporary workers, especially in an era of institutionalized temporary employment? What conditions and policies might enable people to feel that taking temporary jobs was their choice and not something they were forced into? These are just a handful of questions that could give us greater purchase on the other side of the story of the good temp.

Much remains to be done on the front of cultural or discourse analysis. We analyzed business and personnel publications, but there is a substantial genre of self-help, job-search literature that could yield meaningful data about how experts try to persuade people to seek temporary employment. One example would be an analysis of Richard Bolles's annually updated *What Color Is Your Parachute?* which was first published in 1970, has sold nearly ten million copies, and has been translated into twelve different languages. We were not able to do a historical overview of this best-selling career advice book, but our assumption is that Bolles's assuring advice about normative temporary employment has seeped into his writing only in recent years. It would be instructive to analyze the way Bolles has framed employment relations over time, as well as his conceptualization of how it has become acceptable and sometimes desirable to take temporary rather than permanent employment (i.e., when one can't find a full-time, permanent "dream" job, temporary employment is the next best thing). These studies and others have the potential to contribute further to a better understanding of how the employment relationship of the new economy arose and the institutions and beliefs that fertilized its growth.

Our study shows that labor markets are social constructions, guided by the helping (and very visible) hands of economic institutions and the people who lead them. The historically specific labor market we investigated has been created over time by people with the resources and the venues to promulgate new ideas about the best way to employ, control, and cut the costs of labor and to exploit new openings in global economic and institutional conditions.

It is sustained by contemporary profit seekers and daily interactions on the part of individual soldiers in the trenches: those who work for agencies today. Our analysis provides powerful evidence for the argument that the labor market for temporary workers might possibly be reconstructed in a different direction, that we do not have to resign ourselves to letting it take its course without progressive intervention.

Block's conceptualization of how to move toward a moral economy is helpful in thinking about how progressive change might take place. As he and others note, the quality of relations between workers and employers is not preordained. Corporations make choices about pursuing high versus low roads in the way they handle their employment relations (Block 2006; Appelbaum and Batt 1994). Taking the low road by ruthlessly cutting costs and neglecting employees might maximize short-term profits, yet there are obvious costs, such as turning out products that are shoddy and staffing workplaces with employees who are angry and might look for ways to sabotage the company. Taking the high road, on the other hand, by implementing practices in the workplace that are premised on respect for workers and on the belief that companies can benefit from workers' loyalty and expertise, may compromise short-term high profits but yield long-term quality, stability, and consumer loyalty. To achieve the high road with respect to the situation of temporary workers today, many different groups of actors could pressure temporary-help agencies to provide the most beneficial policies possible, all the while working to build alternative community organizations and associations and battling for improvements through the court system.

And in an era when the market increasingly governs management practices, pressure from consumers—whether consumers who purchase goods and services, workers seeking the assistance of labor market intermediaries, or corporations seeking temporary or contract workforces—seems imperative. As we were writing the final pages of this book, the newest iteration of low-road practices, a stunning example of how companies allow markets to shape their management practices, hit the news: in early April 2007, Circuit City, the nation's second largest retailer of electronic products, announced that it would lay off about 3,400 of its most highly paid sales and warehouse workers, publicly stating that they were doing so because these workers' wages, which were the highest in the retail end of their business, constituted a drag on profits (Carr 2007; Leonhardt 2007a).

Circuit City, like many big businesses in the United States, is struggling to maintain profits as other companies manage to outsell them by bringing cheaper products to the market. Circuit City's decision to blatantly slice out its higher-earning workers represents a new and ominous lane in the low road of employment relations. To be sure, companies have been laying off workers for decades because they feel that their large workforces and high payrolls are cutting into profits or because the company is perceived as having a bloated workforce. And these companies have been richly rewarded by Wall Street: when they engage in large-scale layoffs, the value of their stocks typically goes right up. But what is unique about the Circuit City case, why this event should be viewed as a prime example of bad practice, and why it should deeply alarm everyone who is concerned about the condition of labor in the United States today, is that executive management in this corporation made the decision to lay off workers explicitly because this class of employees earned too much money.

Usually, when companies lay off their longer-term workers (some of whom, to be sure, have maxed out in their salaries), they don't baldly flaunt the fact that they are targeting a particular class of employees. It is one thing for a firm to announce that it will lay off a total of 3,000 workers across the board or shut down specific operational units; it is another to single out a class of employees and lay them off because the company is dead-bent on cheapening the cost of its labor by selectively firing highly paid employees. New workers will be hired at entry-level wages, and Circuit City is magnanimously allowing the laid-off workers to reapply for these jobs after ten weeks— at the same entry-level wages as everyone else.

Vowing not to consume the products of companies that take such an immoral stance toward their workers seems like the first and maybe most powerful thing that we—who are not the workers or the stockholders but are the consumers—can do. For the purposes of our study, temporary-help service agencies have consumers on two sides: the companies that hire their temps and the workers that apply to them for temporary jobs. With enough public education, support, and steadfast determination to boycott companies who are actively involved in the contemporary degradation of labor, it is easy to envision that more agencies could come to see the high road of labor practices—adopting a set of best practices around the recruitment, training, and placement of temporary workers—as desirable and profitable.

A final note. Our analysis should not be construed as an endorsement of profitmaking temporary-help service agencies or the industry as a whole. The fact that the practices we have discussed take the edge off temporary employment, in our view, is a byproduct of the explicit profit-seeking strategies of private-sector business, profits created by the labor of temporary workers. Nevertheless, as temporary employment has become widespread, normalized, and arguably permanent, the infrastructure of the temporary-help industry may provide unusual forms of assistance and protections for workers who lack options for better jobs.

In an ideal society, all of us would have reasonable access to a living wage, good working conditions, mobility opportunities, and job security. It is the shame of our society that instead, most workers lack these conditions and assurances and must resort to working in insecure or temporary positions, often both. Given the reality of contemporary labor markets—that corporations today have near-complete latitude to restructure their operations and their workforces, whittle away at permanent employment contracts, and move operations overseas—it seems highly desirable to seek ways to achieve both optimal conditions for pursuing, gaining, and working in temporary and other kinds of jobs, and maximum institutional protection for workers, whether in temporary or permanent positions. Leaning on labor market intermediaries such as Select Labor may take us a big step closer to ensuring such institutional protection for a great many workers.

APPENDIX I

Analyzing the Management Media

To build a database of articles for our content analysis of industry discourse, we began searching the Industrial Arts Index (later the Business Periodicals Index published by the H.W. Wilson Company) in 1945, finding a number of subject headings that showed promise. Because no headings including the word "temporary" appeared there until 1956, we scanned a comprehensive list of other subject headings likely to yield articles that would address the staffing industry: Employees; Employment, management; Employment systems; Labor, casual; Labor, recruitment; Labor, supply; Office management; Office workers; and Woman, employment. In 1956 the subject heading "Office temporaries" appeared in the Industrial Arts Index, and in 1958, when the index's title changed to Business Periodicals Index (BPI), the heading "Employees, temporary" debuted. Still, it was not until the 1960s that the number of articles per topic per year grew to ten or more. In 1968, Manpower gained its very own subject heading ("Manpower, Inc."), a mark of distinction that would be extended to (and sometimes taken away from) several other staffing companies as their fortunes waxed and waned.

The more direct subject headings "Temporary employees" and "Temporary help service agencies" surfaced in 1982, and an explosion of articles on the burgeoning industry ensued, increasing in number each year of our inquiry, which ended with the 1990 edition of the Business Periodicals Index. Because we expected to find more articles than we could reasonably pursue, we limited ourselves to those found through index volumes issued every two years between 1956 and 1990. Even so, we were able to compile a database of some 430 articles on the staffing industry. Since we sampled BPI volumes every two years, we estimate that the 430 articles represent only about half of all articles published in those decades.

Of these articles, we excluded news reports on specific temporary help service firms, articles about firms' in-house temporary programs, profiles of "famous men" (leaders in the industry), articles that tracked industry and economic growth, and articles that addressed temporary employment in other countries. We also excluded articles written in academic management publications because we were less interested in articles based on scholarly research and more interested in the types of ideological and rhetorical claims we expected to find in mass-market, management-oriented publications. Though we ended by excluding about 170 articles from our analysis, the broad search nevertheless had value in that it gave us a sense of the THS industry as a whole. We were able to glean information about its financial status over the years, its profitability and stock market fortunes, and how it positioned itself through its advertisements and executive commentaries.

A few limitations of the search must be noted. First, very few articles on the staffing industry were available between 1945 and 1956, and even then they were scarce until 1962 (see figure 1). There are several plausible reasons for the lack of early articles on what was at that time a new industry. Most simply, there were not as many relevant magazines in these earlier decades (see figure 2). Slim volumes cataloguing two years at a time in the 1940s and 1950s gave way to fat volumes dedicated to single years in the 1970s, and even fatter volumes for half-years in the 1990s. Given fewer magazines, one would expect to see fewer articles in the early years.

Figure 2, however, shows that as more magazines were being published, the density of relevant articles relative to magazine numbers became much thicker in the 1970s and 1980s. In other words, the

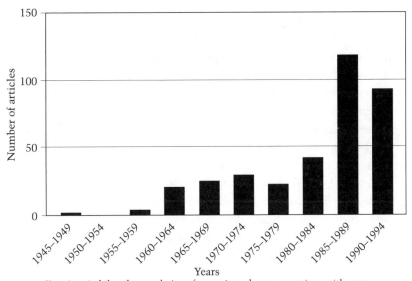

Keep in mind that the population of magazines changes over time, with more magazines being published in recent years than in the past. Also, search terms have changed over time, as the industry itself has changed.

Figure 1. Number of articles on the staffing industry, 1945–1994.

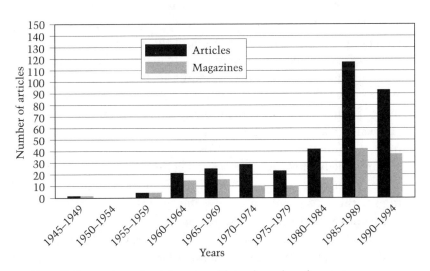

Figure 2. Comparison of article sums with total number of magazines.

increase in number of articles published on this topic wasn't *simply* a function of the increase in the number of magazines being published. As indicated in note 1, chapter 2, we constructed a simple density ratio for average number of articles per magazine issue over time. In the 1960s, on average, 1.5 articles per issue addressed these themes; in the 1970s and 1980s, 2.5 articles per issue. The number of periodicals increased significantly over these decades as well: in the 1960s we were drawing from a population of about 15 different personnel and business magazines, but by the second half of the 1980s we were drawing from some 44 publications.

Another possible limitation is the depth of the search for applicable subject headings. Though we made our pursuit of them as logical as possible (e.g., using later indices and their "see also" notations as guides for finding applicable headings in earlier indices), there are no guides to finding the perfect subject heading. Still, we believe that our search was fairly comprehensive.

Why did we limit our analysis to rhetoric of the 1960s through the 1980s? As noted, there were very few articles from earlier decades, whereas between 1960 and 1969 the number expanded significantly, giving us confidence that we could generalize from them about industry and personnel rhetoric. Starting with 1960 seemed theoretically defensible: we expected to find rhetoric in the '60s about the traditional or "temporary temp," the woman who filled in for a permanent worker who was out of the job for a short time (the "stopgap" paradigm of temporary employment). We had expected to observe a notable shift to the "staffing paradigm" by the late 1970s, slightly preceding the major statistical change in rates of employment of temporary workers in the early 1980s. (The number of articles our search yielded for the 1970s did not increase by much, moving from 46 in the '60s to 52 in the '70s.)

Surprisingly, however, rhetoric reflecting the newer staffing paradigm emerged in the early 1960s: the number of articles working from within this paradigm grew visibly, and the articulation of why companies would want to use temps mirrored contemporary (i.e., 1990s and early twenty-first century) discourse. Clearly, the problem of the costs of labor and of building a labor market for temporary work had preoccupied business practitioners early on.

We coded the articles in the following way. In addition to tracking their frequency, we looked to see how writers addressed the following questions. What was the rationale for new ways of using temporary workers? How did they distinguish the new approach from the traditional approach? What measures were suggested for using temps? And what did authors have to say about the traditional employment model and permanent workers?

We ended the analysis at 1990 because, even though temporary employment continued to grow in the 1990s (paralleling the growth of sociological studies of temporary work, with Parker 1994 being one of the earliest full-blown analyses), the practice of employing people on a temporary basis was widespread by 1990. Assuming that the rhetoric in personnel management literature had to some degree preceded the surge in the 1980s, we expected to observe sufficient evidence of the new paradigm well before the '90s. We assumed that our data would feel "saturated": that by the 1990s the transition to the new paradigm would be marked and told. We were right about this. The articles in the 1980s generated a gold mine of data about business views of temporary employment. Their number tripled that of the 1970s, from 52 to 160. By the end of the 1980s we were not uncovering any new themes.

It is entirely possible that if one conducted content analysis of articles through the early years of the twenty-first century, new themes and concerns would be discovered, but our interest was in historical change during the period when the industry was trying to sell a qualitatively new product—good temporary workers—and a new employment system.

APPENDIX II

Frequently Asked Questions about the Economic and Legal Dimensions of Temporary Employment

Q: The temporary help industry pressed hard for legislation that would make THS agencies the employer of record of temps. But from the perspective of hiring companies, why do employers (hiring companies) want to avoid the impression that temporary workers are their employees?

A: Hiring companies classify temporary workers as nonemployees. If temporary workers were classified as employees, companies may have to give them access to the same benefit, pension, and retirement plans and the same amenities that they make available to their regular employees. Existing labor law protects companies from having to extend these fringe benefits to nonemployees. Under current labor law, companies have to abide by legal statutes (Title VII of the Civil Rights Act, Fair Labor Standards Act, Family and Medical Leave Act, Americans with Disabilities Act) when managing their employees but are not always mandated to abide by them for nonemployees such as temps and contract workers. Finally, under the current interpretation of the National Labor Relations Act, companies can avoid union organizing efforts when they use temporary workers. As "nonemployees," temps do not have the right to bargain collectively with their hiring companies. Further, they lack the right to participate in existing units covered by union agreements without the dual consent of both the temp agency and the hiring company, which in practice is never granted (Befort 2003; Carlson 2001; Freeman and Gonos 2005; Gonos 1997; Kennedy 2005). Befort (2003, 165) claims that as nonemployees, temporary workers often "fall outside the regulatory safety net constructed for the employment relationship"; rather, they fall into a "regulatory black hole," in his terms, because firms have consciously structured their work systems in a manner that classifies the minimum number of workers as employees.

Q: Are there any conditions under which a hiring firm might want to be viewed as the temp's employer?

A: Yes. Most states have laws specifying that if a temporary worker is injured on the job, he or she can receive workers' compensation for injury or time lost but cannot sue her or his employer. As Stone notes, both the temporary-placement agency and the hiring firm have "an interest in being deemed the employer for purposes of workers' compensation because they then get the advantage of the exclusive remedy provision in the law and avoid the prospect of a much more costly judgment in tort" (2006, 267).

Q: What criteria do the courts use to determine whether the THS agency or the hiring company is the temp's employer?

A: Typically, they rely on the Internal Revenue Service's "20 Factor Test," which emphasizes a list of factors that are considered relevant, among them, who has the right to fire, hire, and set daily working conditions; how the worker is paid (by the hour, week, month, year, or a set amount for completing a specific job); whether the worker receives benefits and, if so, who pays for them; who owns the equipment used and the premises in which the work takes place; who controls the temp's work; and what degree of the employee's initiative, judgment, or foresight is involved in carrying out an assignment.

Q: What policies do hiring companies use to make it clear that temporary and contract workers are nonemployees, to avoid any impression of being the employer of either group?

A: Hiring companies do this in a variety of ways. They may put a cap or limit on the number of months that a temporary employee can stay in one job, reflecting a ruling by a U.S. District Court judge in 1998 against Microsoft. In the 1990s, Microsoft had a large population of high-tech contract workers who had been there so long they had earned the informal name of "permatemps." Contract workers at Microsoft (classified as nonemployees) sued on the grounds that they worked side by side with permanent high-tech workers (classified as employees) for long periods of time and performed the same type of work, yet they were not given access to Microsoft's benefits or the company's lucrative stock option plan because they lacked employee status. The Ninth Circuit Court of Appeals ruled that these permatemps were "common law" employees of Microsoft and therefore eligible for the same benefits and rights as permanently employed workers (DuRivage 2001, 386). (Courts can rule that nonemployees are de facto employees if they have a "community of interests" with permanent workers: that is, are in physical promixity to them, are controlled in a similar way, and share mutual interests in work conditions and salary, see Vockrodt 2005.)

Microsoft's response to this ruling was to institute a "break-in-service" policy, requiring that "long-term agency employees who have held one or more continuous assignments at Microsoft for 12 months or more must leave the company for at least 31 consecutive calendar days upon finishing an assignment or ending a contract" (DuRivage 2001, 386). The goal for Microsoft and other companies is to eliminate any ambiguity about temporary workers' employment status, to make clear that they are independent contractors or are employees of an agency, not Microsoft. The ruling that required Microsoft to pay out about $97 million in stock options to these contractors was a sobering lesson to the thousands of companies that hire temporary workers (Kennedy 2005). Many companies now put a limit on the amount of time an individual can work in one position as a temporary worker. CompTech, for example, where Smith conducted fieldwork in the late 1990s, capped the length of time their temps could stay in one temp job at eighteen months, in response to the Microsoft ruling. Often it is the case, however, that an individual can return to work for the same company *as a temp* once a designated period of time has passed.

Companies might impose rules that segregate temporary workers from permanent workers in order to delineate clearly that these are two different workforces: for example, restricting temporaries from attending social events and celebrations that are held for permanent employees; denying them participation in the company's stock option, bonus, or profit-sharing programs; making temporaries wear badges that clearly state they are temps or wear differently colored uniforms or clothing. Sometimes temps work in production settings where they are isolated from permanent workers. Companies impose these rules and practices in order to minimize the appearance that temporary workers are just like regular workers and to avoid their misclassification as employees. The goal is to reduce the likelihood that there will be grounds for temporary workers to sue the hiring company for violating their employee rights.

Q: Using temporary workers seems to be a complex, and possibly financially costly morass. Under these circumstances, what are the specific economic incentives for companies to use temporary workers?

A: (1) The company can let people go when they don't need them and thus keep staffing costs down without fear of suit for wrongful discharge. (2) When a firm places lower-level employees on the payroll of a staffing agency, it may avoid giving them access to the company retirement programs mandated by the 1975 Employee Retirement Income Security Act, which requires that retirement programs for management be made available proportionally to lower-level employees as well. (3) The hiring company does not pay federal insurance contributions, federal unemployment taxes, or social security taxes on temporary workers. (4) The firm does not have to pay temporary employees for sick leave, vacation or holiday pay, health benefits, or life insurance that it may offer to regular employees. Even given these quantifiable savings, however, it is not entirely clear from studying the topic, reading the literature on temporary employment, or reading human resources publications that companies have fine-tuned a cost/benefit analysis with respect to their temporary employment arrangements.

Q: Is it just cost saving that leads companies to use temporary workers, or do corporations have other reasons for holding down the size (head count) of their regular workforces? How does using temporary workers enable them to do this? Are temps counted as part of the company payroll?

A: Companies often feel pressured to hold down the size of their workforces and their payrolls in order to improve investors' and stockholders' assessment of how lean and mean they are. If a company appears to have a bloated workforce, investors can pressure its top managers to lay off large numbers of permanent workers, sell off operating units, and reengineer the business (Useem 1996, chap. 5). Additionally, since human resources managers are often evaluated according to how successfully they keep the head count down in the units for which they are responsible, they attempt to minimize the permanent workforce. Even when companies lay people off and maintain smaller permanent workforces, however, the total size of the workforce may be greater than it looks because of contemporary accounting procedures that pertain to temporary and contract labor. Such procedures can rather artfully understate workforce size.

One way the cost and size of temporary labor forces can be hidden is by not counting them as part of the company's workforce; thus, their presence is obscured and the overall head count is understated. Companies have been known to pay agencies for the labor of their temporary workers from their "materials and supplies," "services," and "overhead" budgets rather than from "personnel and payroll." A second way firms hide the cost of contingent labor is by paying contract workers through invoices that the workers submit to companies rather than through the payroll system (Kennedy 2005, 151). Third, if a manager submits an aggregate operating budget for a unit or a project but does not itemize how the money will be allocated, temporary workers can be obscured because they are not a separate line item in the budget. In these ways, head count and payroll are converted into "overhead" and other nonlabor categories.

Hiding and obscuring—not counting—temporary workers can have meaningful implications for measuring economic output. Estevão and Lach (1999) found that once they adjusted labor counts in manufacturing to include temporary workers, productivity rates were lower than those officially reported (in the late 1990s). Calculation of productivity in manufacturing typically does not factor in the presence of temporary labor—in part because of the Bureau of Labor Statistics' own measurement procedures: employees are counted in the industry by which they are employed, not the industry where they work; thus, temps working outside business services are still counted as part of the business services workforce. But not accounting for temporary labor, according to Estevão and Lach, means that companies overstate increases in average labor productivity.

Q: From the hiring companies' point of view, what is the economic rationale for having long-term temps, or permatemps?

A: Companies save costs using long-term temps for several reasons. We explain the first in chapter 1: once the system of fee splitting was eliminated, companies couldn't profit from repeatedly replacing temps and assigning them only for short periods of time. In an earlier era, each time a new temp was hired, the company would receive a portion of the fee paid by the temp. The markup system removes that economic incentive from hiring companies; there is no need to let go of one temp and hire another, simply to earn the fee. In fact, it probably benefits the company more to have a temp for the long term because that individual's growing experience and insights about the job are developed over time, thus increasing his or her value as a good temp. Another reason relates to conversion policies. Select Labor, for example, once had a policy that if a client firm employed one of its temps for three consecutive months, SL would not charge the client firm to convert the temp to permanent status. SL changed this practice in a way that made it more costly for a client firm to convert a temp at earlier points in the temp's tenure. The new policy required that if a client firm wanted to convert the temp to permanent status before the end of a three-month period, the client would be charged about 30 percent of the worker's annual salary. If the client firm held off and kept the worker on temporary status for up to five months, however, SL charged only a 20 percent conversion fee.

Q: Are temporary workers eligible for unemployment compensation?

A: Technically, yes, but rarely can a temporary worker meet the criteria for unemployment compensation because of the generally brief and transient nature of temp work. Although the exact terms vary by state, eligibility for unemployment is calculated according to a formula that asks whether the individual has earned above a state-determined level of compensation within a specific duration of employment. Temps typically lack the hours or wages necessary to qualify (Stone 2006, 264). Further, according to the regulations in many states, a temp who does not return to his or her agency for another assignment may be classified as a "voluntary quit" and denied coverage.

Q: What can we expect in the future, with respect to legal regulation of temporary employment?

A: The area of law related to temporary employment is highly contested and rapidly changing. None of the above rulings or interpretations are fixed. Thus, much will depend on the efforts of labor activists, the power of the THS industry and large corporations, and the leanings of state and federal courts.

NOTES

Chapter 1. The Temporary Advantage

1. The Bureau of Labor Statistics (BLS) measures the size of the contingent workforce as being from 2 to 4 percent of the entire workforce. The BLS differentiates between contingent workers ("persons who do not expect their jobs to last or who reported that their jobs are temporary") and workers in alternative arrangements (independent contractors, on-call workers, temporary agency workers, and workers provided by contract companies—with independent contractors being the largest and workers from contract companies the smallest), stating that the two groups overlap to some degree but that a contingent job is not necessarily an alternative arrangement (Bureau of Labor Statistics 2005a, 1). This distinction makes it somewhat confusing to provide a definitive estimate for the size of the temporary workforce. Nevertheless, the BLS figures give a working sense of its parameters.

2. We don't address nor do we have data about small, precarious, "fly-by-night" temporary placement agencies that come and go, may violate labor law, or fail to pay wages for work performed (Stone 2006, 259).

3. In 2005, temporary help service agencies (our subject) employed approximately 71 percent of the workers in the employment services industry sector, which also comprises professional employer organizations (accounting for 21 percent of employment services) and employment

agencies (8 percent) (Bureau of Labor Statistics 2005b; Dey, Houseman, and Polivka 2007, 4). The number of temporary help service offices surged from about 600 in the early 1960s to 5,000 by 1981 and nearly 40,000 today. THS industry revenue has likewise exploded over the years, its annual earnings expanding from about $250 million in the early 1960s to $72.3 billion in 2006. Growth in industry earnings was paralleled by growth in the size of the temporary workforce, which was a little over 12 million in 2006 (American Staffing Association 2006a; Fiamingo 1984; Mangum, Mayall, and Nelson 1985; Moore 1965).

4. Virtually all studies have found that, on average, temporary agency workers earn lower wages than do permanent workers, even when they perform the same work. Temporary jobs offer few (if any) benefits and very limited (if any) opportunities for upward mobility.

5. The Bureau of Labor Statistics did not track the size, ratio, or composition of the temporary workforce in the mid–twentieth century, so precise numbers and demographic information for that period are educated guesses. The BLS Current Employment Statistics program has total employment data for temporary help services from 1990 onward. Data on contingent and alternative employment arrangements have been collected periodically in supplements to the Current Population Survey since February 1995 (Bureau of Labor Statistics 2005a; Watson 2007).

6. See Acker 1990; Hochschild 1971; and Kanter 1977.

7. Marriage bars—prohibitions originating from the early 1900s against the employment of married women—kept significant numbers of women out of the labor force and career tracks. Employers both refused to hire married women and sometimes fired single women employees who later married. This marriage bar most likely contributed to making temporary work in the post–World War II era a female-dominated sector and preserved the world of permanent jobs and careers as the domain of male workers. Goldin (1990) argues that employers might retain women whom they valued who had started as single but then married; however, they usually retained them as temporary workers only. Between the relegation of some married women to temp status as a result of the marriage bar, and the exclusion of other married women from permanent jobs, temporary employment became a reliable job enclave for this population. By 1940 the most extensive controls excluding married women from permanent jobs were found in firms that were likely to have well-developed internal labor markets and career ladders where good jobs would have been found: insurance offices, banks, public utilities, and the offices in manufacturing firms and in larger firms in general (Goldin 1990, chap. 6, table 6.2).

8. Women and men are close to equals in temporary agency employment, but this is a case of dubious equality given that jobs in this category are neither well-paid nor secure. Breaking down contingent work into detailed categories reveals a pattern of underlying gender segregation and inequality. Men constitute a much higher percentage of self-employed, independent contractors (66.5 percent) than women do (33.5 percent)— important because contractors tend to earn higher wages (Mishel, Bernstein, and Allegretto 2007, 242, table 4.9). Interestingly, the timing of increases in women's and men's participation in temporary work occurred in different waves: although the overall temporary employment rate roughly quadrupled during the 1980s, the fastest growth for women occurred in the early 1980s, the fastest for men in the later 1980s. Levenson suggests that this is evidence that the "growth in temporary employment among the 'pink-collar' occupations dominated by women preceded the more recent growth in temporary employment in the 'blue-collar' occupations dominated by men" (2000, 359).

9. See Doeringer et al. 1991; Heckscher 1995; Osterman 1999; Sennett 1998; Smith 1997, 2001a; Uchitelle 2006; and many others.

10. Many researchers argue that job stability and security have declined, although there is disagreement about the *degree* of decline. Houseman and Polivka argue that "although the decline in aggregate job stability is itself modest, our results indicate that *the growth in agency temporaries and other flexible staffing arrangements can account for a substantial part of the decline*" (2000, 453; emphasis added). Jacoby (1999) asserts that the hype about declining stability and security is much greater than is warranted by the objective facts. Neumark (2000), editor of a highly influential volume about whether job security and stability were then declining, concluded that the bonds between workers and firms had been "weakened," not broken, and he was skeptical about trends in employment relations in the 1990s being indicative of future employment relations. When Uchitelle interviewed Neumark in 2005, however, he noted that the latter's thinking had shifted considerably (an "about-face," in Uchitelle's words), with Neumark saying that the "people who used to be in the most secure jobs are experiencing less stability" (Uchitelle 2006, 213).

11. Barley and Kunda 2004; Chun 2001; Gottfried 1991; Henson 1996; Lautsch 2003; Rogers 2000; Smith 1998, 2001a, 2001b.

12. Barsness and Uzzi 1998; Benner 2002; Davis-Blake and Uzzi 1993; Harrison and Kelley 1993; Houseman 2001; Kalleberg, Reynolds, and Marsden 2003; Pfeffer and Baron 1988.

13. Gonos 1997, 1998, 2000–2001; Ofstead 1999; Osterman 1999, chap. 6; Peck and Theodore 1998.

14. According to staffing industry figures, office, clerical, and industrial workers constitute 55.5 percent of temporary and contract workers; technical, 6.4 percent; health care, 7.8 percent; professional/managerial, 21 percent; and information technology, 9.3 percent (American Staffing Association 2006a, fig.7). These figures don't show the breakdown between temporary and contract workers per se, but it is highly likely that these sectoral categories coincide with employment categories, such that the first three clusters of workers would be temporary and the last two would be contract workers. Some researchers include part-time workers in their definition of contingent work (Belous 1989; but see also Polivka 1996). We do not include part-timers: the percentage and growth rates of part-time jobs and part-time workers has been on a fairly consistent trajectory since World War II, whereas the size and use of the temporary and contract workforce has experienced a fundamental quantitative change.

15. Labor economists have tried to isolate the factors that make a bad or marginal temp. Posthuma, Campion, and Vargas, for example (2005, 553), found that marginal temps (whose rate of productivity was lower and who were less dependable) were more likely to have been laid off from their previous job, would take any kind of temporary work, had worked for a long time as a temp, and had earned lower-than-average temp wages; in other words, they had a "meaningful pattern of poorer work history." We are wary of efforts to isolate causal factors that might explain good and bad temps without looking at temporary workers in institutional context and historical perspective.

16. When we talk about the companies that hire temporary workers from agencies, we refer to them as "hiring companies" or "client firms"; we refer to temporary help placement agencies as "agencies," "staffing agencies," or THS agencies; and we make every effort to distinguish between the industry and individual agencies. Technically, the term "staffing agency" refers to one that not only places temporary workers but also helps client firms find permanent workers, assists them with their "temp-to-perm" programs, and offers other placement and administrative services. We use "staffing agency" more loosely here, but when we do, we are always talking about an agency whose primary component is placing temporary workers.

17. To be sure, some negative images are based in fact. *Processed World* (PW)—an edgy, critical publication that was started in San Francisco in 1981 and is still published intermittently—valorized the alienated, vengeful temp who became so after suffering through temporary jobs in the city's financial district. The following excerpt is representative

of the narratives, written by downwardly mobile, middle-class young adults, found in *PW:* "I decided to enter the temp world. The next several months were a kaleidoscope of numbing, unbearable days and sabotage at every opportunity....I was always let go without a specific reason. It was frustrating that the hiring and firing hierarchy could have the power to dispose of me and not tell me the truth about why they were doing it; and I would always be left wondering, 'Did they really mean it when they said they had too many people or was it because they saw the sticker I put up in the bathroom and suspected me?' I could never tell. Most supervisors are chickenshit when it comes to letting people go; they do whatever they can to avoid controversy and open resentment....I always preferred the situations when I was at least given a reason for being fired. *Especially if the supervisor or boss was noticeably upset about something that I did; I would feel a sense of accomplishment. I'm the only person I know to actually be fired from a temp agency. I got away with a lot, however, before it caught up with me"* (Noe 1986; emphasis added). These alienated temps advocated pouring soda on their keyboards, duplicating non-work-related papers while on the job, and stealing company time whenever possible.

18. These studies are part of a larger genre of literature that looks at the way labor market intermediaries shape and construct labor markets; see Benner, Leete, and Pastor 2007; Finlay and Coverdill 2002; Indegaard 1999; and Smith, Flynn, and Isler 2006.

19. Many scholars have documented and analyzed the impact of de-industrialization and other changes on our industrial structure. The reader who is interested in exploring the long and sobering downsizing of America, especially its effects on organized labor, might take a look at Bluestone and Harrison 1982; Bowles, Gordon, and Weisskopf 1983; Gordon 1996; Osterman 1988; and Osterman 1999.

20. When Mack Moore did his dissertation research on THS firms in the early 1960s, he discovered that the leading companies offered "temporary warranties." "All contacted," Moore wrote, "guarantee that workers will be satisfactory, but no details were provided by any firms except Manpower and Kelly Girl. Both of them provide new customers with a formal, written warranty, similar in appearance to that provided buyers of durable goods" (1965, 566).

21. Essentially, the THS industry was lobbying for the deregulation of employment services. It needed to establish that temporary help placement firms were different from employment agencies. The latter placed workers but were not their employers and were subject to a different system of legal controls. THS firms, lobbyists argued, actually employed

workers—or so the industry hoped to persuade legislators. Gonos points out that the claim that THS firms are employers and that hiring companies are not is dubious—or, as Stone (2006) calls it, a "legal fiction"—when one scrutinizes the temporary job to determine who controls the work, who provides tools and supplies, and who benefits from the work output (Gonos 1997, 88); nevertheless, the industry succeeded in having temporary workers classified in this way. See also Vosko (2000), who found similar trends in Canadian and international labor law.

22. Autor notes that there are a number of indicators of the existence of an employment contract, even if it is not formalized. Evidence of contracts has been found by the courts in definitions of disciplinary procedures (e.g., when a company guarantees that a worker won't be terminated without advance warning and documentation), when the existence of 401K and retirement programs signal expectations of long-term employment, and when regular workers are placed on probationary status at the inception of their jobs (2003, 7). Thus, courts have ruled that evidence of a "contract" between employer and employee is embedded in any number of organizational artifacts, practices, and policies. See also Katherine Stone's *From Widgets to Digits* (2004, chap. 4).

23. See Appendix II for commonly asked questions and answers about legal, financial, and accounting issues related to temporary employment.

24. According to the Bureau of Labor Statistics, 56.2 percent of temporary agency workers would have preferred "traditional," permanent employment, an increase from 31 percent in 1995 (Bureau of Labor Statistics 2005a; see also 2001, table 10). Others have reported higher rates: according to Carré and Tilly (1998), in the late 1990s, 73 percent of temporary workers reported that they would prefer permanent employment. Analyzing Current Population Survey data, Osterman (1999) notes the gap between independent contractors and temporary workers on this issue. Contractors typically are content with their status, whereas "a substantial fraction" of other contingent employees prefer standard jobs (1999, 85–86, table 3.9). Men's rate of involuntary temporary work tends to be higher than women's (Levenson 2000, 364, table 10.2), although Bernasek and Kinnear (1999, 468) found no meaningful difference between men and women contingent workers in their preference for permanent employment.

25. According to the Bureau of Labor Statistics (2005b), approximately 37,000 of the 64,000 firms in employment services are temporary help placement firms.

26. The increased emphasis on providing quality temps parallels the larger preoccupation with "quality service" that has swept through American

business over several decades. As companies in the same sector have had to compete to survive, they increasingly have struggled to distinguish themselves by the high quality of the services they provide to the public (Korczynski et al. 1999; Leidner 1993; MacDonald and Sirianni 1996).

27. In her study of temporary workers in an assembly plant in Silicon Valley, Chun relates how she discovered who is served by "flexibility." Upon entering the office of an agency that placed temps at FlexTech, which prominently advertised "immediate temporary positions" in its window, Chun explained to the staff person that she was a student seeking a position for the summer and thus wanted a temporary job for its flexibility. The staff person informed her that FlexTech did not offer summer jobs and hired only full-time workers, adding, "Yes, FlexTech hires temporary workers, but that means that *they* decide how long they need workers to work, *not* the other way around. If FlexTech only hired people who wanted summer jobs, then what would happen when they all left at the end of the summer? The company would be stuck with all these empty positions and that would be bad for the company" (2001, 142–43).

28. Cf. Chun 2001, 146–49; Erickcek, Houseman, and Kalleberg 2003, 382–83; Smith 2001a, chap. 4; Smith 2001b.

29. "Soft skills" refers to know-how about interpersonal relations: how to interact, be deferential, and be sympathetic to the needs of others (Capelli 1995; Moss and Tilly 2001).

30. Studies of day labor agencies that specialize in the placement of highly vulnerable and exploited workers have noted that dispatchers who allocate jobs use similar conceptions of good day laborers. Bartley and Roberts (2006), for example, found that dispatchers look for signs of loyalty and reliability on the part of job applicants while the dispatchers that Purser (2007) observed looked for evidence of patience, positive attitude, and self discipline. Their research, along with Peck's and Theodore's (2002), unpacks how day labor agencies' placement strategy of "best match for the dispatch" is encoded with assumptions about job applicants' behavior and capacity for work.

31. We registered this pseudonym, selectlabor.com, as a domain name with Google, after experimenting with probably twenty to thirty different possibilities; it was surprisingly difficult to come up with a memorable pseudonym that a for-profit company had not already taken! Only when writing the final chapter of this book did we discover that there is a temporary help service agency called GoodTemps (http://www.goodtemps.org).

32. Neuwirth worked at Select Labor as an unknown researcher after evaluating potential data sites and fully grappling with the ethical

issues. It was a difficult decision because most researchers who conduct fieldwork do so as known investigators (however, there are important exceptions for those who study workplaces: see Chun 2001; Graham 1995, 13–17; Gottfried and Graham 1993, 611–12; Sallaz 2002, 399; and Williams 2006). Williams did not reveal to her coworkers that she was conducting research or that she planned to write a book based on her work experiences at two toy stores, but she did not hide the fact that she had a Ph.D. or that she was a "teacher." Mindful of the need for confidentiality, an evaluation of risk, and the imperative to do no harm to study subjects, Neuwirth chose this approach to fieldwork in order to achieve intimate familiarity with the staffing industry, a view that would be blocked to someone not actually working in the trenches. In choosing to collect data as an unknown researcher, Neuwirth was following Lofland et al.'s appraisal that "the ethically sensitive, thoughtful, and knowledgeable investigator is the best judge of whether covert research is justified" (2006, 39). In this book we use additional pseudonyms to maintain the confidentiality of individuals, of the agency, and of the companies Neuwirth encountered when researching Select Labor.

33. Here, her identity was known to the study participants, and she conducted her fieldwork with the permission of organizational leaders.

34. The American Staffing Association reports that in 2001, temporary and contract placements accounted for 81.8 percent of total staffing industry sales; in 2005 it was 84.9 percent (2006a, fig. 6)—nearly exactly the figure for Select Labor's temp staffing sales at the time of the research.

35. By thinking about the possibility that some temporary jobs are "good enough," we can acknowledge that although ideally, people would have jobs of the sort and on the terms they want, in fact, some jobs, like those at the heart of this book, are adequate, particularly in light of such alternatives as unemployment, or employment in horrific work sites.

Chapter 2. The Social Construction of New Markets and Products

1. In constructing a simple density ratio for average number of articles per magazine issue over time, we found that in the 1980s there were both more personnel and business magazines and *proportionately* more articles being published on temporary employment than in the 1960s and 1970s. See Appendix I and Figure 2.

2. See Gonos (1998) for extensive analysis of the formation of NATS and its role in establishing temporary employment agencies as employers of temporary workers.

3. Quotations are taken verbatim from magazine articles. If the author used the word temp (rather than temporary) it appears here as temp, but we do not substitute temp for temporary. If parentheses around words or phrases appeared in the original article, we include them here. We inserted brackets around words and phrases we inserted in order to clarify (but not change) the passage. We indicate whether emphasis of words or phrases is original or added by us.

4. We assume that if we were to study academic human resources periodicals of this period, we would see the same preoccupation with the true cost of labor and how to reduce it. It seems very likely that the magazine articles we analyzed reflected ideas and debates from the scholarly business world and probably contributed to them as well. Academics and managerial practitioners constitute two worlds that "exist as separate but interdependent social systems characterized by different traditions, languages, interests and norms.... [T]he direction and degree of influence [of each world upon the other] might vary from issue to issue" (Barley, Meyer, and Gash 1988, 25).

5. The search for every dime spent on labor continues today in the temporary help service industry. Gonos (2001, 601) discusses the chart provided by COMFORCE, a staffing firm, which shows the breakdown of expenses for "regular" labor in the late 1990s.

6. As Peck (1996, 177) points out in his discussion of the social construction of labor markets, "the nature of jobs is shaped by expectations about which social groups will fill them."

7. *Forbes's* 1982 article titled "Kelly Boys" begins, "Everyone knows about Kelly girls, those able-bodied office helpers who jump to the rescue when your secretary comes down with the flu. But what do executives do when they need a specific engineering problem solved, yet find themselves shorthanded? Why, hire a temporary engineer, of course" (October 25, 1982, 114). The article never *names* gender or race but assumes the masculinity and the whiteness of the job holder. Its title is gendered; it features a picture of a mature white man; and the occupation was heavily male dominated at that time. Yet other than in reference to the director of the agency at the center of the story, the article does not use the pronoun he or talk about men (or boys, the analogous term to Kelly Girls), but its different elements report a strongly gendered temporary experience.

8. Interestingly, as far back as the early 1970s THS industry leaders bragged that people of color could benefit by using agency services to

overcome the barrier of racial discrimination in the labor market. Leaders who commented for an article on the advantages of temporary employment claimed that agencies had always been in the forefront of placing "minority groups," that their placement practices were color-blind, insofar as agency representatives did not note race, ethnicity, or whether someone came from an "underprivileged" background on application files. People of color, leaders argued, were eligible for any job for which they possessed appropriate skills. Through temporary employment, they also claimed, minorities could accumulate the skills and experiences necessary to landing a permanent job. Barbara Jones of Western Girl Agency viewed the THS industry as a trendsetter, in that "we have employed minority group members from our agencies beginning twenty-five years ago. We feel we have played an important role in breaking down barriers because companies which accepted the first minority group member as a temporary were much more likely to accept the first minority permanent employee" (*Office,* December 1972, 42–43).

9. One writer, Nathan Picker of Echelons, conveyed the demeaning general impression of women who worked as temps: "One woman in the suburbs had to be reminded that she had a paycheck waiting at our office so she sent her chauffeur for it in the family Cadillac" (*Office,* March 1963, 110). We see this formulation, with its questionable veracity, as being similar to the demeaning term "welfare queen," a negative stereotype that resonates with public ideology and is used as a weapon against disadvantaged groups (Neubeck and Cazenave 2001).

10. Winter wrote seven of the articles we analyzed, was interviewed numerous times for articles on temporary employment, and has been featured in various articles about Manpower, the company.

Chapter 3. "We're Not Body Pushers"

1. Typically, the placement process at Select Labor went as follows (a process that most studies suggest is typical throughout the industry). Job applicants would be screened by staff at SL. If the individual seemed to be appropriate for a job at any given hiring firm, the agency would send that person over to the hiring manager or human resources manager for an interview. Thus, even with the intervention of the agency, managers in the client firm were engaged in the screening process to a certain extent. The claim that agencies fully relieve corporations of the need to screen job applicants is overstated. More accurately, the agency staff prequalify temps for hiring managers. Job applicants who try to start first at the hiring firm are redirected to the agency.

2. Bronson had this to say about the seductiveness of the Valley: "By car, by plane, they come. They just show up. They've given up their lives elsewhere to come *here*. They come for the tremendous opportunity, believing that in no other place in the world right now can one person accomplish so much with talent, initiative, and a good idea. It's a region where who you know and how much money you have have never been less relevant to success. They come because it does not matter that they are young or left college without a degree or have dark skin or speak with an accent. They come even if it is illegal to do so. They come because they feel that they will regret it the rest of their lives if they do not at least give it a try" (1999, 3–4; original emphasis).

3. Job fairs that Neuwirth attended were strikingly similar to a major job fair in Sacramento that Smith, Flynn, and Isler (2006) attended when they studied job search organizations. At all of them, companies with informational tables included those representing blue- and white-collar fields, professional fields, medical and health fields, training schools, and others. Job fairs are curious mixes of optimism and anxiety. On the one hand, they attract throngs of job seekers, most of whom radiate hope and curiosity. After all, you might happen upon *the* opportunity or establish *the* career-making contact with someone. On the other hand, you're surrounded by hundreds of other people with precisely the same hope and ambition. The sense of competition is palpable.

4. The dollar value of the bonus system revealed the way Select Labor valued jobs themselves. At the top of the scale were executive and legal secretaries; a successful referral in these categories would garner a bonus of several hundred dollars for the recommender. At the bottom were general clerical workers and electronic assemblers, worth a bonus of $25 to the recommender.

5. Minimal skills tests were administered in the office: SL had one room in the facility dedicated to testing the computer skills (word processing, graphics, and database management) of some candidates and the soldering skills (for example) of others.

6. Quotes come from Select Labor training literature on how to interview and select workers.

7. Peck and Theodore (1998, 659) found that temporary agencies had a "no return policy" in which clients would inform agency representatives about temps whom the client firm refused to take back. Peck and Theodore also note that in the bottom end of the temp industry in Chicago, agencies used feedback from the clients to skim off their high-quality workers from the undesirable "warm bodies."

8. Powell (2001, 35) notes that in 1999 the mantra swirling around the Silicon Valley region was that "sixty-four millionaires were created daily."

9. One staff member lamented that people who worked in temp agencies were viewed as "slimy and aggressive" by some job seekers.

10. This problem of perceptions of temporary work is pervasive throughout the world of temporary employment. When Smith interviewed a forty-year-old white male temporary assembler at CompTech in the late 1990s, he spoke grimly of the "reality check" he had been served up by working as a temp: "I had the idea that if you work out, you turn into a permanent right away. If you don't, they send you on your way and you go to another place. That's my idea of temporary service; I had no idea that you could be a temporary the rest of your life" (Smith 2001a, 111).

11. As Chun found at FlexTech, temps will work hard and well because they're trying to "score points" to avoid being laid off and to maximize their chances of being offered a permanent job (2001, 139). Others have noted a variety of reasons why temporary workers consent to the conditions of their jobs. Henson found that temps "play the part" (including "looking busy") simply to keep their temp jobs: "Out of necessity, temps soon realize that they must not only possess the skills to produce the required work but also look and play the part if they wish to continue working" (1996, 142). Chun notes that "workers' dependence on employers for their livelihoods provides the material links through which firms are able to elicit workers' compliance to the vagaries and specific needs of subcontracting manufacturing" (2001, 132)—an observation seconded by Peck and Theodore (1998) and others.

12. "We're not Manpower," the trainer added—a disparaging reference. We have no evidence to suggest that Manpower, the largest placement firm for temporary workers in Silicon Valley (not to mention in the world), has any more or less integrity or any less concern for marketing good temporary workers than Select Labor. It is easy to believe that this trainer sees SL as David, positioned against the Goliath of Manpower, and that the former makes a virtue out of its comparatively small size. After all, one could argue, a hiring company might receive more customized treatment from a smaller firm like SL than it would from the behemoth, Manpower. On the other hand, the level of rationalization and efficiency that a large firm like Manpower is capable of achieving undoubtedly can bring its own advantages to workers.

Chapter 4. Softening "Rough and Tough Managers"

1. In 2000, temporary placement agencies and client firms were well aware of the legal risks involved in using temporary workers. The contentious

and relatively successful case of contract workers at Microsoft publicized the delicate dance needed to employ temporary workers without creating grounds for accusations of unfair labor practices (Van Jaarsveld 2004; see Appendix II). But there are many grounds on which temps might sue their agencies and the companies where they labor. Two of the temporary workers that Smith (2001a) interviewed in the late 1990s later sued their supervisor at CompTech as well as the agency that had employed them, claiming that they had been sexually harassed by the supervisor and that agency representatives had ignored their complaints about it.

2. What Burawoy might call "relations of production" in which temps are enmeshed are those "relations of the shop floor into which workers enter, both with one another and with management" (1979, 15).

3. Autor (2001) argues that THS firms invest in their temporary workers by offering general skills training; in part, he asserts, they do so to retain high-quality or high-ability temporary workers and reduce their turnover.

4. The subject of bad practices and employment conditions cropped up regularly in conversations in the Select Labor office. Staff often discussed client companies whose practices could be deleterious to temps. They talked periodically about the difficulties of living in Silicon Valley on an entry-level temp wage. Indeed, low wages brought the endemic problem of capitalism into stark relief: temps found it nearly impossible to live if wages dipped too low or if they couldn't work for a sufficient number of hours. Although the agency staff never used these terms, they were touching on the ability of labor—their product—to reproduce itself. One conversation, centered on the question of how temps could live on $7 an hour, captured the low-grade concern one agency staff member felt about the people who came to him for temporary jobs. Jack, a placement specialist who talked about the high cost of living in the Silicon Valley area, admitted that he couldn't figure out how people made it on temps' wages. Jack lived in a city located on the southeast side of the San Francisco Bay in an apartment complex. He expressed embarrassment over the fact that he and his roommate were the only ones in the complex (that he could think of) who had a two-bedroom apartment housing only two people: "Lots of other units have ten or more people living in them," according to his recollection.

5. It is not the case (although some make this argument) that agency staff are the sole managers of temps. The agency is the employer of record, and its staff are the ones who communicate to temps about jobs. In a typical temp's experience, however, the manager in the client firm to whom the temp is assigned strongly influences the job experiences of the worker. For this reason, it is easy to understand why hiring companies and staffing agencies can be charged as joint employers or

co-employers if a temp has a grievance. The term "joint employment" means that temporary workers have two employers: the staffing agency and the hiring company. Various legal rulings have found that agencies and hiring companies are joint employers. The determination of whether the two parties are co-employers or not (based on criteria such as who hires and fires, who supervises and controls, who determines the rate or method of compensation, and who maintains employment records) can have considerable consequences for legal rulings on the status of temps, particularly whether or not temps are eligible for the same work conditions, benefits, and pay as permanent employees (see chapter 6 and Appendix II). The THS industry has devoted much attention to the ambiguities surrounding joint employment (see Lenz 1997) and many resources to resolving these ambiguities (Gonos 1997, 1998).

6. In contrast, a "good" company such as Hewlett-Packard was considered a desirable work site. Although HP has been criticized for the way it uses temps, it nevertheless had one of the better reputations in Silicon Valley. For the critical view of HP, see the video "Secrets of Silicon Valley," online at http://www.secretsofsiliconvalley.org. For a broad-ranging critical perspective on temporary work in Silicon Valley, see the magazine *De-Bug: The Voice of the Young and Temporary*, at http://www.siliconvalleydebug.org, a publication written by employed and unemployed temporary workers (the more contemporary counterpart to *Processed World:* see chapter 1, note 17).

7. This issue is explored in Smith (2001b). Corporate policies on hiring contingent workers often wedge line managers between a rock and a hard place. When budgets for fixed labor decrease while funds for variable labor increase, managers can be forced to hire temps even though they would prefer permanent workers from the outset. Because time limits on months of employment for temporaries can be imposed by higher levels of management, shop floor managers and supervisors often have to let good temps go when they run up against the limit. Smith found that doing so was costly and frustrating to managers who had to deal with production objectives on a day-to-day basis. See Appendix II for details about these issues.

Chapter 5. Shaping and Stabilizing the Personnel Policy Environment

1. Although for different reasons, trade unions, of course, fought for wages and benefits that similarly constructed "good," committed industrial

workers. In addition, unions had a significant role in pressuring employers for fair and standardized employment practices (Befort 2003).

2. These trends and their implications have been studied extensively. See, for example, Blair and Kochan 2000; Capelli 1999; Jacoby 2005; Osterman 1999; Sennett 1998; and Smith 1997.

3. On the importance of internal labor markets for producing consent, loyalty, and commitment and for reducing worker turnover (quit rates), see Althauser 1989; Burawoy 1979, chap. 12; Doeringer and Piore 1971; Doeringer et al. 1991; Edwards 1979, chap. 8; Fairris 2004; Kalleberg et al. 1996; Kalleberg and Moody 1996; and Osterman 1984, 1996, 1999, among others. "The prevalent internal labor market model of 1950 was designed to encourage career rather than casual employment tenure" (Befort 2003, 156): internal labor markets and bureaucratic control (the foundation of ILMs) were premised on the expectation of long-term corporate stability and corporations' expectations that they could offer their employees job security (Edwards 1979). These intermixed assumptions and premises have virtually collapsed in the new economy, although the verdict is inconclusive about whether anxious and fearful assumptions actually match the reality of what has happened to ILMs. Jacoby (1999) argues that there is a worrisome discrepancy between the rhetoric and reality of change and that internal labor markets are still, in fact, the norm in corporations, as is the spirit of welfare capitalism. This may be true, but the fact that so many people perceive jobs and labor markets to be unstable is quite important (Uchitelle 2006; see also Schmidt 2000). Leonardt hypothesizes that our perceptions of instability and volatility may be higher today because inequality in the United States is unprecedentedly high: "Inequality is probably the real reason that the economy often feels more volatile. When people are stretched—when their pay has been stagnant, when they're worried about health insurance, when they don't know what the future holds—a jolt to their income is harder to handle"— referring to the fact that in 2003, 20 percent of American workers saw their earnings drop 25 percent or more compared with the previous year; 22 percent saw their earnings rise at least 25 percent (2007b, C 12).

4. The vulnerability of human resources management and the view that HR might be dispensable come from other quarters, as well. Capelli argues, for example, that contemporary employment law, which includes a wide array of both federal and state laws and regulations, has made employment administration too costly and burdensome for firms. These laws provide protection for employees, Capelli maintains, by constraining the actions of employers, yet they also impose significant costs on employers. Employers can avoid many of the requirements of

these laws and the administrative burden associated with them if their workers are leased from an agency such as a temporary help firm. Pressure to comply with current employment law has been a significant factor influencing the decision of companies to outsource HR activities (Capelli 1999, 108–9).

Bottom-line concerns about whether in-house human resources departments can efficiently find the right employees also figure into calculations about the disposability of in-house HR management. In this view, jobs have become so specialized that managers need expert help in recruiting and retaining the appropriate workforce. This rationale explains why companies are increasingly likely to use headhunters to find skilled, high-level managers and professionals (Finlay and Coverdill 2002). Headhunters, with their own rules, regulations, educational requirements, and accreditation processes, can develop the expertise to find people for specialized jobs, expertise that traditional HR managers, stretched thin over multiple occupational groups and production units, may lack (Drucker 2002). Under these conditions it can be hard for HR managers to defend themselves against the encroachment of external parties or to protect their turf.

5. Corporations have introduced a number of mechanisms to achieve flexibility in this manner, including employee participation programs, quality circles, worker self-management, just-in-time production programs, and others. The common thread is that they enable workers to respond to changing market conditions more quickly, to bring their judgment and expertise to bear on production processes in order to increase productivity and effectiveness, and to decrease bureaucratic levels so that decisions can be made more quickly and information will have less organizational mileage to travel. See Appelbaum and Batt 1994; Appelbaum et al. 2000; and Smith 1997, 2001a.

6. There is by now extensive automation of the human resource management-staffing agency interface. Cutting-edge software programs in the form of "vendor management" systems enable hiring companies' HR personnel to manage all the agencies they contract with. These programs and management systems ensure that companies are complying with relevant labor law, help HR and top managers standardize staffing procurement, keep the "maverick spending" of line managers under control, monitor headcounts, generate reports on use of different agencies and temporary or contract workforces over time, make projections of staff usage, and, in general, manage the "workforce acquisition cycle." Companies that sell these programs claim that they are "vendor neutral," which ideally keeps HR managers from discriminating against some vendors (staffing agencies) and illegally favoring others, particularly

when agencies bid against one another for a contract with a hiring firm. One company that specializes in these programs, Taleo, calls attention to the dread "hidden costs" of contingent labor as part of its sales pitch. For examples of the alleged advantages that vendor-management programs afford companies, see http://www.beeline.com (Beeline), http://www.taleo.com (Taleo), http://www.stafflogix.com (StaffLogix), or http://www.peopleclick.com (Total Workforce Acquisition's People clickVMS™). Increased use of these systems will further rationalize and codify temporary-employment systems, and in this case we might hypothesize that these systems work to hiring companies' advantage but less to the advantage of temporary help service agencies, since the software takes data acquisition, management, and projections out of the hands of the latter. We might even say that when companies adopt these new software systems, they are fighting back against the expertise of temporary help companies, trying to take back control over contingent workforce management.

7. To be sure, in the community of management scholars, these trends have provoked genuine consternation. Drucker, for example, argues that in today's knowledge economy, workers are not just labor; they are also capital (Drucker 2002, 76), and that in order to ensure success, managers must maintain a strong connection to this important corporate capital. With HR outsourcing, managers are in danger of losing oversight of their employees. And HR outsourcing, others argue, may increase costs and administrative problems because it can mean that personnel matters are undermanaged and poorly monitored (Lepak and Snell 1998, 221). In addition, when internal HR activities are unique to a firm and idiosyncratic, relying upon an external arrangement may prove infeasible or incur excessive costs (Klaas, McClendon, and Gainey 2001, 130; Lepak and Snell 1998, 223).

8. These problems were endemic in the larger HR community. HR managers regularly phoned the Select Labor office, desperate to fill orders for temporary workers. It was not uncommon, however, for SL office workers to pass along some résumés, only to have the HR managers sit on them for long periods of time. SL reps would later be told that HR couldn't find time to review the résumés or the temps, or that the positions had disappeared because of hiring freezes imposed by higher-level management.

9. In 2000, the *Staffing Industry Report*, a leading trade newsletter, stated that vendor-on-premises programs had grown by over 30 percent annually in the previous five years and that VOP business had "settled into a pattern of stable growth" (*Staffing Industry Analysts* 2000). VOP

business accounted for approximately 12 percent of total temp revenue dollars in the industry at large and was expected to keep growing by 10 percent annually.

10. This hospitable treatment on the part of a vendor-on-premises seems to be common in the temporary employment industry. When Smith interviewed staff from Volt (a leading temporary help placement firm) in the late 1990s (just before Neuwirth conducted research) in Silicon Valley, reps reported having "open door policies" wherein temps could come by to chat or ask questions, as well as organizing a celebration with cake for all their temps during National Temporary Help Week (sponsored by the current version of NATS, now National Association of Temporary Help and Staffing Services, now NATSS), which typically takes place in the first month of October.

Smith's earlier research (2001b) also pointed to the way in which constructing the new human resources partnership is a two-way street. Researching CompTech, a progressive, paternalistic company, she found that it carefully scrutinized temporary help placement agencies in order to find those whose practices fit with the paternalistic practices of the company itself. Volt was one of more than a hundred temporary placement firms that had been considered by this very large and profitable company. Volt was chosen because it "customized" its own handling of temps in accordance with CompTech's progressive culture. These Volt reps characterized their firm as a "socially responsible" company.

11. Today there are sophisticated data management programs that human resources personnel can use to manage contingent workforces that comprise temps from different agencies (see chapter 5, note 6).

12. Some articles published in personnel magazines in the 1960s and 1970s (see chapter 2) discussed how companies should manage in-house temporary workers. In such an arrangement, a company directly hired its own temporary workers, and these temps—"floaters," for example— might move about from job to job, as needed. In-house temp programs had essentially disappeared from the pages of these magazines by the 1980s, victims, it would seem, of the very great economies and efficiencies that external THS agencies could provide.

Chapter 6. Do Good Enough Temporary Jobs Make Good Enough Temporary Employment?

1. Findings are mixed about the effects of temporary agency jobs on welfare recipients. Autor and Houseman (2005, 2006) argue that welfare

recipients may experience short-term earnings increases when they use temporary agencies and that agencies can help welfare recipients who have underdeveloped job skills and work experience. They found that long-term outcomes were discouraging, however, and that former welfare recipients do not earn enough to leave welfare and ultimately escape poverty.

2. CompTech's managerial practices were paternalistic, as were the practices of the temporary firms with whom CompTech contracted. The company's selection of agencies was based on how well the latter conformed with its culture. Working with managers who have "superior management skills" can be one bonus of working as a temp, according to Houseman and Erickcek (2002, 3).

3. American Staffing Association 2006a.

4. Mishel, Bernstein, and Allegretto 2007, 241, table 4.8.

5. Brady et al. 2000; Buchmueller and Valletta 1996; Gruber and Madrian 1994; Monheit and Cooper 1994.

6. Glassner 1994; Hacker 2006; Jacoby 1999; Neumark 2000; Rayman 2001; Sennett 1998; Uchitelle 2006; and Wallulis 1998.

7. See http://www.freelancersunion.org; http://www.fastcompany.com/social/2006/statements/working-today.html; http://www.fastcompany.com/social/2007/profiles/profile42.html.

8. On the new organizing model, see Bronfenbrenner et al. 1998; Carré and Joshi 2001; Cobble and Vosko 2001; DuRivage, Carré, and Tilly 1998; Fantasia and Voss 2004; Lichtenstein 2003; Milkman 2006; Milkman and Voss 2004; Rabadán, Milkman, and Wong 2000; and Tait 2005.

9. See Carnevale, Jennings, and Eisenmann (1998) and Freeman and Gonos (2005) on how employment law must be revamped to adapt to the increase of the contingent labor force.

REFERENCES

Abrahamson, Eric. 1996. "Management Fashion." *Academy of Management Review* 21 (1): 254–285.

Acker, Joan. 1990. "Hierarchies, Bodies and Jobs: A Theory of Gendered Organizations." *Gender and Society* 4 (2): 139–158.

Addison, John, and Christopher Surfield. 2006. "The Use of Alternative Work Arrangements by the Jobless: Evidence from the CAEAS/CPS." *Journal of Labor Research* 27 (2): 149–162.

Althauser, Robert. 1989. "Internal Labor Markets." *Annual Review of Sociology* 15: 141–161.

American Staffing Association. 2006a. American Staffing 2006: Annual Economic Analysis. Steven Bercham. http://www.americanstaffing. net/statistics/pdf/American%20staffing%202006.pdf.

——. 2006b. A Profile of Temporary and Contract Employees. Steven Bercham.http://www.americanstaffing.net/statistics/pdf/Staffing_Em ployee_Survey_Executive_Summary.pdf.

Andersson, Fredrik, Harry Holzer, and Julia Lane. 2005. *Moving Up or Moving On: Who Advances in the Low-Wage Labor Market?* New York: Russell Sage Foundation.

Andrews, Linda Wasmer. 2003. "Avoiding HR Burnout." *HR Magazine* 48 (7): 44–49.

Appelbaum, Eileen, Thomas Bailey, Pēter Berg, and Arne Kalleberg. 2000. *Manufacturing Advantage: Why High-Performance Work Systems Pay Off.* Ithaca: Cornell University Press, ILR Press.

Appelbaum, Eileen, and Rosemary Batt. 1994. *The New American Workplace: Transforming Work Systems in the United States.* Ithaca: Cornell University Press, ILR Press.

Appelbaum, Eileen, Annette Bernhardt, and Richard Murnane, eds. 2003. *Low-Wage America: How Employers are Reshaping Opportunity in the Workplace.* New York: Russell Sage Foundation.

Autor, David. 2001. "Why Do Temporary Help Firms Provide Free General Skills Training?" *Quarterly Journal of Economics* 116 (4): 1409–1448.

——. 2003. "Outsourcing at Will: The Contribution of Unjust Dismissal Doctrine and the Growth of Employment Outsourcing." *Journal of Labor Economics* 21 (1): 1–42.

Autor, David, and Susan Houseman. 2005. "Do Temporary Jobs Help Improve Labor Market Outcomes for Low-Skilled Workers? Evidence from Random Assignments." Working Paper 11743, National Bureau of Economic Research. http://www.nber.org/papers/W11743.

——. 2006. "Temporary Agency Employment as a Way out of Poverty." In *Working and Poor: How Economic and Policy Changes Are Affecting Low-Income Workers,* ed. Rebecca Blank, Sheldon Danziger, and Robert Shoemi, 312–337. New York: Russell Sage Foundation.

Barley, Stephen, and Gideon Kunda. 1992. "Design and Devotion: Surges of Rational and Normative Ideologies of Control in Managerial Discourse." *Administrative Science Quarterly* 37 (3): 363–399.

——. 2004. *Gurus, Hired Guns, and Warm Bodies: Itinerant Experts in a Knowledge Economy.* Princeton: Princeton University Press.

Barley, Stephen, Gordon Meyer, and Debra Gash. 1988. "Cultures of Culture: Academics, Practitioners, and the Pragmatics of Normative Control." *Administrative Science Quarterly* 33 (1): 24–60.

Baron, James, Frank Dobbin, and P. Devereaux Jennings. 1986. "War and Peace: The Evolution of Modern Personnel Administration in U.S. Industry." *American Journal of Sociology* 92 (2): 350–383.

Barsness, Zoe, and Brian Uzzi. 1998. "Contingent Employment in British Establishments: Organizational Determinants of Fixed-Term Hires and Part-Time Workers." *Social Forces* 76 (3): 967–1005.

Bartely, Tim, and Wade Roberts. 2006. "Regional Exploitation: The Informal Organization of Day Labor Agencies." *Working USA: The Journal of Labor and Society* 9 (4): 41–58.

Bates, Steve. 2002. "Facing the Future." *HR Magazine* 47 (7): 26–32.

Befort, Stephen. 2003. "Revisiting the Black Hole of Workplace Regulation: A Historical and Comparative Perspective of Contingent Work." *Berkeley Journal of Employment and Labor Relations* 24 (1): 153–178.

Belous, Richard. 1989. *The Contingent Economy: The Growth of the Temporary, Part-Time, and Subcontracted Workforce.* Washington, D.C.: National Planning Association.

Bendix, Reinhart. 1956. *Work and Authority in Industry: Ideologies of Management in the Course of Industrialization.* Berkeley: University of California Press.

Benner, Chris. 2002. *Work in the New Economy: Flexible Labor Markets in Silicon Valley.* Oxford: Blackwell.

Benner, Chris, Laura Leete, and Manuel Pastor. 2007. *Staircases or Treadmills: Labor Market Intermediaries and Economic Opportunity in a Changing Economy.* New York: Russell Sage Foundation.

Berman, Jay. 2005. "Industry Output and Employment Projections to 2014." *Monthly Labor Review* 128 (11): 45–69.

Bernasek, Alexandra, and Douglas Kinnear. 1999. "Workers' Willingness to Accept Contingent Employment." *Journal of Economic Issues* 33 (2): 461–469.

Bickham Mendez, Jennifer. 1998. "Of Mops and Maids: Contradictions and Continuities in Bureaucratized Domestic Work." *Social Problems* 45 (1): 114–135.

Bishop, Todd. 2005. "Microsoft's 'Orange Badge' Culture Gets Forum." *Seattle Post-Intelligencer,* December 29. http://seattlepi.nwsource.com/business/253826_orangebadges29.html.

Blair, Margaret, and Thomas Kochan, eds. 2000. *The New Relationship: Human Capital in the American Corporation.* Washington, D.C.: Brookings Institute Press.

Block, Fred. 1990. *Postindustrial Possibilities: A Critique of Economic Discourse.* Berkeley: University of California Press.

———. 2006. "One Step toward a Moral Economy." June 29. http://www.longviewinstitute.org/news_items/inmex.

Bluestone, Barry, and Bennett Harrison. 1982. *The Deindustrialization of America: Plant Closings, Community Abandonment, and the Dismantling of Basic Industry.* New York: Basic Books.

Bolles, Richard. 2007. *What Color Is Your Parachute?* Berkeley: Ten Speed Press.

Bowles, Samuel, David Gordon, and Thomas Weisskopf. 1983. *Beyond the Wasteland: A Democratic Alternative to Economic Decline.* New York: Doubleday.

Brady, Henry, Kamran Nayeri, Michael Brunetti, and Carlos Dobkin. 2000. "Health Status, Health Insurance, and Worker Mobility: A Study of Job Lock in California." Berkeley: University of California Data/Survey Research Center.

Bronfenbrenner, Kate, Sheldon Friedman, Richard Hurd, Rudolph Oswald, and Ronald Seeber, eds. 1998. *Organizing to Win: New Research in Union Strategies.* Ithaca: Cornell University Press, ILR Press.

Bronson, Po. 1999. *Nudist on the Late Shift and Other True Tales of Silicon Valley.* New York: Random House.

Brown, Clair, John Haltiwanger, and Julia Lane. 2006. *Economic Turbulence: Is a Volatile Economy Good for America?* Chicago: University of Chicago Press.

Buchmueller, Thomas, and Robert Valletta. 1996. "The Effects of Employer-Provided Health Insurance on Worker Mobility." *Industrial and Labor Relations Review* 49 (3): 439–455.

Burawoy, Michael. 1979. *Manufacturing Consent.* Chicago: University of Chicago Press.

Bureau of Labor Statistics. 2001. "Contingent and Alternative Employment Relationships." http://www.bls.gov/news.release/History/conemp-05242001.txt.

——. 2005a. "Contingent and Alternative Employment Arrangements, February 2005." http://www.bls.gov/news.release/pdf/conemp.pdf.

——. 2005b. "Employment Services: Outlook: Employment Services." http://www.bls.gov/oco/cg/cgs039.htm.

Capelli, Peter. 1995. "Is the Skills Gap Really about Attitudes?" *California Management Review* 37 (4): 108–124.

——. 1999. *The New Deal at Work: Managing the Market-Driven Workforce.* Boston: Harvard Business School Press.

——. 2000. "Examining the Incidence of Downsizing and Its Effect on Establishment Performance." In *On the Job: Is Long-Term Employment a Thing of the Past?* ed. David Neumark, 463–516. New York: Russell Sage Foundation.

Carleson, Richard. 2001. "Why the Law Still Can't Tell an Employee When It Sees One and How It Ought to Stop Trying." *Berkeley Journal of Employment and Labor Law* 22 (2): 295–368.

Carnevale, Anthony, Lynn Jennings, and James Eisenmann. 1998. "Contingent Workers and Employment Law." In *Contingent Work: American Employment Relations in Transition,* ed. Kathleen Barker and Kathleen Christensen, 281–305. Ithaca: Cornell University Press, ILR Press.

Carr, David. 2007. "Thousands Are Laid Off: What's New?" *New York Times,* April 2, C1, C7.

Carré, Françoise, Marianne Ferber, Lonnie Golden, and Stephen Herzenberg, eds. 2001. *Nonstandard Work: The Nature and Challenges of Changing Employment Relations.* Champaign: Industrial Relations Research Association and University of Illinois Press.

Carré, Françoise, and Pamela Joshi. 2001. "Looking for Leverage in a Fluid World: Innovative Responses to Temporary and Contracted Work." In *Nonstandard Work: The Nature and Challenges of Changing Employment Relations*, ed. Françoise Carré, Marianne Ferber, Lonnie Golden, and Stephen Herzenberg, 313–339. Champaign: Industrial Relations and Research Association and University of Illinois Press.

Carré, Françoise, and Chris Tilly. 1998. "Part-time and Temporary Work: Flexibility for Whom?" *Dollars and Sense*, no. 215.

Carré, Françoise, Joaquin Herranz, Jr., Dorie Seavey, Carlha Vickers, Ashley Aull, and Rebecca Keegan. 2003. *Alternative Job Brokering: Addressing Labor Market Disadvantages, Improving The Temp Experience and Enhancing Job Opportunities*. Report of The National Study of Alternative Staffing Services. http://www.mccormacktmp.umb.edu/csp/csp_publications.jsp.

Chun, Jennifer JiHye. 2001. "Flexible Despotism: The Intensification of Uncertainty and Insecurity in the Lives of High-Tech Assembly Workers in the Silicon Valley." In *The Critical Study of Work: Labor, Technology, and Global Production*, ed. Rick Baldoz, Charles Koeber, and Philip Kraft, 127–154. Philadelphia: Temple University Press.

——. 2005. "Public Dramas and the Politics of Justice: Comparison of Janitors' Union Struggles in South Korea and the United States." *Work and Occupations* 32 (4): 486–503.

Cobble, Sue, and Leah Vosko. 2001. "Historical Perspectives on Representing Nonstandard Workers." In *Nonstandard Work: The Nature and Challenges of Changing Employment Relations*, ed. Françoise Carré, Marianne Ferber, Lonnie Golden, and Stephen Herzenberg, 291–312. Champaign: Industrial Relations and Research Association and University of Illinois Press.

Cohany, Sharon. 1998. "Workers in Alternative Employment Arrangements: A Second Look." *Monthly Labor Review* 121 (11): 3–21.

Davis-Blake, Alison, and Brian Uzzi. 1993. "Determinants of Employment Externalization: A Study of Temporary Workers and Independent Contractors." *Administrative Science Quarterly* 38 (2): 195–223.

Dempsey, Karen. 2006. "HR Needs to Be Wary of Losing Its Role Altogether." *Personnel Today*, October 17, 12.

Dey, Matthew, Susan Houseman, and Anne Polivka. 2007. "Outsourcing to Staffing Services: How Manufacturers' Use of Staffing Agencies Affects Employment and Productivity Measurement." *Employment Research* 14 (1): 4–6 (Kalamazoo, Mich.: Upjohn Institute for Employment Research).

DiMaggio, Paul, ed. 2001. *The Twenty-First Century Firm: Changing Economic Organization in International Perspective.* Princeton: Princeton University Press.

Dineen, Brian, Raymond Noe, and Chongwei Wang. 2004. "Perceived Fairness of Web-Based Applicant Screening Procedures: Weighing the Rules of Justice and the Role of Individual Differences." *Human Resource Management* 43 (2/3): 127–145.

Dobbin, Frank, and John Sutton. 1998. "The Strength of a Weak State: The Rights Revolution and the Rise of Human Resources Management Divisions." *American Journal of Sociology* 104 (2): 441–476.

Dobbin, Frank, John Sutton, John W. Meyer, and Richard Scott. 1993. "Equal Opportunity Law and the Construction of Internal Labor Markets." *American Journal of Sociology* 99 (2): 396–427.

Doeringer, Peter, and Michael Piore. 1971. *Internal Labor Markets and Manpower Analysis.* Lexington, Mass.: Heath.

Doeringer, Peter, Kathleen Christensen, Patricia Flynn, and Douglas Hall. 1991. *Turbulence in the American Workplace.* Oxford: Oxford University Press.

Drucker, Peter. 2002. "They're Not Employees, They're People." *Harvard Business Review* 80 (2): 70–77.

DuRivage, Virgina. 2001. "CWA's Organizing Strategies: Transforming Contract Work Into Union Jobs." In *Nonstandard Work: The Nature and Challenges of Changing Employment Relations,* ed. Françoise Carré, Marianne Ferber, Lonnie Golden, and Stephen Herzenberg, 377–392. Champaign: Industrial Relations and Research Association and University of Illinois Press.

DuRivage, Virginia, Françoise Carré, and Chris Tilly. 1998. "Making Labor Law for Part-Time and Contingent Workers." In *Contingent Work: American Employment Relations in Transition,* ed. Kathleen Barber and Kathleen Christensen, 263–280. Ithaca: Cornell University Press, ILR Press.

Edelman, Lauren. 1990. "Legal Environments and Organizational Governance: The Expansion of Due Process in the American Workplace." *American Journal of Sociology* 95 (6): 1401–1440.

Edelman, Lauren, Sally Riggs Fuller, and Iona Mara-Drita. 2001. "Diversity Rhetoric and the Managerialization of Law." *American Journal of Sociology* 106 (6): 1589–1641.

Edwards, Richard. 1979. *Contested Terrain.* New York: Basic Books.

Ehrenreich, Barbara. 2001. *Nickeled and Dimed: On (Not) Getting By in America.* New York: Henry Holt, Metropolitan Books.

Ehrenreich, Barbara, and Tamara Draut. 2006. "Downsized but Not Out." *The Nation,* November 6. http://www.thenation.com/doc/20061106/ ehrenreich.

Erickcek, George, Susan Houseman, and Arne Kalleberg. 2003. "The Effects of Temporary Services and Contracting Out on Low-Skilled Workers." In *Low-Wage America: How Employers Are Reshaping Opportunity in the Workplace,* ed. Eileen Appelbaum, Annette Bernhardt, and Richard Murnane, 368–403. New York: Russell Sage Foundation.

Estevão, Marcello, and Saul Lach. 1999. "Measuring Temporary Labor Outsourcing in U.S. Manufacturing." Working Paper 7421, National Bureau of Economic Research. http://www.nber.org/papers/ w7421.

Fairris, David. 2004. "Internal Labor Markets and Worker Quits." *Industrial Relations* 43 (3): 573–594.

Fantasia, Rick, and Kim Voss. 2004. *Hard Work: Remaking the American Labor Movement.* Berkeley: University of California Press.

Farber, Henry. 1999. "Alternative and Part-Time Employment Arrangements as a Response to Job Loss." *Journal of Labor Economics* 17 (4, pt. 2): S142–169.

———. 2000. "Employment Arrangements as a Response to Job Loss." In *On the Job: Is Long-Term Employment a Thing of the Past?* ed. David Neumark, 398–426. New York: Russell Sage Foundation.

Fiamingo, Josephine. 1984. "Need a Pro? Try Temporary Help." *Office Administration and Automation* 45 (August): 48–50, 55, 68, 70.

Fine, Janice. 2006. *Worker Centers: Organizing Communities at the Edge of the Dream.* An Economic Policy Institute Book. Ithaca: Cornell University Press, ILR Press.

Finegold, David, Alec Levenson, and Mark Van Buren. 2003. "A Temporary Route to Advancement? The Career Opportunities for Low-Skilled Workers in Temporary Employment." In *Low-Wage America: How Employers Are Reshaping Opportunity in the Workplace,* ed. Eileen Appelbaum, Annette Bernhardt, and Richard Murnane, 317–367. New York: Russell Sage Foundation.

Finlay, William, and James Coverdill. 2002. *Headhunters: Matchmaking in the Labor Market.* Ithaca: Cornell University Press, ILR Press.

Fiorito, Jack. 2001. "Human Resource Management Practices and Worker Desires for Union Representation." *Journal of Labor Research* 22 (2): 335–354.

Fitzgerald, Joan. 2006. *Moving Up in the New Economy: Career Ladders for U.S. Workers.* Ithaca: Cornell University Press, ILR Press.

Fligstein, Neil. 1990. *The Transformation of Corporate Control.* Cambridge: Harvard University Press.

Foulkes, Fred. 1980. *Personnel Policies in Large Nonunion Firms.* Englewood Cliffs, N.J.: Prentice-Hall.

Freeman, Harris, and George Gonos. 2005. "Regulating The Employment Sharks: Reconceptualizing the Legal Status of the Commercial Temp Agency." *Working USA: The Journal of Labor and Society* 8 (3): 293–314.

French, Wendell. 1998. *Human Resources Management.* Boston: Houghton Mifflin.

Gertner, Jon. 2006. "What Is a Living Wage?" *New York Times Magazine,* January 15, 38–45, 62, 68, 72.

Giloth, Robert, ed. 2003. *Workforce Intermediaries for the Twenty-First Century.* Philadelphia: Temple University Press.

Glassner, Barry. 1994. *Career Crash: America's New Crisis—and Who Survives.* New York: Simon and Schuster.

Goldin, Claudia. 1990. *Understanding the Gender Gap: An Economic History of American Women.* New York: Oxford University Press.

Gonos, George. 1997. "The Contest over 'Employer' Status in the Postwar United States: The Case of Temporary Help Firms." *Law & Society Review* 31 (1): 81–110.

——. 1998. "The Interaction between Market Incentives and Government." In *Contingent Work: American Employment Relations in Transition,* ed. Kathleen Barker and Kathleen Christensen, 170–191. Ithaca: Cornell University Press, ILR Press.

——. 2000–2001. "Never a Fee! The Miracle of the Postmodern Temporary Help and Staffing Agency." *Working USA* 4 (3): 9–36.

——. 2001. "Fee-Splitting Revisited: Surplus Value in the Temporary Employment Relationship." *Politics and Society* 29 (4): 589–611.

Gordon, David. 1996. *Fat and Mean: The Corporate Squeeze of Working Americans and the Myth of Managerial Downsizing.* New York: Free Press.

Gottfried, Heidi. 1991. "Mechanisms of Control in the Temporary Help Service Industry." *Sociological Forum* 6 (4): 699–713.

Gottfried, Heidi, and Laurie Graham. 1993. "Constructing Difference: The Making of Gendered Subcultures in a Japanese Automobile Assembly Plant." *Sociology* 27 (4): 611–628.

Graham, Laurie. 1995. *On the Line at Subaru-Isuzu: The Japanese Model and the American Worker.* Ithaca: Cornell University Press, ILR Press.

Granovetter, Mark. 1995. *Getting a Job: A Study of Contacts and Careers.* Chicago: University of Chicago Press.

Greengard, Samuel. 2003. "Evolution, Not Revolution." *Workforce Management* 82 (10): 43–46.

Gruber, Jonathan, and Brigitte Madrian. 1994. "Health Insurance and Job Mobility: The Effects of Public Policy on Job Lock." *Industrial and Labor Relations Review* 48 (1): 86–102.

Hacker, Jacob. 2006. *The Great Risk Shift: The Assault on American Jobs, Families, Health Care, and Retirement, and How You Can Fight Back.* Oxford: Oxford University Press.

Harrison, Bennett, and Mary Ellen Kelley. 1993. "Outsourcing and the Search for 'Flexibility.'" *Work, Employment, and Society* 7 (2): 213–235.

Hayes, Sharon. 2003. *Flat Broke with Children: Women in the Age of Welfare Reform.* Oxford: Oxford University Press.

Heckscher, Charles. 1995. *White-Collar Blues: Management Loyalties in an Age of Corporate Restructuring.* New York: Basic Books.

——. 2001. "HR Strategy and Nonstandard Work: Dualism versus True Mobility." In *Nonstandard Work: The Nature and Challenges of Changing Employment Relations,* ed. Françoise Carré, Marianne Ferber, Lonnie Golden, and Stephen Herzenberg, 267–290. Champaign: Industrial Relations and Research Association and University of Illinois Press.

Heinrich, Carolyn. 2005. "Temporary Employment Experiences of Women on Welfare." *Journal of Labor Research* 26 (2): 335–350.

Hely, Michael. 2003. "The Impact of *Sturgis* on Bargaining Power for Contingent Workers in the U.S. Labor Market." *Washington University Journal of Law and Policy* 11: 295–322.

Hempel, Paul. 2004. "Preparing the HR Profession for Technology and Information Work." *Human Resource Management* 43 (2/3): 163–177.

Henson, Kevin. 1996. *Just a Temp.* Philadelphia: Temple University Press.

Hewitt Associates. 2002. "Survey Findings: CFOs' Views on Outsourcing in 2002." Lincolnshire, Ill. http://www.hewitt.com.

Hirschman, Carolyn. 2003. "Fiduciary Fitness." *HR Magazine* 48 (9): 60–64.

——. 2004. "Are Your Contractors Legal?" *HR Magazine* 49 (3): 58–63.

Hochschild, Arlie. 1971. "Inside the Clockwork of the Male Career." In *Women and the Power to Change,* ed. Florence Howe, 47–80. New York: McGraw-Hill.

——. 1983. *The Managed Heart.* Berkeley: University of California Press.

Hodson, Randy. 2001. *Dignity at Work.* Cambridge: Cambridge University Press.

Holzer, Harry. 1996. *What Employers Want: Job Prospects for Less-Educated Workers.* New York: Russell Sage Foundation.

Houseman, Susan. 2001. "Why Employers Use Flexible Staffing Arrangements: Evidence from an Establishment Survey." *Industrial and Labor Relations Review* 55 (1): 149–170.

Houseman, Susan, and George Erickcek. 2002. "Temporary Services and Contracting Out: Effects on Low-Skilled Workers." *Employment Research* 9 (3): 1–3. http://www.upjohninst.org/publications/newsletter/SNH_702.pdf.

Houseman, Susan, Arne Kalleberg, and George Erickcek. 2003. "The Role of Temporary Agency Employment in Tight Labor Markets." *Industrial and Labor Relations Review* 57 (1): 105–127.

Houseman, Susan, and Anne E. Polivka. 2000. "The Implications of Flexible Staffing Arrangements for Job Stability." In *On the Job: Is Long-Term Employment a Thing of the Past?* ed. David Neumark, 427–462. New York: Russell Sage Foundation.

Indegaard, Michael. 1999. "Retrainers as Labor Market Brokers: Constructing Networks and Narratives in the Detroit Area." *Social Problems* 46 (1): 67–87.

Jacoby, Sanford. 1985. *Employing Bureaucracy: Managers, Unions, and the Transformation of Work in American Industry, 1900–1945.* New York: Columbia University Press.

——. 1997. *Modern Manors: Welfare Capitalism since the New Deal.* Princeton: Princeton University Press.

——. 1999. "Are Career Jobs Headed for Extinction?" *California Management Review* 42 (1): 123–145.

——. 2005. *The Embedded Corporation: Corporate Governance and Employment Relations in Japan and the United States.* Princeton: Princeton University Press.

Kalleberg, Arne. 2006. *The Mismatched Worker.* New York: W. W. Norton.

Kalleberg, Arne, Peter Marsden, David Knoke, and Joe Spaeth. 1996. "Formalizing the Employment Relation." In *Organizations in America: Analyzing Their Structures and Human Resource Practices,* ed. Arne Kalleberg, David Knoke, Peter Marsden, and Joe Spaeth, 87–112. Thousand Oaks, Calif.: Sage.

Kalleberg, Arne, and James Moody. 1996. "Human Resource Management and Organizational Perfomance." In *Organizations in America: Analyzing Their Structures and Human Resource Practices,* ed. Arne Kalleberg, David Knoke, Peter Marsden, and Joe Spaeth, 113–129. Thousand Oaks, Calif.: Sage.

Kalleberg, Arne, Barbara Reskin, and Ken Hudson. 2000. "Bad Jobs in America: Standard and Nonstandard Employment Relations and Job Quality in the United States." *American Sociological Review* 65 (2): 256–278.

Kalleberg, Arne, Jeremy Reynolds, and Peter Marsden. 2003. "Externalizing Employment: Flexible Staffing Arrangements in U.S. Organizations." *Social Science Research* 32 (4): 525–552.

Kanter, Rosabeth Moss. 1977. *Men and Women of the Corporation.* New York: Basic Books.

Kennedy, Elizabeth. 2005. "Freedom from Independence: Collective Bargaining Rights for Dependent Contractors." *Berkeley Journal of Employment and Labor Law* 26 (1): 143–180.

Ketter, Paula. 2007. "HR Outsourcing." *T + D* (Training and Development) 61 (2): 12–13.

Kilcoyne, Patrick. 2004. "Occupations in the Temporary Help Services Industry." U.S. Department of Labor. Bureau of Labor Statistics, Occupational Employment and Wages. http://www.bls.gov/oes/2004/may/temp.pdf.

Klaas, Brian, John McClendon, and Thomas Gainey. 2001. "Outsourcing HR: The Impacts of Organizational Characteristics." *Human Resource Management* 40 (2): 125–138.

Klaff, Leslie Gross. 2003. "A Cure for Contingent Costs." *Workforce Management* 82 (8): 51–53.

Korczynski, Marek, Karen Shire, May Tam, and Stephen Frenkel. 1999. *On the Front Line: Organization of Work in the Information Economy.* Ithaca: Cornell University Press, ILR Press.

Krippner, Greta. 2001. "The Organization of Disorganization in Agricultural Labor Markets." *Politics and Society* 29 (3): 363–383.

Lafer, Gordon. 2002. *The Job Training Charade.* Ithaca: Cornell University Press, ILR Press.

Lane, Julia, Kelly Mikelson, Pat Sharkey, and Doug Wissoker. 2003. "Pathways to Work for Low-Income Workers: The Effect of Work in the Temporary Help Industry." *Journal of Policy Analysis and Management* 22 (4): 581–598.

Lautsch, Brenda. 2002. "Uncovering and Explaining Variance in the Features and Outcomes of Contingent Work." *Industrial and Labor Relations Review* 56 (1): 23–43.

——. 2003. "The Influence of Regular Work Systems on Compensation for Contingent Workers." *Industrial Relations* 42 (4): 565–588.

Leidner, Robin. 1993. *Fast Food/Fast Talk: Service Work and the Routinization of Everyday Life.* Berkeley: University of California Press.

Lenz, Edward. 1997. *Co-Employment: Employer Liability Issues in Third-Party Staffing Arrangements.* Alexandria, Va.: National Association of Temporary and Staffing Services.

Leonard, Bill. 2002. "Access Denied." *HR Magazine* 47 (10): 38–41.

Leonhardt, David. 2007a. "3,400 Layoffs Send a Message to Millions." *New York Times*, April 4, C1, C7.

——. 2007b. "Middle-Class Squeeze Comes with Nuances." *New York Times*, April 25, C1, C12.

Lepak, David, and Scott Snell. 1998. "Virtual HR: Strategic Human Resource Management in the 21st Century." *Human Resource Management Review* 8 (3): 215–234.

Levenson, Alec. 2000. "Long-Run Trends in Part-Time and Temporary Employment: Toward an Understanding." In *On the Job: Is Long-Term Employment a Thing of the Past?* ed. David Neumark, 335–397. New York: Russell Sage Foundation.

Levenson, Alec, and David Finegold. 2001. "The Employment Outcomes and Advancement of Temporary Workers." CEO Publication T 01–19 (409), Center for Effective Organizations, Marshall School of Business, University of Southern California.

Licht, Walter. 2000. *Getting Work: Philadelphia, 1840–1950.* Philadelphia: University of Pennsylvania Press.

Lichtenstein, Nelson. 2003. *State of the Union: A Century of American Labor.* Princeton: Princeton University Press.

Lofland, John, David Snow, Leon Anderson, and Lyn Lofland. 2006. *Analyzing Social Settings: A Guide to Qualitative Observation and Analysis.* Belmont, Calif.: Wadsworth/Thomson.

Luce, Stephanie. 2004. *Fighting for a Living Wage.* Ithaca: Cornell University Press, ILR Press.

——. 2005. "Lessons from Living-Wage Campaigns." *Work and Occupations* 32 (4): 423–440.

MacDonald, Cameron, and Carmen Sirianni, eds. 1996. *Working in the Service Society.* Philadelphia: Temple University Press.

Mangum, Garth, Donald Mayall, and Kristin Nelson. 1985. "The Temporary Help Industry: A Response to the Dual Internal Labor Market." *Industrial and Labor Relations Review* 38 (4): 599–611.

Marks, Mitchell Lee. 2003. "Surviving Madness." *HR Magazine* 48 (6): 86–92.

McAllister, Jean. 1998. "Sisyphus at Work in the Warehouse: Temporary Employment in Greenville, South Carolina." In *Contingent Work: American Employment Relations in Transition*, ed. Kathleen Barker and Kathleen Christensen, 221–242. Ithaca: Cornell University Press, ILR Press.

Milkman, Ruth. 2006. *L.A. Stories: Immigrant Workers and the Future of the U.S. Labor Movement.* New York: Russell Sage Foundation.

Milkman, Ruth, and Kim Voss. 2004. *Rebuilding Labor: Organizing and Organizers in the New Union Movement.* Ithaca: Cornell University Press, ILR Press.

Millner, Guy. 1972. Quoted in *Office* (December), 40.

Mishel, Lawrence, Jared Bernstein, and Sylvia Allegretto. 2007. *The State of Working America: 2006/2007.* An Economic Policy Institute Book. Ithaca: Cornell University Press, ILR Press.

Monheit, Alan, and Philip Cooper. 1994. "Health Insurance and Job Mobility: Theory and Evidence." *Industrial and Labor Relations Review* 48 (1): 68–85.

Moore, Mack. 1965. "The Temporary Help Service Industry: Historical Development, Operation, and Scope." *Industrial and Labor Relations Review* 18 (4): 554–569.

Morris, Michael, and Alexander Vekker. 2001. "An Alternative Look at Temporary Workers, Their Choices, and the Growth in Contingent Employment." *Journal of Labor Research* 22 (2): 373–390.

Moss, Philip, and Chris Tilly. 2001. *Stories Employers Tell: Race, Skill, and Hiring in America.* New York: Russell Sage Foundation.

Neubeck, Kenneth, and Noel Cazenave. 2001. *Welfare Racism: Playing the Race Card against America's Poor.* New York: Routledge.

Neumark, David, ed. 2000. *On the Job: Is Long-Term Employment a Thing of the Past?* New York: Russell Sage Foundation.

Neuwirth, Esther. 2004. "Blurring Corporate Boundaries: Staffing Agencies, Human Resource Practices, and Unions in the New Employment Relationship." Ph.D. dissertation, University of California, Davis.

——. 2006. "Opportunities and Challenges Facing New Workforce Institutions: A Close-Up Analysis of an Alternative Staffing Service." In *Worker Participation: Practices and Possibilities,* ed. Vicki Smith. Special issue of *Research in the Sociology of Work* 16: 319–342. Oxford: JAI, Elsevier Press.

Noble, David. 1977. *America by Design: Science, Technology, and the Rise of Corporate Capitalism.* Oxford: Oxford University Press.

Noe, Zoe. 1986. "Lose Jobs Now! Ask Me How!" *Processed World* 17 (August). http://www.processedworld.com.

Nollen, Stanley, and Helen Axel. 1998. "Benefits and Costs to Employers." In *Contingent Work: American Employment Relations in Transition,* ed. Kathleen Barker and Kathleen Christensen, 126–143. Ithaca: Cornell University Press, ILR Press.

Ofstead, Cynthia. 1999. "Temporary Help Firms as Entrepreneurial Actors." *Sociological Forum* 14 (2): 273–294.

Osterman, Paul, ed. 1984. *Internal Labor Markets.* Cambridge, Mass.: MIT Press.

——. 1988. *Employment Futures: Reorganization, Dislocation, and Public Policy.* New York: Oxford University.

——. 1996. *Broken Ladders: Managerial Careers in the New Economy.* New York: Oxford University Press.

——. 1999. *Securing Prosperity: The American Labor Market; How It Has Changed and What to Do about It.* Princeton: Princeton University Press.

——. 2002. *Gathering Power: The Future of Progressive Politics in America.* Boston: Beacon Press.

Parker, Robert. 1994. *Flesh Peddlers and Warm Bodies: The Temporary Help Industry and Its Workers.* New Brunswick, N.J.: Rutgers University Press.

Peck, Jamie. 1996. *Work-Place: The Social Regulation of Labor Markets.* New York: Guilford Press.

Peck, Jamie, and Nikolas Theodore. 1998. "The Business of Contingent Work: Growth and Restructuring in Chicago's Temporary Employment Industry." *Work, Employment, and Society* 12 (4): 655–674.

——. 2002. "Temped Out? Industry Rhetoric, Labor Regulation and Economic Restructuring in the Temporary Staffing Business." *Economic and Industrial Democracy* 23 (2): 143–175.

Pfeffer, Jeffrey, and James Baron. 1988. "Taking the Workers Back Out: Recent Trends in the Structuring of Employment." *Research in Organizational Behavior* 10: 257–303.

Polivka, Anne. 1996. "A Profile of Contingent Workers." *Monthly Labor Review* 119 (10): 10–21.

Posthuma, Richard, Michael Campion, and Amber Vargas. 2005. "Predicting Counterproductive Performance among Temporary Workers: A Note." *Industrial Relations* 44 (3): 550–554.

Powell, Walter. 2001. "The Capitalist Firm in the Twenty-First Century." In *The Twenty-First Century Firm: Changing Economic Organization in International Perspective,* ed. Paul DiMaggio, 33–68. Princeton: Princeton University Press.

Purser, Gretchen. 2007. "Flexploitation: Time and Power in a Day Labor Industry." Unpublished Paper. Department of Sociology. University of California, Berkeley. Presented at The Annual American Sociological Association Meetings, New York.

Rabadán, Luis Escala, Ruth Milkman, and Kent Wong. 2000. *Voices from the Front Lines: Organizing Immigrant Workers in Los Angeles.* Los Angles: UCLA, Center for Labor Research and Education.

Rassuli, Ali. 2005. "Evolution of the Professional Contingent Workforce." *Journal of Labor Research* 26 (4): 689–710.

Rayman, Paula. 2001. *Beyond the Bottom Line: The Search for Dignity at Work.* New York: Palgrave.

Reich, Robert. 2000. *The Future of Success: Working and Living in the New Economy.* New York: Vintage.

"Revamping the 'Employment Contract.'" 2003. *HR Focus* 80 (12): 1, 11–15.

Riesman, David. 1965. *The Lonely Crowd: A Study of the Changing American Character.* New Haven: Yale University Press.

Robb, Drew. 2003. "Data Overload." *HR Magazine* 48 (10): 70–76.

Rogers, Jackie Krasas. 2000. *Temps: The Many Faces of the Changing Workplace.* Ithaca: Cornell University Press, ILR Press.

Rogers, Jackie Krasas, and Kevin Henson. 1997. "Hey, Why Don't You Wear a Shorter Skirt?: Structural Vulnerability and the Organization of Sexual Harassment in Temporary Clerical Employment." *Gender and Society* 11 (2): 215–237.

Rosenfeld, David. 2006. "Worker Centers: Emerging Labor Organizations— Until They Confront the National Labor Relations Act." *Berkeley Journal of Employment and Labor Law* 27 (2): 469–513.

Sallaz, Jeffrey. 2002. "The House Rules: Autonomy and Interests among Service Workers in the Contemporary Casino Industry." *Work and Occupations* 29 (4): 394–427.

Saxenian, AnnaLee. 1994. *Regional Networks: Industrial Adaptation in Silicon Valley and Route 128.* Cambridge: Harvard University Press.

——. 2000. "The Origins and Dynamics of Production Networks in Silicon Valley." In *Understanding Silicon Valley: The Anatomy of an Entrepreneurial Region,* ed. Martin Kenney, 141–164. Stanford, Calif.: Stanford University Press.

Schmidt, Stefanie. 2000. "Job Security Beliefs in the General Social Survey: Evidence on the Long-Run Trends and Comparability with Other Surveys." In *On the Job: Is Long-Term Employment a Thing of the Past?* ed. David Neumark, 300–331. New York: Russell Sage Foundation.

Schoch-Spana, Monica. 1998. "National Security and Radiological Control: Worker Discipline in the Nuclear Weapons Complex." In *More than Class: Studying Power in U.S. Workplaces,* ed. Ann Kingsolver, 21–53. Albany: State University of New York Press.

Schultz, Howard, and Dori Jones Yang. 1997. *Pour Your Heart into It: How Starbucks Built a Company One Cup at a Time.* New York: Hyperion.

Sennett, Richard. 1998. *The Corrosion of Character: The Personal Consequences of Work in the New Capitalism.* New York: Norton.

Shelgren, Diane. 2001. "HR Outsourcing." *Journal of Business Strategy* 4 (July/August): 4.

Shipley, David. 2004. *The Working Poor: Invisible in America.* New York: Vintage.

Shrivastava, Samir, and James Shaw. 2003. "Liberating HR through Technology." *Human Resource Management* 42 (3): 201–222.

Shuit, Douglas. 2003. "Passing the Bucks." *Workforce Management* 82 (10): 43–46.

Sirianni, Carmen, and Lewis Friedland. 2001. *Civic Innovation in America: Community Empowerment, Public Policy, and the Movement for Civic Renewal.* Berkeley: University of California Press.

Smith, Sandra. 2005. "'Don't Put My Name on It': (Dis)Trust and Job-Finding Assistance among the Black Urban Poor." *American Journal of Sociology* 111 (1): 1–57.

Smith, Vicki. 1994. "Institutionalizing Flexibility in a Service Firm: Multiple Contingencies and Hidden Hierarchies." *Work and Occupations* 21 (3): 284–307.

——. 1997. "New Forms of Work Organization." *Annual Review of Sociology* 23:315–339.

——. 1998. "The Fractured World of the Temporary Worker." *Social Problems* 45 (4): 411–430.

——. 1999. "'Postmodern' Manors: Welfare Capitalism at the End of the Century." *Industrial Relations* 38 (2): 135–140.

——. 2001a. *Crossing the Great Divide: Worker Risk and Opportunity in the New Economy.* Ithaca: Cornell University Press, ILR Press.

——. 2001b. "Teamwork vs. Tempwork: Managers and the Dualisms of Workplace Restructuring." In *Working in Restructured Workplaces: New Directions for the Sociology of Work,* ed. Karen Campbell, Daniel Cornfield, Holly McCammon, 7–28. Thousand Oaks, Calif.: Sage.

Smith, Vicki, Heather Kohler Flynn, and Jonathan Isler. 2006. "Finding Jobs and Building Careers: Reproducing Inequality in State-Sponsored Job Search Organizations." In *Worker Participation: Practices and Possibilities,* ed. Vicki Smith. Special issue of *Research in the Sociology of Work* 16:381–409. Oxford: JAI, Elsevier Press.

Stacey, Judith. 1990. *Brave New Families: Stories of Domestic Upheaval in Late Twentieth Century America.* Basic Books.

Staffing Industry Analysts, Inc. 2000. "Vendor on Premises Business Expected to Grow 100% in 2000." *Staffing Industry Report* (Los Altos, Calif.), 11 (15/16): 14.

Stone, Katherine. 2004. *From Widgets to Digits: Employment Regulation for the Changing Workplace.* Cambridge: Cambridge University Press.

——. 2006. "Legal Protections for Atypical Employees: Employment Law for Workers without Workplaces and Employees without Employers." *Berkeley Journal of Employment and Labor Law* 27 (2): 251–286.

Sutton, John, Frank Dobbin, John Meyer, and W. Richard Scott. 1994. "The Legalization of the Workplace." *American Journal of Sociology* 99 (4): 944–971.

Tait, Vanessa. 2005. *Poor Workers' Unions: Rebuilding Labor from Below.* Boston: South End Press.

Temp Workers Alliance of the North American Alliance for Fair Employment (33 Harrison Ave., Boston). 2003. "Best Practices, Temp Agencies." *Consumer Guide.* 12, September. http://academic.shu.edu/ccs/work/pdf/consguide_sep03.pdf.

Tilly, Chris, and Charles Tilly. 1994. "Capitalist Work and Labor Markets." In *The Handbook of Economic Sociology,* ed. Neil Smelser and Richard Swedberg, 283–312. Princeton: Princeton University Press; New York: Russell Sage Foundation.

Tyler, Kathryn. 2004. "Carve Out Training?" *HR Magazine* 49 (2): 53–57.

Tyson, Shaun. 2007. "Why HR Management Will Never Be the Same Again." *Personnel Today,* January 9, 13.

Uchitelle, Louis. 2006. *The Disposable American: Layoffs and Their Consequences.* New York: Knopf.

Useem, Michael. 1996. *Investor Capitalism: How Money Managers Are Changing the Face of Corporate America.* New York: Basic Books.

Van Jaarsveld, Danielle. 2004. "Collective Representation among High-Tech Workers at Microsoft and Beyond: Lessons from WashTech/CWA." *Industrial Relations* 43 (2): 364–385.

Vockrodt, Jeff. 2005. "Realizing the Need For and Logic of an Equal Pay Act for Temporary Workers." *Berkeley Journal of Employment and Labor Law* 26 (2): 583–606.

Vosko, Leah. 2000. *Temporary Work: The Gendered Rise of a Precarious Employment Relationship.* Toronto, Ont.: University of Toronto Press.

Waldinger, Roger, and Michael Lichter. 2003. *How the Other Half Lives: Immigration and the Social Organization of Labor.* Berkeley: University of California Press.

Wallulis, Jerald. 1998. *The New Insecurity: The End of the Standard Job and Family.* Albany: State University of New York Press.

Waters, Mary. 1999. *Black Identities: West Indian Immigrant Dreams and American Realities.* Cambridge: Harvard University Press.

Watson, Audrey. 2007. Economist, Occupational Employment Statistics, Bureau of Labor Statistics. Personal communication.

Weber, Max. 1958. *The Protestant Ethic and the Spirit of Capitalism.* New York: Scribner.

Whyte, William H. 1956. *The Organization Man.* New York: Doubleday.

Wiatrowski, William. 1995. "Who Really Has Access to Employer-Provided Health Benefits?" *Monthly Labor Review* 118 (6): 36–44.

——. 2004. "Medical and Retirement Plan Coverage: Exploring the Decline in Recent Years." *Monthly Labor Review* 127 (8): 29–35.

Williams, Christine. 2006. *Inside Toyland: Working, Shopping, and Social Inequality.* Berkeley: University of California Press.

INDEX

Note: Page numbers with an *f* indicate figures; those with a *t* indicate tables.

Abrahamson, Eric, 34
academic lecturers, 5
adaptability, 22–23, 61, 128
Addison, John, 151
African Americans, 6, 59, 75, 152, 154–155, 199n8
See also race/ethnicity
agricultural workers, 5, 149
Allied Chemical Corporation, 58–59
American Staffing Association, 19
Americans with Disabilities Act, 183
Andersson, Fredrik, 153
Apple Computers, 9, 12
Association of Temporary Personnel Contractors, 42
at-will employment, 16, 22, 82
AutoMate Corporation, 139–140
Autor, David, 16, 17
on employment contracts, 196n22
on temp-to-perm programs, 113
on training programs, 203n3

BackTreks Corporation, 141–142
Barley, Stephen, 8, 20, 30, 33, 169
Baron, James, 141

Befort, Stephen, 184
Bendix, Reinhart, 34
benefits
for permanent workers, 46–47, 118, 124t, 127–129, 183
for temps, 20–21, 142, 163–171, 186, 192n4
See also specific types, e.g., health care
Benner, Chris, 27, 153, 171
Bernasek, Alexandra, 196n24
best practices, 169–172
Bickham Mendez, Jennifer, 77, 91–92
Block, Fred, 174
"boardhouses" (for computer components), 110
Bolles, Richard, 18–19, 173
Bredeson, Sharon, 50, 56, 61–62
Bronson, Po, 72, 201n2
Building Blocks (BB) Corporation, 108
Built to Order (BTO) Corporation, 71, 86, 133–136, 138, 140–141
Burawoy, Michael, 203n2
burnout, 49, 129
Business Periodicals Index (BPI), 178